The Contemporary American Poets

American Poetry Since 1940

Edited by MARK STRAND

A MENTOR BOOK from
NEW AMERICAN LIBRARY
TIMES MIRROR
New York and Scarborough, Ontario
The New English Library Limited, London

Acknowledgments and Copyright Notices

*(The following pages constitute a continuation of this
copyright page.)*

The Rebirth of Poetry

One of the most remarkable facts of American cultural life during the past three decades has been the reemergence of poetry as an important artistic force with a wide and dramatically expanding audience. American poets once again found they could speak to their society, and joyously set about to do so.

The 92 poets selected for this anthology reflect no single artistic school or geographical region. Instead they represent the rich variety that characterizes the new American poetry, as well as the exuberant vitality and self-confidence that has made this one of the most exciting of all generations of poets.

ABOUT THE EDITOR: *Mark Strand was born in Summerside, Prince Edward Island, Canada, and attended Antioch College and Yale University. Himself a distinguished younger poet, Mr. Strand has published three volumes of poetry,* Sleeping with One Eye Open, Reasons for Moving *and, most recently,* Darker. *Among the several honors he has received have been grants from The National Council on the Arts and from the Rockefeller Foundation.*

MENTOR Poetry Titles

BOWERS, EDGAR: "The Stoic: for Laura von Courten" from *The Form of Loss* by Edgar Bowers, Denver: Alan Swallow, copyright © 1956 by Edgar Bowers. Reprinted by permission of The Swallow Press Incorporated.

CLARK, TOM: "Sonnet" copyright © 1967 by Tom Clark. Reprinted by permission of Tom Clark.

CORSO, GREGORY: "Marriage," from Gregory Corso, *The Happy Birthday of Death*. Copyright © 1960 by New Directions. Reprinted by permission of New Directions Publishing Corporation and Eyre & Spottiswoode Ltd.

COULETTE, HENRI: "The Black Angel" and "At the Telephone Club" are reprinted with the permission of Charles Scribner's Sons from *The War of the Secret Agents* by Henri Coulette. Copyright © 1966 by Henri Coulette. "The Family Goldschmitt" copyright © 1968 by Henri Coulette. Reprinted by permission of Henri Coulette.

CREELEY, ROBERT: "The Pool" and "The Rain" are reprinted with the permission of Charles Scribner's Sons and Calder and Boyars, Ltd., from *For Love* by Robert Creeley. Copyright © 1962 Robert Creeley.

CUNNINGHAM, J. V.: "For My Contemporaries" and "Meditation on Statistical Method" copyright © 1959 by J. V. Cunningham from *Exclusions of Rhyme*. Reprinted by permission of The Swallow Press Incorporated.

DICKEY, JAMES: "The Performance," copyright © 1960 by James Dickey. Reprinted from *Poems 1957-1967*, by James Dickey, by permission of Wesleyan University Press. "The Heaven of Animals" and "Armor" copyright © 1961, 1962 by James Dickey, reprinted from *Drowning with Others* by James Dickey by permission of Wesleyan University Press. "The Heaven of Animals" first appeared in *The New Yorker*. "Cherrylog Road" copyright © 1963 by James Dickey. Reprinted from *Helmets* by James Dickey, published by Wesleyan University Press and Longmans, Green & Co., Ltd., by permission of Wesleyan University Press. This poem first appeared in *The New Yorker*. "The Common Grave" copyright © 1964 by James Dickey. Reprinted from *Buckdancer's Choice*, by James Dickey, by permission of Wesleyan University Press. The poem first appeared in *The New Yorker*.

DICKEY, WILLIAM: "Canonical Hours" from *Of the Festivity* by William Dickey. Copyright © 1959 by Yale University Press. Reprinted by permission of Yale University Press.

DUGAN, ALAN: "How We Heard the Name," "On Hurricane Jackson," and "Wall, Cave, and Pillar Statements, After Asôka" copyright © 1956, 1961 by Alan Dugan. Reprinted by permission of Alan Dugan.

FEINMAN, ALVIN: "November Sunday Morning" from *Preambles and Other Poems* by Alvin Feinman. Copyright © 1964 by Alvin Feinman. Reprinted by permission of Oxford University Press, Inc.

FIELD, EDWARD: "The Dirty Floor" and "An Event" from *Stand Up, Friend, with Me*. Copyright © 1963 by Edward Field. Reprinted by permission of Grove Press, Inc. "The Bride of Frankenstein" from *Variety Photoplays* copyright © 1967 by Edward Field. Reprinted by permission of Grove Press, Inc.

SIGNET, SIGNET CLASSICS, MENTOR, PLUME AND MERIDIAN BOOKS are published *in the United States* by
The New American Library, Inc.,
1301 Avenue of the Americas, New York, New York 10019,
in Canada by The New American Library of Canada Limited,
81 Mack Avenue, Scarborough, 704, Ontario,
in the United Kingdom by The New English Library Limited,
Barnard's Inn, Holborn, London, E.C. 1, England

FIRST MENTOR PRINTING, JULY, 1971

3 4 5 6 7 8 9 10 11

PRINTED IN THE UNITED STATES OF AMERICA

I would like to thank Philip Flayderman, Ben La Farge, and Frank Derby for their help in putting together this book. I would especially like to thank Lea Forsman and Roz Heller, with whom I worked longest, for their willingness to give up so much of their own time to see this project through; without their help this book would not have been possible.

M. S.

EDITOR'S PREFACE

By 1940 the revolution we call Modernism had run its course; the battle against the nineteenth century had been won with time's help, and the poetry of experimentation was so secure that it became a new academicism. Whereas we had gone out of our way in earlier decades to make a pact with the most radical poet of the nineteenth century, Walt Whitman, we accepted quite matter-of-factly our association with and, occasionally, our debt to figures like Poe and even Longfellow. In fact, it is part of the character of American poetry since 1940 to have made friends with everyone. Many different sorts of poetry seem to have co-existed more or less peacefully except for a brief skirmish at the end of the 1950s when we experienced what has been glamorously called "the war of the anthologies" and when it seemed that only two kinds of poetry were being written— the "beat" and the "academic" or, as some wished to call them, the "raw" and the "cooked." But that seems more a part of the sociology of poetry than an accurate description of what in fact was being written. It is one of the points of this anthology to demonstrate the variety in American poetry since 1940 and, in those cases where careers extend from that time, to demonstrate their development.

Many of today's poets have made, if not a cult, at least a lifetime's work of the self, a self defined usually by circumstances that would tend to set it apart. In their energetic pursuit of an individual manner that would reflect a sense of self-definition, they have used what they wanted from various literary traditions. Helped on in recent years by the abundance of translations from almost every language, there are poets in the United States whose imaginative roots seem to have sprung from Neruda or Char or Cavafy or from Arthur Waley's versions of Chinese poetry quite as much as they have from Emerson or Whitman.

It should also be noted that with the growing international-ism of American poetry, there has been a lessening of the influence of British verse in this country. In fact, increasingly since 1940, the influence has worked the other way around.

Poets who published books before 1940 will not be found in this anthology, nor will poems that appeared in periodicals prior to that date. The editor would like to have made exceptions for Robert Penn Warren, Stanley Kunitz, and Josephine Miles, who continue to be outstanding poets, but once certain exceptions are made, other exceptions are created and the year 1940 and the consequent program of this book might cease to have any meaning or relevance. By the same token, the editor would like to have included John Berryman's poem, "Winter Landscape" and Elizabeth Bishop's poem, "A Miracle For Breakfast," both of which appeared in periodicals before 1940.

Editorial policy has been a question of editorial taste; the editor has attempted to present the reader with a broad sampling of recent American poetry, and in an effort not to call too much attention to a few poets at the expense of the many others included, he has limited individual representation to no more than seven poems. It is hoped therefore that more concern will be given the poems than the poets. To provide the reader with a sense of the directions American poetry has taken since 1940, each poem has been dated with its first appearance.

MARK STRAND

New York City
April 1969

CONTENTS

A. R. AMMONS

Bridge

A tea garden shows you how:

    you sit in rhododendron shade

at table
on a pavilion-like lawn

    the sun midafternoon through the blooms
and you

watch lovers and single people
go over the steep moonbridge at the pond's narrows

where flies nip circles

    in the glass
and vanish in the widening sight except for an uncertain

    gauze memory of wings

and as you sip from the small thick cup
    held bird-warm
    in the hands

    you watch
the people
rising on the bridge

descend into the pond,
    where bridge and mirrorbridge merge

    at the bank
returning their images to themselves:
    a grove
of pepper trees (sgraffito)
    screens them into isolations of love or loneliness:

it is enough from this to think in the green tea scent
and turn to farther things:

when the spirit comes to the bridge of consciousness
and climbs higher and higher
    toward the peak no one reaches live
but where ascension
    and descension meet
completing the idea of a bridge

think where the body is,
    that going too deep

it may lose touch,
    wander a ghost in hell
    sing irretrievably in gloom,
and think

how the spirit silvery with vision may
break loose in high wind

    and go off weightless

body never to rise or spirit fall again to unity,
to lovers strolling through pepper-tree shade:

    paradise was when
Dante
regathered from height and depth
    came out onto the soft, green, level earth

into the natural light, come, sweat, bloodblessings,
    and thinning sheaf of days.

                                 (1960)

Gravelly Run

I don't know somehow it seems sufficient
to see and hear whatever coming and going is,
losing the self to the victory
    of stones and trees,
of bending sandpit lakes, crescent
round groves of dwarf pine:

for it is not so much to know the self
as to know it as it is known
    by galaxy and cedar cone,
as if birth had never found it
and death could never end it:

the swamp's slow water comes
down Gravelly Run fanning the long
    stone-held algal
hair and narrowing roils between
the shoulders of the highway bridge:

holly grows on the banks in the woods there,
and the cedars' gothic-clustered
    spires could make
green religion in winter bones:

so I look and reflect, but the air's glass
jail seals each thing in its entity:

no use to make any philosophies here:
    I see no
god in the holly, hear no song from
the snowbroken weeds: Hegel is not the winter
yellow in the pines: the sunlight has never
heard of trees: surrendered self among
    unwelcoming forms: stranger,
hoist your burdens, get on down the road.

(1960)

Visit

It is not far to my place:
you can come smallboat,
pausing under shade in the eddies
    or going ashore
        to rest, regard the leaves

or talk with birds and
shore weeds: hire a full-grown man not
late in years to oar you
    and choose a canoe-like thin ship;
        (a dumb man is better and no

costlier; he will attract
the reflections and silences under leaves:)
travel light: a single book, some twine:
    the river is muscled at rapids with trout
        and a laurel limb

will make a suitable spit: if you
leave in the forenoon, you will arrive
with plenty of light
    the afternoon of the third day: I will
        come down to the landing

(tell your man to look for it,
the dumb have clear sight and are free of
visions) to greet you with some made
    wine and a special verse:
        or you can come by shore:

choose the right: there the rocks
cascade less frequently, the grade more gradual:
treat yourself gently: the ascent thins both
    mind and blood and you must
        keep still a dense reserve

of silence we can poise against
conversation: there is little news:
I found last month a root with shape and
have heard a new sound among
    the insects: come.

(1962)

Corsons Inlet

I went for a walk over the dunes again this morning
to the sea,
then turned right along
    the surf

                         rounded a naked headland
                         and returned

    along the inlet shore:

it was muggy sunny, the wind from the sea steady and high,
crisp in the running sand,
    some breakthroughs of sun
  but after a bit

continuous overcast:

the walk liberating, I was released from forms,
from the perpendiculars,
    straight lines, blocks, boxes, binds
of thought
into the hues, shadings, rises, flowing bends and blends
        of sight:
                I allow myself eddies of meaning:
yield to a direction of significance
running
like a stream through the geography of my work:
    you can find
in my sayings

                swerves of action
                like the inlet's cutting edge:
            there are dunes of motion,
organizations of grass, white sandy paths of remembrance
in the overall wandering of mirroring mind:
but Overall is beyond me: is the sum of these events
I cannot draw, the ledger I cannot keep, the accounting
beyond the account:

in nature there are few sharp lines: there are areas of
primrose
    more or less dispersed;
disorderly orders of bayberry; between the rows
of dunes,
irregular swamps of reeds,

though not reeds alone, but grass, bayberry, yarrow, all . . .
predominantly reeds:

I have reached no conclusions, have erected no boundaries,
shutting out and shutting in, separating inside
        from outside: I have
        drawn no lines:
        as

manifold events of sand
change the dune's shape that will not be the same shape
tomorrow,

so I am willing to go along, to accept
the becoming
thought, to stake off no beginnings or ends, establish
        no walls:

by transitions the land falls from grassy dunes to creek
to undercreek: but there are no lines, though
    change in that transition is clear
    as any sharpness: but "sharpness" spread out,
allowed to occur over a wider range
than mental lines can keep:

the moon was full last night: today, low tide was low:
black shoals of mussels exposed to the risk
of air
and, earlier, of sun,
waved in and out with the waterline, waterline inexact,
caught always in the event of change:
    a young mottled gull stood free on the shoals
    and ate
to vomiting: another gull, squawking possession, cracked a
                                crab,
picked out the entrails; swallowed the soft-shelled legs,
                              a ruddy
turnstone running in to snatch leftover bits:

risk is full: every living thing in
siege: the demand is life, to keep life: the small
white blacklegged egret, how beautiful, quietly stalks and
    spears
        the shallows, darts to shore
                    to stab—what? I couldn't

see against the black mudflats—a frightened
fiddler crab?

the news to my left over the dunes and
reeds and bayberry clumps was
fall: thousands of tree swallows
gathering for flight:
an order held
in constant change: a congregation
rich with entrophy: nevertheless, separable, noticeable
as one event,
not chaos: preparations for
flight from winter,
cheet, cheet, cheet, cheet, wings rifling the green clumps,
beaks
at the bayberries:
a perception full of wind, flight, curve,
sound:
the possibility of rule as the sum of rulelessness:
the "field" of action
with moving, incalculable center:

in the smaller view, order tight with shape:
blue tiny flowers on a leafless weed: carapace of crab:
snail shell:
pulsations of order
in the bellies of minnows: orders swallowed,
broken down, transferred through membranes
to strengthen larger orders: but in the large view, no
lines or changeless shapes: the working in and out, together
and against, of millions of events: this,
so that I make
no form of
formlessness:

orders as summaries, as outcomes of actions override
or in some way result, not predictably (seeing me gain
the top of a dune,
the swallows
could take flight—some other fields of bayberry
could enter fall
berryless) and there is serenity:

no arranged terror: no forcing of image, plan,
or thought:
no propaganda, no humbling of reality to precept:

terror pervades but is not arranged, all possibilities
of escape open: no route shut, except in
    the sudden loss of all routes:

        I see narrow orders, limited tightness, but will
not run to that easy victory:
       still around the looser, wider forces work:
       I will try
to fasten into order enlarging grasps of disorder, widening
scope, but enjoying the freedom that
Scope eludes my grasp, that there is no finality of vision,
that I have perceived nothing completely,
            that tomorrow a new walk is a new walk.

                                  (1963)

ALAN ANSEN

Tennyson

The lawns darken, evening broods in the black.
Juiceless heroic phantoms wander in pain
Whispering, sighing threnodies for a lack,
For a luck, for a look, for a likeness they sought in vain
As they slithered and wraithed over a rotting plain
To the Faceless City where kindly exorcists
By playing house banish the hoarse refrain
Of a vatic Sybil ululating in mists
Woe, woe, woe to the bowler hats and the spats.
The Muse, a Fury with her nine-lashed whip,
Beats us in tears of refusal to the acid vats
Where the decomposing somatic lies steadily fulsomely drip.
Oh you who in spite of yourself have shown us the end,
Help us to break like oaks in the soughing bacterial wind.

(1959)

Fatness

aleph

1. How comely glisten the rounded cheeks and the swelling
   thighs! Blessed the sinews, auspicious the tissues that
   prosper to the benediction of amplitude.

37

2. Rejoice, ye beholders, in the nutritive steaks and comforting sauces, the delights of the palate and the strength-giving proteins.

3. The chiming bowels give thanks to their Maker and broadcast the incense of life lived well.

4. Bear witness, O body in bloom, to the goodness of the Lord and to the wealthiness with which He endowed thee.

5. The people dance in the streets, fulfilled with my fullness.

6. Just are the ways of God to men! A proof, let me communicate gladness.

7. In the day of my rising up, low I give thanks: Thou hast heaped up my treasure, Thou hast exalted my horn—to Thee be the glory.

8. Not for us alone, O Lord, not for us alone; but let Thy bounteousness extend to all: soften the hearts of the princes that they endue even the meanest, especially the meanest, with the fruits of benevolent earth.

9. I rest not from celebrating the goodness of the All-Highest: my heart never wearies in hymns of thanksgiving.

10. Grow to the height of blessing: there are giants on the face of the earth in these days.

beth

11. Stately and calm, the mature body serene studies quietness.

12. The due and regular refection soothes the stomach with punctual beauty.

13. Punctual, too, the bowels' outpourings betoken the sanctity of the measured life.

14. Roseate repletion hallows my accomplished torso.

15. Solid in a world of solids, I exist a landmark to the more fluid.

16. Unshaken, I contemplate unmoved the variations of behavior.

17. My spirit, if it does not rejoice, it snoozes complacent.

18. Content you, turbulent minds, with the portion meted out to you: lest a worse thing befall.

19. Conform yourselves to the established rite: in a multitude of worships only the will is adored.

20. Peace! Peace! Let us imprecate peace on the living, the dead and the resting.

gimel

21. An inert mass groans to its Creator: can this dead fat live?
22. Shovel in the pork, the oils and the butters: so much the less for sneering starvelings.
23. Bowels, laboratories of decay, infect the unjudging air with the poison gases of your spiteful superfluity.
24. Sweaty flesh, gravid with itself, overlays my life.
25. Mine enemies hiss at me, a ridiculous monster, a laughable roadblock in the path of their impatience.
26. Their mockery I answer with my mightiest curse, my continued existence.
27. My vacuously frenzied spirits tears and rends in vain the meaty clogs of static adiposity.
28. Jacob, I lie immobilized in possession: why troublest thou thyself?
29. Beyond this bed and this trough is nothing: blind and deaf, I am conscious only of weight and pain.
30. Heaviness is all.

daleth

31. Let us fly then, my corpulent soul, to the hot lands, the black lands, the simple and starved lands,
32. Where adoring the woolly-haired natives proclaim the steatopygous and the beautiful one.
33. Up! Up and away.

(1961)

JOHN ASHBERY

Last Month

No changes of support—only
Patches of gray, here where sunlight fell.
The house seems heavier
Now that they have gone away.
In fact it emptied in record time.
When the flat table used to result
A match recedes, slowly, into the night.
The academy of the future is
Opening its doors and willing
The fruitless sunlight streams into domes
The chairs piled high with books and papers.

The sedate one is this month's skittish one
Confirming the property that,
A timeless value, has changed hands.
And you could have a new automobile
Ping pong set and garage, but the thief
Stole everything like a miracle.
In his book there was a picture of treason only
And in the garden, cries and colors.

(1963)

Rivers and Mountains

On the secret map of assasins
Cloistered, the Moon River was marked
Near the eighteen peaks and the city

Of humiliation and defeat—wan ending
Of the trail among dry, papery leaves
Gray-brown quills like thoughts
In the melodious but vast mass of today's
Writing through fields and swamps
Marked, on the map, with little bunches of weeds.
Certainly squirrels lived in the woods
But devastation and dull sleep still
Hung over the land, quelled
The rioters turned out of sleep in the peace of prisons
Singing on marble factory walls
Deaf consolation of minor tunes that pack
The air with heavy invisible rods
Pent in some sand valley from
Which only quiet walking ever instructs.
The bird flew over and
Sat—there was nothing else to do.
Do not mistake its silence for pride or strength
Or the waterfall for a harbor
Full of light boats that is there
Performing for thousands of people
In clothes some with places to go
Or games. Sometimes over the pillar
Of square stones its impact
Makes a light print.

So going around cities
To get to other places you found
It all on paper but the land
Was made of paper processed
To look like ferns, mud or other
Whose sea unrolled its magic
Distances and then rolled them up
Its secret was only a pocket
After all but some corners are darker
Than these moonless nights spent as on a raft
In the seclusion of a melody heard
As though through trees
And you can never ignite their touch
Long but there were homes
Flung far out near the asperities
Of a sharp, rocky pinnacle
And other collective places

Shadows of vineyards whose wine
Tasted of the forest floor
Fisheries and oyster beds
Tides under the pole
Seminaries of instruction, public
Places for electric light
And the major tax assessment area
Wrinkled on the plan
Of election to public office
Sixty-two years old bath and breakfast
The formal traffic, shadows
To make it not worth joining
After the ox had pulled away the cart.

Your plan was to separate the enemy into two groups
With the razor-edged mountains between.
It worked well on paper
But their camp had grown
To be the mountains and the map
Carefully peeled away and not torn
Was the light, a tender but tough bark
On everything. Fortunately the war was solved
In another way by isolating the two sections
Of the enemy's navy so that the mainland
Warded away the big floating ships.
Light bounced off the ends
Of the small gray waves to tell
Them in the observatory
About the great drama that was being won
To turn off the machinery
And quietly move among the rustic landscape
Scooping snow off the mountains rinsing
The coarser ones that love had
Slowly risen in the night to overflow
Wetting pillow and petal
Determined to place the letter
On the unassassinated president's desk
So that a stamp could reproduce all this
In detail, down to the last autumn leaf
And the affliction of June ride
Slowly into the sun-blackened landscape.

(1964)

The Bungalows

I

Impatient as we were for all of them to join us,
The land had not yet risen into view: gulls had swept the
    gray steel towers away
So that it profited less to go searching, away over the hum-
    ming earth
Than to stay in immediate relation to these other things—
    boxes, store parts, whatever you call them—
Whose installedness was the price of further revolutions, so
    you knew this combat was the last.
And still the relationship waxed, billowed like scenery on the
    breeze.

II

They are the same aren't they,
The presumed landscape and the dream of home
Because the people are all homesick today or desperately
    sleeping,
Trying to remember how those rectangular shapes
Became so extraneous and so near
To create a foreground of quiet knowledge
In which youth had grown old, chanting and singing wise
    hymns that
Will sign for old age
And so lift up the past to be persuaded, and be put down
    again.

III

The warning is nothing more than an aspirate "h";
The problem is sketched completely, like fireworks mounted
    on poles:
Complexion of evening, the accurate voices of the others.
During Coca Cola lessons it becomes patent
Of noise on the left, and we had so skipped a stage that
The great wave of the past, compounded in derision,
Submerged idea and non-dreamer alike
In falsetto starlight like "purity"
Of design that had been the first danger sign
To wash the sticky, icky stuff down the drain—pfui!

How does it feel to be outside and inside at the same time,
The delicious feeling of the air contradicting and secretly
  abetting
The interior warmth? But the land curdles the dismay in
  which it's written
Bearing to a final point of folly and doom
The wisdom of these generations.
Look at what you've done to the landscape—
The ice-cube, the olive—
There is a perfect tri-city mesh of things
Extending all the way along the river on both sides
With the end left for thoughts on construction
That are always turning to alps and thresholds
Above the tide of others, feeding a European moss rose
  without glory.

We shall very soon have the pleasure of recording
A period of unanimous tergiversation in this respect
And to make that pleasure the greater, it is worth while
And the risk of tedious iteration, to put first upon record a
  final protest:
Rather decaying art, genius, inspiration to hold to
An impossible "calque" of reality, than
"The new school of the trivial, rising up on the field of
  battle,
Something of sludge and leaf-mold," and life
Goes trickling out through the holes, like water through a
  sieve,
All in one direction.

You who were directionless, and thought it would solve
  everything if you found one,
What do you make of this? Just because a thing is immortal
Is that any reason to worship it? Death, after all, is im-
  mortal.
But you have gone into your houses and shut the doors,
  meaning
There can be no further discussion.
And the river pursues its lonely course
With the sky and the trees cast up from the landscape
For green brings unhappiness—*le verte porte malheur.*
"The chartreuse mountain on the absinthe plain
Makes the strong man's tears tumble down like rain."

All this came to pass eons ago.
Your program worked out perfectly. You even avoided

The monotony of perfection by leaving in certain flaws:
A backward way of becoming, a forced handshake,
An absent-minded smile, though in fact nothing was left to
 chance.
Each detail was startlingly clear, as though seen through a
 magnifying glass,
Or would have been to an ideal observer, namely yourself—
For only you could watch yourself so patiently from afar
The way God watches a sinner on the path to redemption,
Sometimes disappearing into valleys, but always *on the way,*
For it all builds up into something, meaningless or mean-
 ingful
As architecture, because planned and then abandoned when
 completed,
To live afterwards, in sunlight and shadow, a certain amount
 of years.
Who cares about what was there before? There is no going
 back,
For standing still means death, and life is moving on,
Moving on towards death. But sometimes standing still is
 also life.

(1967)

Farm Implements and
Rutabagas in a Landscape

The first of the undecoded messages read: "Popeye sits in
 thunder,
Unthought of. From that shoebox of an apartment,
From livid curtain's hue, a tangram emerges: a country."
Meanwhile the Sea Hag was relaxing on a green couch:
 "How pleasant
To spend one's vacation *en la casa de Popeye,*" she scratched
Her cleft chin's solitary hair. She remembered spinach

And was going to ask Wimpy if he had bought any spinach.
"M'love," he intercepted, "the plains are decked out in
 thunder

Today, and it shall be as you wish." He scratched
The part of his head under his hat. The apartment
Seemed to grow smaller. "But what if no pleasant
Inspiration plunge us now to the stars? *For this is my
   country."*

Suddenly they remembered how it was cheaper in the
   country.
Wimpy was thoughtfully cutting open a number 2 can of
   spinach
When the door opened and Swee'pea crept in. "How pleas-
   ant!"
But Swee'pea looked morose. A note was pinned to his bib.
   "Thunder
And tears are unavailing," it read. "Henceforth shall Pop-
   eye's apartment
Be but remembered space, toxic or salubrious, whole or
   scratched."

Olive came hurtling through the window; its geraniums
   scratched
Her long thigh. "I have news!" she gasped. "Popeye, forced
   as you know to flee the country
One musty gusty evening, by the schemes of his wizened,
   duplicate father, jealous of the apartment
And all that it contains, myself and spinach
In particular, heaves bolts of loving thunder
At his own astonished becoming, rupturing the pleasant

Arpeggio of our years. No more shall pleasant
Rays of the sun refresh your sense of growing old, nor the
   scratched
Tree-trunks and mossy foliage, only immaculate darkness
   and thunder."
She grabbed Swee'pea. "I'm taking the brat to the country."
"But you can't do that—he hasn't even finished his spinach,"
Urged the Sea Hag, looking fearfully around at the apart-
   ment.

But Olive was already out of earshot. Now the apartment
Succumbed to a strange new hush. "Actually it's quite pleas-
   ant
Here," thought the Sea Hag. "If this is all we need fear from
   spinach
Then I don't mind so much. Perhaps we could invite Alice
the Goon over"—she scratched

One dug pensively—"but Wimpy is such a country
Bumpkin, always burping like that." Minute at first, the
   thunder

Soon filled the apartment. It was domestic thunder,
The color of spinach. Popeye chuckled and scratched
His balls: it sure was pleasant to spend a day in the country.

(1967)

MARVIN BELL

Things We Dreamt We Died For

Flags of all sorts.
The literary life.
Each time we dreamt we'd done
the gentlemanly thing,
covering our causes
in closets full of bones
to remove ourselves forever
from dearest possibilities,
the old weapons re-injured us,
the old armies conscripted us,
and we gave in to getting even,
a little less like us
if a lot less like others.
Many, thus, gained fame
in the way of great plunderers,
retiring to the university
to cultivate grand plunder-gardens
in the service of literature,
the young and no more wars.
Their continuing tributes
make them our greatest saviours,
whose many fortunes are followed
by the many who have not one.

(1965)

Communication on His Thirtieth Birthday

You didn't have to travel to become an airplane,
nor fly to get high. Considerable numbers languished
in your exclusive calculations. You would wind up abroad.
You chose home entertainment and the mechanical society.

The machine had machines which told machines all about it.
The machine knew, for example, of sensational airwaves.
The machine knew how to go up and how to drop down.
The machine knew all the exits, and the best exits.

Then your metabolism changed and you entered energy:
model-making glue, carbon tet., solder, a piezo-electric
crystal-controlled oscillator smelled like the real thing,
and gave you the advantage of interchangeable frequencies.

You were calibrating fame and the landscapes you entered.
You could prove forty-eight states and Britain
and at dusk you could prove the small isles of the Atlantic.
You spoke to every radio on St. Pierre and Miquelon Islands!

Fifteen years later, you abandoned your license,
just as the next generation was entering chemicals.
You were writing, compulsively, but nothing fashionable.
A poem on your birthday seemed out of the question.

Yet here you are, celebrating, speaking openly as if
the moral of aesthetics is that the parable convinces.
The easy way out, you concluded, is through the village,
under the antenna, down the long path intended for your feet.

(1967)

The Perfection of Dentistry

Guanajuato, Mexico

Here I am, an industry without chimneys,
looking for an alternative
to abandoning privilege,
looking out from my long floral porch
which is not a porch but an expatriate
way of life (he hates her, she hates
him, but they can't leave), leaning
over the intricate stone railing,
over the caretaker asleep on the ground,
toward the haciendas on the opposite hill
which seems so luxurious without cactus.

Surviving "turistas," the physics of the fiesta
and the intimacy of our schizophrenia,
we have arrived, not without mercy,
to render unto trees and flowers and hills
our unnatural, filling-laden homage.
Across the way, they may be watching,
mineral water in hand, the spectacle-clad vermin.
But we do not think ourselves unhealthy,
if afflicted. We do not think ourselves visited
but visitors, without undue recompense.
If the trees bow slightly, that is alright. And

if the flowers bloom indiscriminately,
we can accept such favors. We knew before coming
we must restore to its altar the spine of the tree,
and the ebullient blooming to its rightful position.
We knew before coming that notoriety was wrong
everywhere, though trusting the wealthy North American.
But the causes of suffering are like impure water,
which one must walk beside and ingest
until one is covered completely in the sweaty afternoon.
And the momentum of the rains is like the momentum
of the bells, penetrating and cleansing the lush cover.

Here, every workday is part of a pilgrimage
for which the church tolls the approximate hours.
It's true, we have paid too much attention to our mouths.
We have the expression, "like pulling teeth";
we have words for the cabinets of our emotions.
But the caretaker has pulled his bad tooth
without fuss, and now weathers his senses in sleep.
And we, compensating witnesses, lead his concurrent
lives, take place in the garden of his salvation,
in the hierarchy of anonymity, and in
the masterful units of his siesta, and always did.

(1968)

MICHAEL BENEDIKT

Divine Love

A lip which had once been stolid, now moving
Gradually around the side of the head
Eye-like
The eye twisted on the end of somebody's finger and spinning
Around the sun, its ear,
And the brain aloft over the lake of the face—
Near the cataract of the body—
Like a cumulus cloud enlarged before a rainstorm:

A sound
That grows gradually in the East
Driving everything before it: cattle and rainbows and lovers
Swept on
To the table of the body at which five men and two women
    are casually sitting down to eat

(1966)

Some Litanies

1.
Was the arrangement made between the two couples legal?

No.

Did they spread the word around?

No.

51

Have you visited the two couples lately? Did you have an
   interesting time? Was it illegal?

No.

What was the decoration like?

It was furnished in Swedish "modern." Strings were hanging
   down in the living room. A bird flew in the window
   once and out again.

Will you ever marry?

No.

Have you ever been married?

I don't remember.

Do you love your husband?

Yes.

2.
May I please have this dance?

No.

May I please have that dance?

No.

Aren't you going to wear anything to the dance?

Yes.

Are you a good dancer?

Yes.

Do you know how to dance?

No.

May I in that case have your company during the dance
   they decide to play exactly at midnight, whatever it is?

I have fallen in love with your eyes, lips, hands
and hair.

No.

3.

During the lapse of several years, during which I spent
    most of my time in Barcelona, was the magazine
    published?

Yes.

During the lapse of several years, during which I spent
    most of my time in Barcelona, was the magazine
    published?

No.

Aren't you absolutely sure?

No.

Aren't you absolutely sure?

Yes.

Will you ever come to Barcelona with me?

No. I am afraid to leave behind the business affairs
    of the magazine, of which I am general manager.

Are you really that conscientious?

No.

4.

Would you care to deal him the death-dealing blow?

No.

Would you care to pay him a little visit?

No.

Would you care to improve his laundry service by
    making persistent inquiries?

No.

Are you really his legal guardian?

No.

Would you care to hand him this large can of
    fortified beeswax?

No.

Do you have a favorite hobby?

Yes. Devoting myself entirely to that boy.

(1967)

JOHN BERRYMAN

The Moon and the Night and the Men

On the night of the Belgian surrender the moon rose
Late, a delayed moon, and a violent moon
For the English or the American beholder;
The French beholder. It was a cold night,
People put on their wraps, the troops were cold
No doubt, despite the calendar, no doubt
Numbers of refugees coughed, and the sight
Or sound of some killed others. A cold night.

On Outer Drive there was an accident:
A stupid well-intentioned man turned sharp
right and abruptly he became an angel
Fingering an unfamiliar harp,
Or screamed in hell, or was nothing at all.
Do not imagine this is unimportant.
He was a part of the night, part of the land,
Part of the bitter and exhausted ground
Out of which memory grows.

                  Michael and I
Stared at each other over chess, and spoke
As little as possible, and drank and played.
The chessmen caught in the European eye,
Neither of us I think had a free look
Although the game was fair. The move one made
It was difficult at last to keep one's mind on.
'Hurt and unhappy' said the man in London.
We said to each other, The time is coming near

55

When none shall have books or music, none his dear,
And only a fool will speak aloud his mind.
History is approaching a speechless end,
As Henry Adams said. Adams was right.

All this occurred on the night when Leopold
Fulfilled the treachery four years before
Begun—or was he well-intentioned, more
Roadmaker to hell than king? At any rate,
The moon came up late and the night was cold,
Many men died—although we know the fate
Of none, nor of anyone, and the war
Goes on, and the moon in the breast of man is cold.

(1940)

Canto Amor

Dream in a dream the heavy soul somewhere
struck suddenly & dark down to its knees.
A griffin sighs off in the orphic air.

If (Unknown Majesty) I not confess
praise for the wrack the rock the live sailor
under the blue sea,—yet I may You bless

always for hér, in fear & joy for hér
whose gesture summons ever when I grieve
me back and is my mage and minister.

—Muses: whose worship I may never leave
but for this pensive woman, now I dare,
teach me her praise! with her my praise receive.—

Three years already of the round world's war
had rolled by stoned & disappointed eyes
when she and I came where we were made for.

Pale as a star lost in returning skies,
more beautiful than midnight stars more frail
she moved towards me like chords, a sacrifice;

entombed in body trembling through the veil
arm upon arm, learning our ancient wound,
we see our one soul heal, recovering pale.

Then priestly sanction, then the drop of sound.
Quickly part to the cavern ever warm
deep from the march, body to body bound,

descend (my soul) out of dismantling storm
into the darkness where the world is made.
. . Come back to the bright air. Love is multiform.

Heartmating hesitating unafraid
although incredulous, she seemed to fill
the lilac shadow with light wherein she played,

whom sorry childhood had made sit quite still,
an orphan silence, unregarded sheen,
listening for any small soft note, not hopeful:

caricature: as once a maiden Queen,
flowering power comeliness kindness grace,
shattered her mirror, wept, would not be seen.

These pities moved. Also above her face
serious or flushed, swayed her fire-gold
not earthly hair, now moonless to unlace,

resistless flame, now in a sun more cold
great shells to whorl about each secret ear,
mysterious histories, white shores, unfold.

New musics! One the music that we hear,
this is the music which the masters make
out of their minds, profound solemn & clear.

And then the other music, in whose sake
all men perceive a gladness but we are drawn
less for that joy than utterly to take

our trial, naked in the music's vision,
the flowing ceremony of trouble and light,
all Loves becoming, none to flag upon.

Such Mozart made,—an ear so delicate
he fainted at a trumpet-call, a child
so delicate. So merciful that sight,

so stern, we follow rapt who ran a-wild.
Marriage is the second music, and thereof
we hear what we can bear, faithful & mild.

Therefore the streaming torches in the grove
through dark or bright, swiftly & now more near
cherish a festival of anxious love.

Dance for this music, Mistress to music dear,
more, that storm worries the disordered wood
grieving the midnight of my thirtieth year

and only the trial of our music should
still this irresolute air, only your voice
spelling the tempest may compel our good:

Sigh then beyond my song: whirl & rejoice!

(1946)

The Song of the Tortured Girl

After a little I could not have told—
But no one asked me this—why I was there.
I asked. The ceiling of that place was high
And there were sudden noises, which I made.
I must have stayed there a long time today:
My cup of soup was gone when they brought me back.

Often "Nothing worse now can come to us"
I thought, the winter the young men stayed away,
My uncle died, and mother broke her crutch.
And then the strange room where the brightest light
Does not shine on the strange men: shines on me.
I feel them stretch my youth and throw a switch.

Through leafless branches the sweet wind blows
Making a mild sound, softer than a moan;
High in a pass once where we put our tent,
Minutes I lay awake to hear my joy.
—I no longer remember what they want.—
Minutes I lay awake to hear my joy.

(1948)

The Ball Poem

What is the boy now, who has lost his ball,
What, what is he to do? I saw it go
Merrily bouncing, down the street, and then
Merrily over—there it is in the water!
No use to say 'O there are other balls':
An ultimate shaking grief fixes the boy
As he stands rigid, trembling, staring down
All his young days into the harbour where
His ball went. I would not intrude on him,
A dime, another ball, is worthless. Now
He senses first responsibility
In a world of possessions. People will take balls,
Balls will be lost always, little boy,
And no one buys a ball back. Money is external.
He is learning, well behind his desperate eyes,
The epistemology of loss, how to stand up
Knowing what every man must one day know
And most know many days, how to stand up
And gradually light returns to the street,
A whistle blows, the ball is out of sight,
Soon part of me will explore the deep and dark
Floor of the harbour . . I am everywhere,
I suffer and move, my mind and my heart move
With all that move me, under the water
Or whistling, I am not a little boy.

(1948)

Dream Song 40

I'm scared a lonely. Never see my son,
easy be not to see anyone,
combers out to sea
know they're goin somewhere but not me.
Got a little poison, got a little gun,
I'm scared a lonely.

I'm scared a only one thing, which is me,
from othering I don't take nothin, see,
for any hound dog's sake.
But this is where I livin, where I rake
my leaves and cop my promise, this' where we
cry oursel's awake.

Wishin was dyin but I gotta make
it all this way to that bed on these feet
where peoples said to meet.
Maybe but even if I see my son
forever never, get back on the take,
free, black & forty-one.

(1964)

Dream Song 61

Full moon. Our Narragansett gales subside
and the land is celebrating men of war
more or less, less or more.
In valleys, thin on headlands, narrow & wide
our targets rest. In us we trust. Far, near,
the bivouacs of fear

are solemn in the moon somewhere tonight,
in turning time. It's late for gratitude,
an annual, rude
roar of a moment's turkey's 'Thanks'. Bright & white
their ordered markers undulate away
awaiting no day.

Away from us, from Henry's feel or fail,
campaigners lie with mouldered toes, disarmed,
out of order,
with whom we will one. The war is real,
and a sullen glory pauses over them harmed,
incident to murder.

(1964)

ELIZABETH BISHOP

Little Exercise

Think of the storm roaming the sky uneasily
like a dog looking for a place to sleep in,
listen to it growling.

Think how they must look now, the mangrove keys
lying out there unresponsive to the lightning
in dark, coarse-fibred families,

where occasionally a heron may undo his head,
shake up his feathers, make an uncertain comment
when the surrounding water shines.

Think of the boulevard and the little palm trees
all stuck in rows, suddenly revealed
as fistfuls of limp fish-skeletons.

It is raining there. The boulevard
and its broken sidewalks with weeds in every crack,
are relieved to be wet, the sea to be freshened.

Now the storm goes away again in a series
of small, badly lit battle-scenes,
each in "Another part of the field."

Think of someone sleeping in the bottom of a row-boat
tied to a mangrove root or the pile of a bridge;
think of him as uninjured, barely disturbed.

(1946)

At the Fishhouses

Although it is a cold evening,
down by one of the fishhouses
an old man sits netting,
his net, in the gloaming almost invisible
a dark purple-brown,
and his shuttle worn and polished.
The air smells so strong of codfish
it makes one's nose run and one's eyes water.
The five fishhouses have steeply peaked roofs
and narrow, cleated gangplanks slant up
to storerooms in the gables
for the wheelbarrows to be pushed up and down on.
All is silver: the heavy surface of the sea,
swelling slowly as if considering spilling over,
is opaque, but the silver of the benches,
the lobster pots, and masts, scattered
among the wild jagged rocks,
is of an apparent translucence
like the small old buildings with an emerald moss
growing on their shoreward walls.
The big fish tubs are completely lined
with layers of beautiful herring scales
and the wheelbarrows are similarly plastered
with creamy iridescent coats of mail,
with small iridescent flies crawling on them.
Up on the little slope behind the houses,
set in the sparse bright sprinkle of grass,
is an ancient wooden capstan,
cracked, with two long bleached handles
and some melancholy stains, like dried blood,
where the ironwork has rusted.

The old man accepts a Lucky Strike.
He was a friend of my grandfather.
We talk of the decline in the population
and of codfish and herring
while he waits for a herring boat to come in.
There are sequins on his vest and on his thumb.
He has scraped the scales, the principal beauty,
from unnumbered fish with that black old knife,
the blade of which is almost worn away.

Down at the water's edge, at the place
where they haul up the boats, up the long ramp
descending into the water, thin silver
tree trunks are laid horizontally
across the gray stones, down and down
at intervals of four or five feet.

Cold dark deep and absolutely clear,
element bearable to no mortal,
to fish and to seals . . . One seal particularly
I have seen here evening after evening.
He was curious about me. He was interested in music;
like me a believer in total immersion,
so I used to sing him Baptist hymns.
I also sang "A Mighty Fortress Is Our God."
He stood up in the water and regarded me
steadily, moving his head a little.
Then he would disappear, then suddenly emerge
almost in the same spot, with a sort of shrug
as if it were against his better judgment.
Cold dark deep and absolutely clear,
the clear gray icy water . . . Back, behind us,
the dignified tall firs begin.
Bluish, associating with their shadows,
a million Christmas trees stand
waiting for Christmas. The water seems suspended
above the rounded gray and blue-gray stones.
I have seen it over and over, the same sea, the same,
slightly, indifferently swinging above the stones,
icily free above the stones,
above the stones and then the world.
If you should dip your hand in,
your wrist would ache immediately,
your bones would begin to ache and your hand would burn
as if the water were a transmutation of fire
that feeds on stones and burns with a dark gray flame.
If you tasted it, it would first taste bitter,
then briny, then surely burn your tongue.
It is like what we imagine knowledge to be:
dark, salt, clear, moving, utterly free,
drawn from the cold hard mouth
of the world, derived from the rocky breasts
forever, flowing and drawn, and since
our knowledge is historical, flowing, and flown.

(1947)

The Prodigal

The brown enormous odor he lived by
was too close, with its breathing and thick hair,
for him to judge. The floor was rotten; the sty
was plastered halfway up with glass-smooth dung.
Light-lashed, self-righteous, above moving snouts,
the pigs' eyes followed him, a cheerful stare—
even to the sow that always ate her young—
till, sickening, he leaned to scratch her head.
But sometimes mornings after drinking bouts
(he hid the pints behind a two-by-four),
the sunrise glazed the barnyard mud with red;
the burning puddles seemed to reassure.
And then he thought he almost might endure
his exile yet another year or more.

But evenings the first star came to warn.
The farmer whom he worked for came at dark
to shut the cows and horses in the barn
beneath their overhanging clouds of hay,
with pitchforks, faint forked lightnings, catching light,
safe and companionable as in the Ark.
The pigs stuck out their little feet and snored.
The lantern—like the sun, going away—
laid on the mud a pacing aureole.

Carrying a bucket along a slimy board,
he felt the bats' uncertain staggering flight,
his shuddering insights, beyond his control,
touching him. But it took him a long time
finally to make his mind up to go home.

(1951)

Visits to St. Elizabeths

1950

This is the house of Bedlam.

This is the man
that lies in the house of Bedlam.

This is the time
of the tragic man
that lies in the house of Bedlam.

This is a wristwatch
telling the time
of the talkative man
that lies in the house of Bedlam.

This is a sailor
wearing the watch
that tells the time
of the honored man
that lies in the house of Bedlam.

This is the roadstead all of board
reached by the sailor
wearing the watch
that tells the time
of the old, brave man
that lies in the house of Bedlam.

These are the years and the walls of the ward,
the winds and clouds of the sea of board
sailed by the sailor
wearing the watch
that tells the time
of the cranky man
that lies in the house of Bedlam.

This is a Jew in a newspaper hat
that dances weeping down the ward
over the creaking sea of board
beyond the sailor
winding his watch
that tells the time
of the cruel man
that lies in the house of Bedlam.

This is a world of books gone flat.
This is a Jew in a newspaper hat
that dances weeping down the ward
over the creaking sea of board
of the batty sailor
that winds his watch
that tells the time
of the busy man
that lies in the house of Bedlam.

This is a boy that pats the floor
to see if the world is there, is flat,
for the widowed Jew in the newspaper hat
that dances weeping down the ward
waltzing the length of a weaving board
by the silent sailor
that hears his watch
that ticks the time
of the tedious man
that lies in the house of Bedlam.

These are the years and the walls and the door
that shut on a boy that pats the floor
to feel if the world is there and flat.
This is a Jew in a newspaper hat
that dances joyfully down the ward
into the parting seas of board
past the staring sailor
that shakes his watch
that tells the time
of the poet, the man
that lies in the house of Bedlam.

This is the soldier home from the war.
These are the years and the walls and the door
that shut on a boy that pats the floor
to see if the world is round or flat.
This is a Jew in a newspaper hat
that dances carefully down the ward,
walking the plank of a coffin board
with the crazy sailor
that shows his watch
that tells the time
of the wretched man
that lies in the house of Bedlam.

                                                            (1957)

First Death in Nova Scotia

In the cold, cold parlor
my mother laid out Arthur
beneath the chromographs:

Edward, Prince of Wales,
with Princess Alexandra,
and King George with Queen Mary.
Below them on the table
stood a stuffed loon
shot and stuffed by Uncle
Arthur, Arthur's father.

Since Uncle Arthur fired
a bullet into him,
he hadn't said a word.
He kept his own counsel
on his white, frozen lake,
the marble-topped table.
His breast was deep and white,
cold and caressable;
his eyes were red glass,
much to be desired.

"Come," said my mother,
"Come and say goodbye
to your little cousin Arthur."
I was lifted up and given
one lily of the valley
to put in Arthur's hand.
Arthur's coffin was
a little frosted cake,
and the red-eyed loon eyed it
from his white, frozen lake.

Arthur was very small.
He was all white, like a doll
that hadn't been painted yet.
Jack Frost had started to paint him
the way he always painted
the Maple Leaf (Forever).
He had just begun on his hair,
a few red strokes, and then
Jack Frost had dropped the brush
and left him white, forever.

The gracious royal couples
were warm in red and ermine;
their feet were well wrapped up
in the ladies' ermine trains.

They invited Arthur to be
the smallest page at court.
But how could Arthur go,
clutching his tiny lily,
with his eyes shut up so tight
and the roads deep in snow ?

(1962)

ROBERT BLY

The Executive's Death

Merchants have multiplied more than the stars of heaven.
Half the population are like the long grasshoppers
That sleep in the bushes in the cool of the day:
The sound of their wings is heard at noon, muffled, near
    the earth.
The crane handler dies, the taxi-driver dies, slumped over
In his taxi. Meanwhile, high in the air, executives
Walk on cool floors, and suddenly fall:
Dying they dream they are lost in a snowstorm in moun-
    tains,
On which they crashed, carried at night by great machines.
As he lies on the wintry slope, cut off and dying,
A pine stump talks to him of Goethe and Jesus.
Commuters arrive in Hartford at dusk like moles
Or hares flying from a fire behind them,
And the dusk in Hartford is full of their sighs;
Their trains come through the air like a dark music,
Like the sound of horns, the sound of thousands of small
    wings.

(1960)

After the Industrial Revolution,

All Things Happen at Once

Now we enter a strange world, where the Hessian Christmas
Still goes on, and Washington has not reached the other
    shore;

69

The Whiskey Boys
Are gathering again on the meadows of Pennsylvania
And the Republic is still sailing on the open sea.

I saw a black angel in Washington dancing
On a barge, saying, Let us now divide kennel dogs
And hunting dogs; Henry Cabot Lodge, in New York,
Talking of sugar cane in Cuba; Ford,
In Detroit, drinking mother's milk;
Henry Cabot Lodge, saying, "Remember the Maine!"
Ford, saying, "History is bunk!"
And Wilson saying, "What is good for General Motors . . ."

Who is it, singing? Don't you hear singing?
It is the dead of Cripple Creek;
Coxey's army
Like turkeys are singing from the tops of trees!
And the Whiskey Boys are drunk outside Philadelphia.

(1962)

Watching Television

Sounds are heard too high for ears,
From the body cells there is an answering bay;
Soon the inner streets fill with a chorus of barks.

We see the landing craft coming in,
The black car sliding to a stop,
The Puritan killer loosening his guns.

Wild dogs tear off noses and eyes
And run off with them down the street—
The body tears off its own arms and throws them into the
    air.

The detective draws fifty-five million people into his
    revolver,
Who sleep restlessly as in an air raid in London;
Their backs become curved in the sloping dark.

The filaments of the soul slowly separate;
The spirit breaks, a puff of dust floats up;
Like a house in Nebraska that suddenly explodes.

(1963)

Those Being Eaten by America

The cry of those being eaten by America,
Others pale and soft being stored for later eating

And Jefferson
Who saw hope in new oats

The wild houses go on
With long hair growing from between their toes
The feet at night get up
And run down the long white roads by themselves

The dams reverse themselves and want to go stand alone in
    the desert

Ministers who dive headfirst into the earth
The pale flesh
Spreading guiltily into new literatures

That is why these poems are so sad
The long dead running over the fields

The mass sinking down
The light in children's faces fading at six or seven

The world will soon break up into small colonies of the
    saved

(1966)

The Day the Tide

The day the tide went out,
and stayed, not just at Mean
Low Water or Spring Ebb,
but out, cut all the way
perhaps as far as Spain,
until the bay was empty,

it left us looking down
at what the sea, and our
reflections on it, had
(for generations of
good fish, and wives fair
as vessels) saved us from.

We watched our fishboats ground
themselves, limp-chained in mud;
careened, as we still are
(though they lie far below us)
against this sudden slope
that once looked like a harbor.

We're level, still, with islands,
or what's still left of them
now that treelines invert:
the basin foothills rock
into view like defeated castles,
with green and a flagpole on top.

Awkward as faith itself,
herons still stand on one leg
in trenches the old tide cut;

maybe they know what the moon's
about, working its gravity
off the Atlantic shelf.

Blind as starfish, we
look into our dried reservoir
of disaster: fouled trawls, old
ships hung-up on their mon-
ument ribs; the skeletons
of which our fathers were master.

We salt such bones down with self-
consolation, left to survive,
if we will, on this emptied slope.
Réunion Radio keeps reporting
how our ebb finally flooded
the terrible Cape of Good Hope.

(1966)

Hard Country

In hard
country each white
house, separated
by granite outcrop
from each white
house, pitches
its roofline
against the hard sky.
Hand-split
shakes, fillet
and face plank, clap-
board, flashing
and lintel: every
fit part over-
laps from the ridge
board on down, wind
tight and water
tight, down
to the sideyard back
door, shut against
eavesdrop.

Nobody
takes storm windows
off: each blank
pane, framed by
its own sharp
moulding, looks out
without shutters at
juniper, granite,
and hackmatack.
Granite takes
nothing for granted,
hackmatack's spiney;
junipers mind their
ledged roots. Save
for a day when its back
door opens on lilac,
there isn't a house
in this country
that sleeps or
wakes.

In hard
country Orion,
come summer, hunts
late; but belts its
prime stars all
winter when sun
is short: each white
house, separated
by granite outcrop
from each white
house, pitches
its private roof
against horizon
and season; each white
clapboard, wind
tight and water
tight, juts
against weather
its own four inches
of shadow and
light.

(1967)

EDGAR BOWERS

The Stoic: for Laura von Courten

All winter long you listened for the boom
Of distant cannon wheeled into their place.
Sometimes outside beneath a bombers' moon
You stood alone to watch the searchlights trace

Their careful webs against the boding sky,
While miles away on Munich's vacant square
The bombs lunged down with an unruly cry
Whose blast you saw yet could but faintly hear.

And might have turned your eyes upon the gleam
Of a thousand years of snow, where near the clouds
The Alps ride massive to their full extreme,
And season after season glacier crowds

The dark, persistent smudge of conifers.
Or seen beyond the hedge and through the trees
The shadowy forms of cattle on the furze,
Their dim coats white with mist against the freeze.

Or thought instead of other times than these,
Of other countries and of other sights:
Eternal Venice sinking by degrees
Into the very water that she lights;

Reflected in canals, the lucid dome
Of Maria dell' Salute at your feet, —
Her triple spires disfigured by the foam.
Remembered in Berlin the parks, the neat

Footpaths and lawns, the clean spring foliage,
Where just short weeks before, a bomb, unaimed,
Released a frightened lion from its cage,
Which in the mottled dark that trees enflamed

Killed one who hurried homeward from the raid.
And by yourself there standing in the chill
You must, with so much known, have been afraid
And chosen such a mind of constant will,

Which, though all time corrode with constant hurt,
Remains, until it occupies no space,
That which it is; and passionless, inert,
Becomes at last no meaning and no place.

(1956)

TOM CLARK

Sonnet

The orgasm completely
Takes the woman out of her
Self in a wave of ecstasy
That spreads through all of her body.
Her nervous, vascular and muscular
Systems participate in the act.
The muscles of the pelvis contract
And discharge a plug of mucus from the cervix
While the muscular sucking motions of the cervix
Facilitate the incoming of the semen.
At the same time the constriction of the pelvic
Muscles prevents the loss of the semen. The discharge
Makes the acid vaginal lubricant
Alkaline, so as not to destroy the spermatozoa.

(1967)

GREGORY CORSO

Marriage

Should I get married? Should I be good?
Astound the girl next door with my velvet suit and faustus
    hood?
Don't take her to movies but to cemeteries
tell all about werewolf bathtubs and forked clarinets
then desire her and kiss her and all the preliminaries
and she going just so far and I understanding why
not getting angry saying You must feel! It's beautiful to
    feel!
Instead take her in my arms lean against an old crooked
    tombstone
and woo her the entire night the constellations in the sky—

When she introduces me to her parents
back straightened, hair finally combed, strangled by a tie,
should I sit knees together on their 3rd degree sofa
and not ask Where's the bathroom?
How else to feel other than I am,
often thinking Flash Gordon soap—
O how terrible it must be for a young man
seated before a family and the family thinking
We never saw him before! He wants our Mary Lou!
After tea and homemade cookies they ask What do you do
    for a living?
Should I tell them? Would they like me then?
Say All right get married, we're losing a daughter
but we're gaining a son—
And should I then ask Where's the bathroom?

O God, and the wedding! All her family and her friends
and only a handful of mine all scroungy and bearded
just wait to get at the drinks and food—
And the priest! he looking at me as if I masturbated
asking me Do you take this woman for your lawful wedded
    wife?
And I trembling what to say say Pie Glue!
I kiss the bride all those corny men slapping me on the
    back
She's all yours, boy! Ha-ha-ha!
And in their eyes you could see some obscene honeymoon
    going on—
Then all that absurd rice and clanky cans and shoes
Niagara Falls! Hordes of us! Husbands! Wives! Flowers!
    Chocolates!
All streaming into cozy hotels
All going to do the same thing tonight
The indifferent clerk he knowing what was going to happen
The lobby zombies they knowing what
The whistling elevator man he knowing
The winking bellboy knowing
Everybody knowing! I'd be almost inclined not to do any-
    thing!
Stay up all night! Stare that hotel clerk in the eye!
Screaming: I deny honeymoon! I deny honeymoon!
running rampant into those almost climactic suites
yelling Radio belly! Cat shovel!
O I'd live in Niagara forever! in a dark cave beneath the
    Falls
I'd sit there the Mad Honeymooner
devising ways to break marriages, a scourge of bigamy
a saint of divorce—

But I should get married I should be good
How nice it'd be to come home to her
and sit by the fireplace and she in the kitchen
aproned young and lovely wanting my baby
and so happy about me she burns the roast beef
and comes crying to me and I get up from my big papa
    chair
saying Christmas teeth! Radiant brains! Apple deaf!
God what a husband I'd make! Yes, I should get married!
So much to do! like sneaking into Mr. Jones' house late at
    night
and cover his golf clubs with 1920 Norwegian books
Like hanging a picture of Rimbaud on the lawnmower

like pasting Tannu Tuva postage stamps all over the picket
    fence
like when Mrs. Kindhead comes to collect for the Com-
    munity Chest
grab her and tell her There are unfavorable omens in the
    sky!
And when the mayor comes to get my vote tell him
When are you going to stop people killing whales!
And when the milkman comes leave him a note in the
    bottle
Penguin dust, bring me penguin dust, I want penguin
    dust—

Yet if I should get married and it's Connecticut and snow
and she gives birth to a child and I am sleepless, worn,
up for nights, head bowed against a quiet window, the past
    behind me,
finding myself in the most common of situations a trem-
    bling man
knowledged with responsibility not twig-smear nor Roman
    coin soup—
O what would that be like!
Surely I'd give it for a nipple a rubber Tacitus
For a rattle a bag of broken Bach records
Tack Della Francesca all over its crib
Sew the Greek alphabet on its bib
And build for its playpen a roofless Parthenon

No, I doubt I'd be that kind of father
not rural not snow no quiet window
but hot smelly tight New York City
seven flights up, roaches and rats in the walls
a fat Reichian wife screeching over potatoes Get a job!
And five nose running brats in love with Batman
And the neighbors all toothless and dry haired
like those hag masses of the 18th century
all wanting to come in and watch TV
The landlord wants his rent
Grocery store Blue Cross Gas & Electric Knights of
    Columbus
Impossible to lie back and dream Telephone snow, ghost
    parking—
No! I should not get married I should never get married!
But—imagine If I were married to a beautiful sophisticated
    woman
tall and pale wearing an elegant black dress and long black
    gloves

holding a cigarette holder in one hand and a highball in the
  other
and we lived high up in a penthouse with a huge window
from which we could see all of New York and even farther
  on clearer days
No, can't imagine myself married to that pleasant prison
  dream—

O but what above love? I forget love
not that I am incapable of love
it's just that I see love as odd as wearing shoes—
I never wanted to marry a girl who was like my mother
And Ingrid Bergman was always impossible
And there's maybe a girl now but she's already married
And I don't like men and—
but there's got to be somebody!
Because what if I'm 60 years old and not married,
all alone in a furnished room with pee stains on my under-
  wear
and everybody else is married! All the universe married but
  me!

Ah, yet well I know that were a woman possible as I am
  possible
then marriage would be possible—
Like SHE in her lonely alien gaud waiting her Egyptian lover
so I wait—bereft of 2,000 years and the bath of life.

(1960)

HENRI COULETTE

The Black Angel

Where are the people as beautiful as poems,
As calm as mirrors,
With their oceanic longings—
The idler whom reflection loved,
The woman with the iridescent brow?
For I would bring them flowers.

I think of that friend too much moved by music
Who turned to games
And made a game of boredom,
Of that one too much moved by faces
Who turned his face to the wall, and of that marvelous liar
Who turned at last to truth.

They are the past of what was always future.
They speak in tongues,
Silently, about nothing.
They are like old streetcars buried at sea,
In the wrong element, with no place to go. . . .
I will not meet *her* eye,

Although I shall, but here's a butterfly,
And a white flower,
And the moon rising on my nail.
This is the presence of things present,
Where flying woefully is like closing sweetly,
And there is nothing else.

(1963)

At the Telephone Club

We sit, crookbacked, at the bar,
each with his own telephone,
all of us with the same itch.
The tight-assed operator
in the opera stockings
—the only one worth having—
hovers, wisely, out of reach.
She has got all our numbers.

My phone rings: it's the matron
with lost eyes and a horse jaw.
I get rid of her: I have
an ugliness within me,
whole as I am not, a kind
of sleeping cancer. Who needs more?
I listen to the broken
English of an Amsterdam

blonde, seduced in her twelfth year—
it was summer!—by a man
in a Silver Cloud, but I
can have her now for the price
of a taxi ride. I can
have her in a Murphy bed,
while the roaches on the sink
stiffen their fine antennae.

I would, I would, dear lady,
but I have a plane to catch,
one piloted by a sly
Tibetan. I have a date
with some porters in the snow.
I buy her a Grasshopper,
and slip out into the night.
How cold the stars are, how clear!

(1964)

The Family Goldschmitt

Punctual as bad luck,
The aerogramme comes sliding
Under the door, mornings,

Addressed to the Family Goldschmitt.
My landlady puts it there.

My landlady—that blonde aura
Of everything Nordic, Clairol
And kroner, the Dowager Queen
Of Inner and Outer Chaos—
Insists that I am Goldschmitt.

Coulette, I tell her, Coulette,
Fumbling my money-green passport.
I'm American, gentile,
And there's gas escaping somewhere.
She nods and mutters, Goldschmitt.

There is gas escaping somewhere,
And what does that evil stain
On the mattress signify?
Are you sure, are you damned sure,
This isn't the train to Deutschland?

Suddenly, unaccountably,
I sit down and write a letter
To the world, no! to the people
I love, no! to my family, yes!
The Family Goldschmitt.

(1968)

ROBERT CREELEY

The Rain

All night the sound had
come back again,
and again falls
this quiet, persistent rain.

What am I to myself
that must be remembered,
insisted upon
so often? Is it

that never the ease,
even the hardness,
of rain falling
will have for me

something other than this,
something not so insistent—
am I to be locked in this
final uneasiness.

Love, if you love me,
lie next to me.
Be for me, like rain,
the getting out

of the tiredness, the fatuousness, the semi-
lust of intentional indifference.
Be wet
with a decent happiness.

(1959)

The Pool

My embarrassment at his nakedness,
at the pool's edge,
and my wife, with his,
standing, watching—

this was a freedom
not given me who am
more naked,
less contained

by my own white flesh
and the ability
to take quietly
what comes to me.

The sense of myself
separate, grew
a white mirror
in the quiet water

he breaks with his hands
and feet, kicking,
pulls up to land
on the edge by the feet

of these women
who must know
that for each
man is a speech

describes him, makes
the day grow white
and sure, a quietness of water
in the mind,

lets hang, descriptive
as a risk, something
for which he cannot find
a means or time.

(1962)

J. V. CUNNINGHAM

For My Contemporaries

How time reverses
The proud in heart!
I now make verses
Who aimed at art.

But I sleep well.
Ambitious boys
Whose big lines swell
With spiritual noise,

Despise me not!
And be not queasy
To praise somewhat:
Verse is not easy.

But rage who will.
Time that procured me
Good sense and skill
Of madness cured me.

(1942)

Meditation on Statistical Method

Plato, despair!
We prove by norms
How numbers bear
Empiric forms,

How random wrong
Will average right
If time be long
And error slight,

But in our hearts
Hyperbole
Curves and departs
To infinity.

Error is boundless.
Nor hope nor doubt,
Though both be groundless,
Will average out.

(1947)

JAMES DICKEY

The Performance

The last time I saw Donald Armstrong
He was staggering oddly off into the sun,
Going down, of the Philippine Islands.
I let my shovel fall, and put that hand
Above my eyes, and moved some way to one side
That his body might pass through the sun,

And I saw how well he was not
Standing there on his hands,
On his spindle-shanked forearms balanced,
Unbalanced, with his big feet looming and waving
In the great, untrustworthy air
He flew in each night, when it darkened.

Dust fanned in scraped puffs from the earth
Between his arms, and blood turned his face inside out,
To demonstrate its suppleness
Of veins, as he perfected his role.
Next day, he toppled his head off
On an island beach to the south,

And the enemy's two-handed sword
Did not fall from anyone's hands
At that miraculous sight,
As the head rolled over upon
Its wide-eyed face, and fell
Into the inadequate grave

He had dug for himself, under pressure.
Yet I put my flat hand to my eyebrows

Months later, to see him again
In the sun, when I learned how he died,
And imagined him, there,
Come, judged, before his small captors,

Doing all his lean tricks to amaze them—
The back somersault, the kip-up—
And at last, the stand on his hands,
Perfect, with his feet together,
His head down, evenly breathing,
As the sun poured up from the sea

And the headsman broke down
In a blaze of tears, in that light
Of the thin, long human frame
Upside down in its own strange joy,
And, if some other one had not told him,
Would have cut off the feet

Instead of the head,
And if Armstrong had not presently risen
In kingly, round-shouldered attendance,
And then knelt down in himself
Beside his hacked, glittering grave, having done
All things in this life that he could.

                                        (1958)

The Heaven of Animals

Here they are. The soft eyes open.
If they have lived in a wood
It is a wood.
If they have lived on plains
It is grass rolling
Under their feet forever.

Having no souls, they have come,
Anyway, beyond their knowing.
Their instincts wholly bloom
And they rise.
The soft eyes open.

To match them, the landscape flowers,
Outdoing, desperately
Outdoing what is required:
The richest wood,
The deepest field.

For some of these,
It could not be the place
It is, without blood.
These hunt, as they have done
But with claws and teeth grown perfect,

More deadly than they can believe.
They stalk more silently,
And crouch on the limbs of trees,
And their descent
Upon the bright backs of their prey

May take years
In a sovereign floating of joy.
And those that are hunted
Know this as their life,
Their reward: to walk

Under such trees in full knowledge
Of what is in glory above them,
And to feel no fear,
But acceptance, compliance.
Fulfilling themselves without pain

At the cycle's center,
They tremble, they walk
Under the tree,
They fall, they are torn,
They rise, they walk again.

(1961)

Armor

When this is the thing you put on
The world is pieced slowly together
In the power of the crab and the insect.

The make of the eyeball changes
As over your mouth you draw down
A bird's bill made for a man.

As your weight upon earth is redoubled
There is no way of standing alone
More, or no way of being
More with the bound, shining dead.
You have put on what you should wear,
Not into the rattling of battle,

But into a silence where nothing
Threatens but Place itself: the shade
Of the forest, the strange, crowned
Motionless sunlight of Heaven,
With the redbird blinking and shooting
Across the nailed beam of the eyepiece.

In that light, in the wood, in armor,
I look in myself for the being
I was in a life before life
In a glade more silent than breathing,
Where I took off my body of metal
Like a brother whose features I knew

By the feel of their strength on my face
And whose limbs by the shining of mine.
In a vision I fasten him there,
The bright locust shell of my strength
Like a hanged man waiting in Heaven,
And then steal off to my life.

In my home, a night nearer death,
I wake with no shield on my breastbone,
Breathing deep through my sides like an insect,
My closed hand falling and rising
Where it lies like the dead on my heart.
I cannot remember my brother;

Before I was born he went from me
Ablaze with the meaning of typhoid.
In a fever I see him turn slowly
Under the strange, perfect branches
Where somehow I left him to wait
That I might be naked on earth,

His crowned face dazzlingly closed,
His curving limbs giving off
Pure energy into the leaves.
When I give up my hold on my breath
I long to dress deeply at last
In the gold of my waiting brother

Who shall wake and shine on my limbs
As I walk, made whole, into Heaven.
I shall not remember his face
Or my dazed, eternal one
Until I have opened my hand
And touched the grave glow of his breast

To stop the gaunt turning of metal:
Until I have let the still sun
Down into the stare of the eyepiece
And raised its bird's beak to confront
What man is within to live with me
When I begin living forever.

(1962)

Cherrylog Road

Off Highway 106
At Cherrylog Road I entered
The '34 Ford without wheels,
Smothered in kudzu,
With a seat pulled out to run
Corn whiskey down from the hills,

And then from the other side
Crept into an Essex
With a rumble seat of red leather
And then out again, aboard
A blue Chevrolet, releasing
The rust from its other color,

Reared up on three building blocks.
None had the same body heat;

I changed with them inward, toward
The weedy heart of the junkyard,
For I knew that Doris Holbrook
Would escape from her father at noon

And would come from the farm
To seek parts owned by the sun
Among the abandoned chassis,
Sitting in each in turn
As I did, leaning forward
As in a wild stock-car race

In the parking lot of the dead.
Time after time, I climbed in
And out the other side, like
An envoy or movie star
Met at the station by crickets.
A radiator cap raised its head,

Become a real toad or a kingsnake
As I neared the hub of the yard,
Passing through many states,
Many lives, to reach
Some grandmother's long Pierce-Arrow
Sending platters of blindness forth

From its nickel hubcaps
And spilling its tender upholstery
On sleepy roaches,
The glass panel in between
Lady and colored driver
Not all the way broken out,

The back-seat phone
Still on its hook.
I got in as though to exclaim,
"Let us go to the orphan asylum,
John; I have some old toys
For children who say their prayers."

I popped with sweat as I thought
I heard Doris Holbrook scrape
Like a mouse in the southern-state sun
That was eating the paint in blisters
From a hundred car tops and hoods.
She was tapping like code,

Loosening the screws,
Carrying off headlights,
Sparkplugs, bumpers,
Cracked mirrors and gear-knobs,
Getting ready, already,
To go back with something to show

Other than her lips' new trembling
I would hold to me soon, soon,
Where I sat in the ripped back seat
Talking over the interphone,
Praying for Doris Holbrook
To come from her father's farm

And to get back there
With no trace of me on her face
To be seen by her red-haired father
Who would change, in the squalling barn,
Her back's pale skin with a strop,
Then lay for me

In a bootlegger's roasting car
With a string-triggered 12-gauge shotgun
To blast the breath from the air.
Not cut by the jagged windshields,
Through the acres of wrecks she came
With a wrench in her hand,

Through dust where the blacksnake dies
Of boredom, and the beetle knows
The compost has no more life.
Someone outside would have seen
The oldest car's door inexplicably
Close from within:

I held her and held her and held her,
Convoyed at terrific speed
By the stalled, dreaming traffic around us,
So the blacksnake, stiff
With inaction, curved back
Into life, and hunted the mouse

With deadly overexcitement,
The beetles reclaimed their field
As we clung, glued together,
With the hooks of the seat springs

Working through to catch us red-handed
Amidst the gray, breathless batting

That burst from the seat at our backs.
We left by separate doors
Into the changed, other bodies
Of cars, she down Cherrylog Road
And I to my motorcycle
Parked like the soul of the junkyard

Restored, a bicycle fleshed
With power, and tore off
Up Highway 106, continually
Drunk on the wind in my mouth,
Wringing the handlebar for speed,
Wild to be wreckage forever.

(1963)

The Common Grave

I

Some sit and stare
In an unknown direction, though most lie still,
Knowing that every season
Must be wintered.

II

The mover of mists and streams
Is usually in the weeds
By twilight, taking slowly
A dark dedicated field-shape.

III

Of all those who are under,
Many are looking over
Their shoulder, although it is only one leap
To beyond-reason gold, only one
Breath to the sun's great city.
All ages of mankind unite
Where it is dark enough.

IV

The midstrides of out-of-shape runners,
The discarded strokes of bad swimmers,
Open-mouthed at the wrong time—
All these are hooked wrongly together.
A rumor runs through them like roots:
They must try even harder
To bring into their vast,
Indiscriminate embrace
All of humanity.

V

In someone's hand an acorn
Pulses, thinking
It is only one leap,
Only one.

VI

In the field by twilight are
The faller in leaves through October,
The white-headed flyer in thistles
Finding out secret currents of air,
The raiser of mists from the creekbed,
A fish extending his body
Through all the curves of the river,
The incredible moon in the voice box
Of dogs on All Souls' Night.

VII

All creatures tumbled together
Get back in the wildest arms
No single thing but each other,
Hear only sounds like train sounds,
Cattle sounds, earth-shakers.

VIII

The mover of all things struggles
In the green-crowded, green-crowned nightmare
Of a great king packed in an acorn.
A train bends round a curve
Like a fish. An oak tree breaks
Out and shoves for the moonlight,
Bearing leaves which shall murmur for years,
Dumfoundedly, like mouths opened all at once
At just the wrong time to be heard,
    Others, others.

                                                   (1964)

WILLIAM DICKEY

Canonical Hours

The ladies of the morning gauze their mouths
With little filmy napkins and are still.
Their husbands live in shells of simple truths,
Perennial explosions of the will.

And through the morns the ample ladies gather
The ribbons of their lives and press them clear.
They are intrinsic selves and need no other
Posture to arrive and interfere.

So through the layers of the afternoons
They warm themselves like giant oven cakes,
And at the patter of enamel spoons
Each stirs and momentarily awakes,

Joining herself in union with her kind,
Feeling the comfortable corset of their thought;
She moves like pilot fish among her mind
Seeking the aboriginal cachalot.

The ladies sit at evening satiate.
Their husbands carve the dressing and the bird,
The day, the napkin, and the carving plate
To bits that are too little to be heard.

(1959)

ALAN DUGAN

On Hurricane Jackon

Now his nose's bridge is broken, one eye
will not focus and the other is a stray;
trainers whisper in his mouth while one ear
listens to itself, clenched like a fist;
generally shadow-boxing in a smoky room,
his mind hides like the aching boys
who lost a contest in the Pan-Hellenic games
and had to take the back roads home,
but someone else, his perfect youth,
laureled in newsprint and dollar bills,
triumphs forever on the great white way
to the statistical Sparta of the champs.

(1956)

How We Heard the Name

The river brought down
dead horses, dead men
and military debris,
indicative of war
or official acts upstream,
but it went by, it all
goes by, that is the thing
about the river. Then
a soldier on a log

99

went by. He seemed drunk
and we asked him Why
had he and this junk
come down to us so
from the past upstream.
"Friends," he said, "the great
Battle of Granicus
has just been won
by all of the Greeks except
the Lacedaemonians and
myself: this is a joke
between me and a man
named Alexander, whom
all of you ba-bas
will hear of as a god."

(1956)

Wall, Cave, and Pillar Statements, After Asôka

In order to perfect all readers
the statements should be carved
on rock walls, on cave walls,
and on the sides of pillars so
the charm of their instruction can
affect the mountain climbers near
the cliffs, the plainsmen near
the pillars, and the city people near
the caves they go to on vacations.

The statements should, and in a fair
script, spell out the right text and gloss
of the Philosopher's jocular remark. Text:
"Honesty is the best policy." Gloss:
"He means not 'best' but 'policy,'
(this is the joke of it) whereas in fact
        Honesty is Honesty, Best
        is Best, and Policy is Policy,
        the three terms being not
        related, but here loosely allied.

What is more important is that 'is'
is, but the rock-like truth of the text
resides in the 'the'. The 'the' is The.
      By this means the amusing sage
      has raised or caused to be raised
      the triple standard in stone:
the single is too simple for life,
the double is mere degrading hypocrisy,
but the third combines the first two
in a possible way, and contributes
something unsayable of its own:
this is the pit, nut, seed or stone
of the fruit when the fruit has been
digested: It is good to do good for the wrong
      reason, better to do good for the good
      reason, and best of all to do good
      good: i.e.: when the doer and doee
      and whatever passes between them
      are beyond all words like 'grace'
      or 'anagogic insight,' or definitions like
      'particular instance of a hoped-at-law,'
      and which the rocks alone can convey.
This is the real reason for the rock walls,
the cave walls and pillars, and not the base
desires for permanence and display
that the teacher's conceit suggests."

      That is the end of the statements, but,
      in order to go on a way after the end
      so as to make up for having begun
      after the beginning, and thus to come around
      to it in order to include the whole thing,
add: "In some places the poignant slogan,
'Morality is a bad joke like everything else'
may be written or not, granted that space
exists for the vulgar remarks, the dates,
initials and hearts of lovers, and all
other graffiti of the prisoners of this world."

(1961)

ALVIN FEINMAN

November Sunday Morning

And the light, a wakened heyday of air
Tuned low and clear and wide,
A radiance now that would emblaze
And veil the most golden horn
Or any entering of a sudden clearing
To a standing, astonished, revealed . . .

That the actual streets I loitered in
Lay lit like fields, or narrow channels
About to open to a burning river;
All brick and window vivid and calm
As though composed in a rigid water
No random traffic would dispel . . .

As now through the park, and across
The chill nailed colors of the roofs,
And on near trees stripped bare,
Corrected in the scant remaining leaf
To their severe essential elegance,
Light is the all-exacting good,

That dry, forever virile stream
That wipes each thing to what it is,
The whole, collage and stone, cleansed
To its proper pastoral . . .

                          I sit
And smoke, and linger out desire.

(1963)

EDWARD FIELD

The Dirty Floor

The floor is dirty:
Not only the soot from the city air
But a surprising amount of hair litters the room.
It is hard to keep up with. Even before
The room is all swept up it is dirty again.

We are shedding more than we realize.
The amount of hair I've shed so far
Could make sixty of those great rugs
The Duke of China killed his weavers for,
And strangle half the sons of Islam.

Time doesn't stop even while I scrub the floor
Though it seems that the mind empties like a bathtub,
That all the minds of the world go down the drain
Into the sewer; but hair keeps falling
And not for a moment can the floor be totally clean.

What is left of us after years of shitting and shedding?
Are we whom our mothers bore or some stranger now
With the name of son, but nameless,
Continually relearning the same words
That mean, with each retelling, less.

He whom you knew is a trail of leavings round the world.
Renewal is a lie: Who I was has no more kisses.
Barbara's fierce eyes were long ago swept up from her floor.
A stranger goes by the name of Marianne; it is not she,
Nor for that matter was the Marianne I knew

The floor having accumulated particles of myself
I call it dirty; dirty, the streets thick with the dead;
Dirty, the thick air I am used to breathing.
I am alive at least. Quick, who said that?
Give me the broom. The leftovers sweep the leavings away.

(1960)

An Event

Before the blond horsemen rode into our village
We held a hasty council to decide how to greet them.
It was planned that we would hide the women in the woods,
Cover our weapons with our sleeping mats in the huts
And greeting them politely
Neither encourage them to stay nor leave.

But when the hoofs raised a sudden dust in the square
Our hearts were beating so wildly
That nothing happened as we had planned it.
We came out all smiles throwing our weapons at their feet
And we feasted them, offering them our gods
And brought them our women
Whom they accepted with thin curved smiles.
And in the morning they drew a map of the area,
Counted the inhabitants and livestock,
And rode away with our silver ornaments.

Life went on as before and yet
Did we imagine it or were there fewer births than before?
The corn grew smaller
And not that things had been prosperous
(Our living had always been a scratching in the dust)
But year by year things seemed to diminish.
Now the young men go off to work in the factories
Putting on tight outlandish trousers and cutting their hair.
Even the women leave: They slip off at night
And return to visit later, slim and strangely garbed,
Talking without opening their mouths wide.

Perhaps now this is only a place to come home to,
To repeat the stories that everyone knows by heart,

And to look at the dusty flowers
And the children who will be going away soon
Playing naked and dirty among the chickens.

(1961)

The Bride of Frankenstein

The Baron has decided to mate the monster,
to breed him perhaps,
in the interests of pure science, his only god.

So he goes up into his laboratory
which he has built in the tower of the castle
to be as near the interplanetary forces as possible,
and puts together the prettiest monster-woman you ever saw
with a body like a pin-up girl
and hardly any stitching at all
where he sewed on the head of a raped and murdered beauty
    queen.

He sets his liquids burping, and coils blinking and buzzing,
and waits for an electric storm to send through the equip-
    ment
the spark vital for life.
The storm breaks over the castle
and the equipment really goes crazy
like a kitchen full of modern appliances
as the lightning juice starts oozing right into that pretty
    corpse.

He goes to get the monster
so he will be right there when she opens her eyes,
for she might fall in love with the first thing she sees
as ducklings do.
That monster is already straining at his chains and slurping
ready to go right to it:
He has been well prepared for coupling
by his pinching leering keeper who's been saying for weeks,
"You gonna get a little nookie, kid,"
or "How do you go for some poontag, baby."
All the evil in him is focused on this one thing now
as he is led into her very presence.

She awakens slowly,
she bats her eyes,
she gets up out of the equipment,
and finally she stands in all her seamed glory,
a monster princess with a hairdo like a fright-wig,
lightning flashing in the background
like a halo and a wedding veil,
like a photographer snapping pictures of great moments.

She stands and stares with her electric eyes,
beginning to understand that in this life too
she was just another body to be raped.

The monster is ready to go:
He roars with joy at the sight of her,
so they let him loose and he goes right for those knockers.
And she starts screaming to break your heart
and you realize that she was just born:
In spite of her big tits she was just a baby.

But her instincts are right—
rather death than that green slobber:
She jumps off the parapet.
And then the monster's sex drive goes wild.
Thwarted, it turns to violence, demonstrating sublimation
    crudely,
and he wrecks the lab, those burping acids and buzzing coils,
overturning the control panel so the equipment goes off like
    a bomb,
the stone castle crumbling and crashing in the storm
destroying them all . . . perhaps.

Perhaps somehow the Baron got out of that wreckage of his
    dreams
with his evil intact if not his good looks
and more wicked than ever went on with his thrilling career.

And perhaps even the monster lived
to roam the earth, his desire still ungratified,
and lovers out walking in shadowy and deserted places
will see his shape loom up over them, their doom—
and children sleeping in their beds
will wake up in the dark night screaming
as his hideous body grabs them.

                                        (1966)

DONALD FINKEL

Hunting Song

The fox he came lolloping, lolloping,
Lolloping. His eyes were bright,
His ears were high.
He was like death at the end of a string
When he came to the hollow
Log. He ran in one side
And out of the other. O
He was sly.

The hounds they came tumbling, tumbling,
Tumbling. Their heads were low,
Their eyes were red.
The sound of their breath was louder than death
When they came to the hollow
Log. They boiled at one end
But a bitch found the scent. O
They were mad.

The hunter came galloping, galloping,
Galloping. All damp was his mare
From her hooves to her mane.
His coat and his mouth were redder than death
When he came to the hollow
Log. He took in the rein
And over he went. O
He was fine.

The log he just lay there, alone in
The clearing. No fox nor hound

Nor mounted man
Saw his black round eyes in their perfect disguise
(As the ends of a hollow
Log). He watched death go through him,
Around him and over him. O
He was wise.

(1955)

Letter to My Daughter
at the End of Her Second Year

Now it is only hours before you wake
to your third year and to the gifts that lie
piled on the coffee-table, yet I keep
the only gift that it is mine to make.

But how can I offer, among the paper hats,
among the balloons and coloring books and dolls
gleaming with golden hair and the sweet primaries,
this shabby vision of myself seeking,
among these gestures and images, myself?
My gift is wrought, not in the fire of love,
but in the consuming egotism of night
that blots out daughter, lover, wife and friend,
a time to take, my darling, not to give.

So smear this book with the sweetness of your fingers,
and mock with your eyes the brightness of this doll;
come learn our urgent language and put on
mask after mask to match our smiling faces,
seeking what gestures and images may serve
to charm the tall world down from which we smile.

Standing there in the shadow of our gifts,
may you forgive the love that lugged them home,
then turn and take the gift I could not give—
the language of childhood looking for itself
under a mountain of masks and dolls—the poem.

(1962)

The Flagpole Sitter

1

Slowly the world contracts about my ears.
First morality goes, then love, then fear
of my death; then beauty, which is bearable truth,
then truth unbearable; then pleasure, then pain.
Rocking at last in the irreducible sun,
slowly, more slow, more slow, I leave behind
even the memory that I was ever a man.

2

Like a shadow passing over the brain, from back to front,
a cool silver, a heat that looks like coolness as it runs,
molten, over the dipping ladle; this is not sleep,
but a gliding darkness, a shadow conscious of nothing
but itself, yet knowing that so intensely, it is bright.

3

When the wind blows,
a few leaves fall to the ground;
where have I been?

4

From those fat green burghers, nodding their hundred chins
at the wind's words, conspiratorial whispers,
I purchased nothing; I passed among their wares
taking nothing, wanting nothing, looking for the exit.
How did I find that city of mossy gutters?
Keeping always to my room, I was poorly prepared,
soothed by the safety of angles, the wisdom of corners
where three unruffled surfaces agree.
One moment of absence, and down the alley,
before me and behind, that army of
obscene salesmen, vegetable, complacent,
plucking at my shirt with their green fingers.

5

Seeing it, I am no longer part of it.
Part of it no longer, I forfeit the right
to be a paradigm. Forfeiting that right,
I became totally free.

6

I have begun to know the true weight of my body.
Slowly the fluid settles in my legs;
it seeps into my shoes, great blisters form,
my final illness. My rivers run into the air;
at the last, a dry leaf on a barren tree,
I shall release my hold, and be blown away.

(1964)

A Joyful Noise

Let each man first seek out his proper totem;
let each man come in his turn, with his cross and his treasure,
let him cleave to his wife, or his enemy, or his car,
let him praise the holy fool who first introduced them;
for whom Christopher has joined together, let no man sunder,
for he has packed us cheek to cheek like tiles on a bathroom floor,
Job by his worm, Balaam by his ass, our scrubbed and gleaming faces turned toward heaven.

Let Christopher praise with a cat,
for it sits on idols;
let Jeoffry praise with Christopher, poor Christopher!
for he loved his prank, nor spat without provocation, and the rat has bit him;
let Samuel Johnson pray in the street with a tambourine.

Let Gogol pray with his nose,
let Van Gogh pray with an ear,
let Poe praise with his liver,
let Pound praise with a curse,
let Blake praise with a handful of dust in our faces,
let Finkel praise with ashes, for his fire is out.

Let Finkel's wife bless patiently with Finkel,
for a high little star provoketh wonder;
let Finkel's children bless with the best they can get:

let all men's children bless,
let them choke the streets, and the balconies, and the
    squares,
for the churches will be packed, no room for kneeling;
let them fill their lungs as they can, under the circumstances,
let them all begin to holler at once, according to their
    custom, like one vast apocalyptic Recess,
let each one and his brother turn up his scrubbed, gleam-
    ing face to the sun, and yell.

(1966)

Hands

The poem makes truth a little more disturbing,
like a good bra, lifts it and holds it out
in both hands. (In some of the flashier stores
there's a model with the hands stitched on, in red or black.)

Lately the world you wed, for want of such hands,
sags in the bed beside you like a tired wife.
For want of such hands, the face of the moon is bored,
the tree does not stretch and yearn, nor the groin tighten.

Devious or frank, in any case,
the poem is calculated to arouse.
Lean back and let its hands play freely on you:
there comes a moment, lifted and aroused,
when the two of you are equally beautiful.

(1966)

ISABELLA GARDNER

Nightmare

A sleeping woman dreams she wakes
Into a surging room of shrieks
and shapes. In the frantic room a red
haired woman looms . . . on her bent arm
there sleeps a girl's carved wooden head
A doll-sized nursing bottle nipples her huge palm
Both head and bottle drop and leeringly she
beckons. The dreamer screams her hatred
of the leering shape. Scrabbling for safety
the dreamer flounders on the floor.
The leerer pounces from behind the door.
The struggling dreamer stands
The dreamer lifts and clenches both her hands
The dreamer rips the red curls
in handfuls from that hateful head and hurls
the hairy gobbets at those manic eyes
The leerer dreadfully diminishes in size
She shrinks and shrinks into a little child.
The screaming dreamer beats the dwindling child.
The dreamer lifts a chair to smash that leering child.
Nothing at all remains. Not hag nor child.
No traces and no tokens.
The red-haired dreamer wakens.

(1961)

JACK GILBERT

The Abnormal Is Not Courage

The Poles rode out from Warsaw against the German
Tanks on horses. Rode knowing, in sunlight, with sabers.
A magnitude of beauty that allows me no peace.
And yet this poem would lessen that day. Question
The bravery. Say it's not courage. Call it a passion.
Would say courage isn't that. Not at its best.
It was impossible, and with form. They rode in sunlight.
Were mangled. But I say courage is not the abnormal.
Not the marvelous act. Not Macbeth with fine speeches.
The worthless can manage in public, or for the moment.
It is too near the whore's heart: the bounty of impulse,
And the failure to sustain even small kindness.
Not the marvelous act, but the evident conclusion of being.
Not strangeness, but a leap forward of the same quality.
Accomplishment. The even loyalty. But fresh.
Not the Prodigal Son, nor Faustus. But Penelope.
The thing steady and clear. Then the crescendo.
The real form. The culmination. And the exceeding.
Not the surprise. The amazed understanding. The marriage,
Not the month's rapture. Not the exception. The beauty
That is of many days. Steady and clear.
It is the normal excellence, of long accomplishment.

(1962)

113

ALLEN GINSBERG

A Supermarket in California

What thoughts I have of you tonight, Walt Whitman, for I walked down the sidestreets under the trees with a headache self-conscious looking at the full moon.

In my hungry fatigue, and shopping for images, I went into the neon fruit supermarket, dreaming of your enumerations!

What peaches and what penumbras! Whole families shopping at night! Aisles full of husbands! Wives in the avocados, babies in the tomatoes—and you, García Lorca, what were you doing down by the watermelons?

I saw you, Walt Whitman, childless, lonely old grubber, poking among the meats in the refrigerator and eyeing the grocery boys.

I heard you asking questions of each: Who killed the pork chops? What price bananas? Are you my Angel?

I wandered in and out of the brilliant stacks of cans following you, and followed in my imagination by the store detective.

We strode down the open corridors together in our solitary fancy tasting artichokes, possessing every frozen delicacy, and never passing the cashier.

Where are we going, Walt Whitman? The doors close in an hour. Which way does your beard point tonight?

(I touch your book and dream of our odyssey in the supermarket and feel absurd.)

Will we walk all night through solitary streets? The trees add shade to shade, lights out in the houses, we'll both be lonely.

Will we stroll dreaming of the lost America of love past blue automobiles in driveways, home to our silent cottage?

Ah, dear father, graybeard, lonely old courage-teacher, what America did you have when Charon quit poling his ferry and you got out on a smoking bank and stood watching the boat disappear on the black waters of Lethe?

Berkeley 1955

(1956)

America

America I've given you all and now I'm nothing.
America two dollars and twentyseven cents January 17, 1956.
I can't stand my own mind.
America when will we end the human war?
Go fuck yourself with your atom bomb.
I don't feel good don't bother me.
I won't write my poem till I'm in my right mind.
America when will you be angelic?
When will you take off your clothes?
When will you look at yourself through the grave?
When will you be worthy of your million Trotskyites?
America why are your libraries full of tears?
America when will you send your eggs to India?
I'm sick of your insane demands.
When can I go into the supermarket and buy what I need with my good looks?
America after all it is you and I who are perfect not the next world.
Your machinery is too much for me.
You made me want to be a saint.
There must be some other way to settle this argument.
Burroughs is in Tangiers I don't think he'll come back it's sinister.
Are you being sinister or is this some form of practical joke?
I'm trying to come to the point.

I refuse to give up my obsession.
America stop pushing I know what I'm doing.
America the plum blossoms are falling.
I haven't read the newspapers for months, everyday some-
    body goes on trial for murder.
America I feel sentimental about the Wobblies.
America I used to be a communist when I was a kid I'm
    not sorry.
I smoke marijuana every chance I get.
I sit in my house for days on end and stare at the roses
    in the closet.
When I go to Chinatown I get drunk and never get laid.
My mind is made up there's going to be trouble.
You should have seen me reading Marx.
My psychoanalyst thinks I'm perfectly right.
I won't say the Lord's Prayer.
I have mystical visions and cosmic vibrations.
America I still haven't told you what you did to Uncle Max
    after he came over from Russia.

I'm addressing you.
Are you going to let your emotional life be run by Time
    Magazine?
I'm obsessed by Time Magazine.
I read it every week.
Its cover stares at me every time I slink past the corner
    candystore.
I read it in the basement of the Berkeley Public Library.
It's always telling me about responsibility. Businessmen are
    serious. Movie producers are serious. Everybody's seri-
    ous but me.
It occurs to me that I am America.
I am talking to myself again.

Asia is rising against me.
I haven't got a chinaman's chance.
I'd better consider my national resources.
My national resources consist of two joints of marijuana
    millions of genitals an unpublished private literature that
    goes 1400 miles an hour and twentyfive-thousand mental
    institutions.
I say nothing about my prisons nor the millions of under-
    privileged who live in my flowerpots under the light of
    five hundred suns.
I have abolished the whorehouses of France, Tangiers is
    the next to go.

My ambition is to be President despite the fact that I'm a Catholic.

America how can I write a holy litany in your silly mood?

I will continue like Henry Ford my strophes are as individual as his automobiles more so they're all different sexes.

America I will sell you strophes $2500 apiece $500 down on your old strophe

America free Tom Mooney

America save the Spanish Loyalists

America Sacco & Vanzetti must not die

America I am the Scottsboro boys.

America when I was seven momma took me to Communist Cell meetings they sold us garbanzos a handful per ticket a ticket costs a nickel and the speeches were free everybody was angelic and sentimental about the workers it was all so sincere you have no idea what a good thing the party was in 1935 Scott Nearing was a grand old man a real mensch Mother Bloor made me cry I once saw Israel Amter plain. Everybody must have been a spy.

America you don't really want to go to war.

America it's them bad Russians.

Them Russians them Russians and them Chinamen. And them Russians.

The Russia wants to eat us alive. The Russia's power mad. She wants to take our cars from out our garages.

Her wants to grab Chicago. Her needs a Red Readers' Digest. Her wants our auto plants in Siberia. Him big bureaucracy running our fillingstations.

That no good. Ugh. Him make Indians learn read. Him need big black niggers. Hah. Her make us all work sixteen hours a day. Help.

America this is quite serious.

America this is the impression I get from looking in the television set.

America is this correct?

I'd better get right down to the job.

It's true I don't want to join the Army or turn lathes in precision parts factories, I'm nearsighted and psychopathic anyway.

America I'm putting my queer shoulder to the wheel.

(1956)

Sunflower Sutra

I walked on the banks of the tincan banana dock and sat
  down under the huge shade of a Southern Pacific loco-
  motive to look at the sunset over the box house hills
  and cry.
Jack Kerouac sat beside me on a busted rusty iron pole,
  companion, we thought the same thoughts of the soul,
  bleak and blue and sad-eyed, surrounded by the gnarled
  steel roots of trees of machinery.
The oily water on the river mirrored the red sky, sun sank
  on top of final Frisco peaks, no fish in that stream, no
  hermit in those mounts, just ourselves rheumy-eyed and
  hungover like old bums on the riverbank, tired and wily.
Look at the Sunflower, he said, there was a dead gray
  shadow against the sky, big as a man, sitting dry on top
  of a pile of ancient sawdust—
—I rushed up enchanted—it was my first sunflower, memo-
  ries of Blake—my visions—Harlem
and Hells of the Eastern rivers, bridges clanking Joes
  Greasy Sandwiches, dead baby carriages, black treadless
  tires forgotten and unretreaded, the poem of the river-
  bank, condoms & pots, steel knives, nothing stainless,
  only the dank muck and the razor sharp artifacts pass-
  ing into the past—
and the gray Sunflower poised against the sunset, crackly
  bleak and dusty with the smut and smog and smoke of
  olden locomotives in its eye—
corolla of bleary spikes pushed down and broken like a bat-
  tered crown, seeds fallen out of its face, soon-to-be-
  toothless mouth of sunny air, sunrays obliterated on its
  hairy head like a dried wire spiderweb,
leaves stuck out like arms out of the stem, gestures from
  the sawdust root, broke pieces of plaster fallen out of
  . the black twigs, a dead fly in its ear,
Unholy battered old thing you were, my sunflower O my
  soul, I loved you then!
The grime was no man's grime but death and human loco-
  motives,
all that dress of dust, that veil of darkened railroad skin,
  that smog of cheek, that eyelid of black mis'ry, that
  sooty hand or phallus or protuberance of artificial worse-
  than-dirt—industrial—modern—all that civilization
  spotting your crazy golden crown—

and those blear thoughts of death and dusty loveless eyes
and ends and withered roots below, in the home-pile
of sand and sawdust, rubber dollar bills, skin of ma-
chinery, the guts and innards of the weeping coughing
car, the empty lonely tincans with their rusty tongues
alack, what more could I name, the smoked ashes of
some cock cigar, the cunts of wheelbarrows and the
milky breasts of cars, wornout asses out of chairs &
sphincters of dynamos—all these

entangled in your mummied roots—and you there standing
before me in the sunset, all your glory in your form!

A perfect beauty of a sunflower! a perfect excellent lovely
sunflower existence! a sweet natural eye to the new hip
moon, woke up alive and excited grasping in the sunset
shadow sunrise golden monthly breeze!

How many flies buzzed round you innocent of your grime,
while you cursed the heavens of the railroad and your
flower soul?

Poor dead flower? when did you forget you were a flower?
when did you look at your skin and decide you were an
impotent dirty old locomotive? the ghost of a locomo-
tive? the specter and shade of a once powerful mad
American locomotive?

You were never no locomotive, Sunflower, you were a
sunflower!

And you Locomotive, you are a locomotive, forget me not!

So I grabbed up the skeleton thick sunflower and stuck it
at my side like a scepter.

and deliver my sermon to my soul, and Jack's soul too, and
anyone who'll listen,

—We're not our skin of grime, we're not our dread bleak
dusty imageless locomotive, we're all beautiful golden
sunflowers inside, we're blessed by our own seed &
golden hairy naked accomplishment-bodies growing into
mad black formal sunflowers in the sunset, spied on by
our eyes under the shadow of the mad locomotive river-
bank sunset Frisko hilly tincan evening sitdown vision.

                                                Berkeley 1955

                                                    (1956)

LOUISE GLÜCK

Cottonmouth Country

Fish bones walked the waves off Hatteras.
And there were other signs
That Death wooed us, by water, wooed us
By land: among the pines
An uncurled cottonmouth that rolled on moss
Reared in the polluted air.
Birth, not death, is the hard loss.
I know. I also left a skin there.

(1967)

PAUL GOODMAN

The Lordly Hudson

"Driver, what stream is it?" I asked, well knowing
it was our lordly Hudson hardly flowing,
"It is our lordly Hudson hardly flowing,"
he said, "under the green-grown cliffs."

Be still, heart! no one needs your passionate
suffrage to select this glory,
this is our lordly Hudson hardly flowing
under the green-grown cliffs.

"Driver! has this a peer in Europe or the East?"
"No no!" he said. Home! home!
be quiet, heart! this is our lordly Hudson
and has no peer in Europe or the East,

this is our lordly Hudson hardly flowing
under the green-grown cliffs
and has no peer in Europe or the East.
Be quiet, heart! home! home!

(1940)

Wellfleet Harbor

Visibly here the tide
Creeps onto shore, almost
which particular lapping

wavelet is the utmost
and then the sea recedes.
The sun in my burning-glass
has moved a millimeter
off-center. Mars is rising
a little further west.
On on the summer
is hurrying away.
Next Thursday is my birthday.
I have already reached
a still point where I stand
hearing my heart pumping
my interior river round,
my friends drifting away,
the shoreline drifting away,
like a ship standing (as we say)
out to sea to sea.
Venus is not so high
when first at dusk she shines
descending with the sun
into the jaws of night.
All days are different days
monotonously flickering
past and faster by,
but there is one single night
and she is called the Night
starlit or dark the Night
my black brain, I have wrapped
myself around me like a coat
yet I am shivering in the night
though flaming like a werewolf in the night.

(1959)

JOHN HAINES

If the Owl Calls Again

at dusk
from the island in the river,
and it's not too cold,

I'll wait for the moon
to rise,
then take wing and glide
to meet him.

We will not speak,
but hooded against the frost
soar above
the alder flats, searching
with tawny eyes.

And then we'll sit
in the shadowy spruce and
pick the bones
of careless mice,

while the long moon drifts
toward Asia
and the river mutters
in its icy bed.

And when morning climbs
the limbs
we'll part without a sound,

fulfilled, floating
homeward as
the cold world awakens.

(1961)

Into the Glacier

With the green lamp of the spirit
of sleeping water
taking us by the hand ...

Deeper and deeper,
A luminous blackness opening
like the wings of a raven—

as though a heavy wind
were rising through all the houses
we ever lived in—

the cold rushing in,
our blankets flying away
into the darkness,
and we, naked and alone,
awakening forever ...

(1964)

DONALD HALL

The Wives

If I said, "Little wives,
shut in your dark
houses, an enormous
tiger lily splits
the roof of each house

in the night, and arranges
the moon to itself,
and only withdraws
just at dawn,"
you would smile,

and think about bright
flowers, and forget
the money and the shopping,
but if I went on, "I only
see your lilies grow

in my happy sleep,
because you have made no gardens
in your blocks of houses
for flowers that come
in the dark night,"

you would suddenly
cry, or pick up a book,
or walk by yourselves
for a long time
on the white sidewalks.

(1962)

KENNETH O. HANSON

Before the Storm

One summer, high in Wyoming
we drove nine miles and paid
to see the great whale, pickled
and hauled on a flatcar crosscountry.
"Throat no bigger'n a orange,"
the man said, in a smell to high
heaven. I wondered how Jonah
could weather that rubbery household
tangled in fish six fathoms down.
Now, beached by the sun and
shunted to a siding, the gray
beast lay dissolving in chains.

It was none of my business
late in the day, while overhead
Stars and Stripes Forever played
in a national breeze, to sidle
past ropes and poke with a ginger
finger, nostril and lip and eye
till Hey! said the man, keep away
from my whale! But too late,
too late. I had made my mark.
The eye in its liquid socket swung,
the jaw clanged shut, and all the way home
through the bone-dry gullies I could
hear the heart as big as a bushel
beat. O weeks I went drowned
while red-winged grasshoppers span
like flying fish, and the mile-high
weather gathered its forces.

(1960)

126

West Lake

Exuberant, restless
Nature, itself unformed
gave form to the lake
and the landscape—
distinctive as
color on plain ground.

In April the water
is jade green, clear
as a monk's eye.
Blue evening hangs
on the hills like dust
on a ripened plum.

The garfish moving
moves its shadow
on the whitewashed wall.
All things are one.
Gull's feather falls
to the fisherman's float.
Small winds. Slant rain.

Far off, the sound
of "Walkin' the Dog"

fading.

(1963)

Take It from Me

Plain truth would never serve
Axarídes. The goddam Greeks
he'd say are a no good people.
You gotta be careful—
a line I'd heard somewhere before
and slowly I got the picture.

I have beautiful eyes for see with
he said almost running down
the bandoleered policeman outside Megalópolis.
Why don't you drive like an American I said.
These village people are stupid he said.
They don't know the tomb of Agamemnon.
Neither did he.

One time I had a fever he said
my mother she took me to a witch
who cut my tongue.
You take me to this witch I said
I'd like to know.
She's outside Phársala he said.

In Phársala then it was *halvas*
we gotta have *halvas*.
Too sweet I said, I don't like sweet.
But it's something we gotta *do* he said
so we stopped and he got six boxes
one for his mother his sister his cousin his girl
and two for him. My money of course.

Greeks never fill the tank he said
so I pushed the car uphill
round a mountain curve at midnight
down into Lárissa.
You stick with me he said
and I stuck, through Argos and Lindos
Lárissa, Phársala and Megalópolis.
It seemed like a month of Sundays
neurasthenics falling from all the olive trees
and the late king coming and going
along Poseidon Street on his way to the airport.

That was the winter
I watched them knocking the old house down.
The Athens News said wolves
ranged the villages in Thessaly.
Friends said the swans on the Thames
were dying by thousands.
You stick with me he said
I'll teach you thinking like a Greek
and I got the picture—pure *paramythy*
nothing but the best and me to pay.
It was the land of opportunity.

But look at it my way.
Here was a new geography
a mind where anything that grows
grows by a kind of tour de force
requiring only unconditional surrender.
Here was the pure perfection of an art.
Nothing like it in the British Museum.

(1965)

ANTHONY HECHT

Third Avenue in Sunlight

Third Avenue in sunlight. Nature's error.
Already the bars are filled and John is there.
Beneath a plentiful lady over the mirror
He tilts his glass in the mild mahogany air.

I think of him when he first got out of college,
Serious, thin, unlikely to succeed;
For several months he hung around the Village,
Boldly T-shirted, unfettered but unfreed.

Now he confides to a stranger, "I was first scout,
And kept my glimmers peeled till after dark.
Our outfit had as its sign a bloody knout,
We met behind the museum in Central Park.

Of course, we were kids." But still those savages,
War-painted, a flap of leather at the loins,
File silently against him. Hostages
Are never taken. One summer, in Des Moines,

They entered his hotel room, tomahawks
Flashing like barracuda. He tried to pray.
Three years of treatment. Occasionally he talks
About how he almost didn't get away.

Daily the prowling sunlight whets its knife
Along the sidewalk. We almost never meet.
In the Rembrandt dark he lifts his amber life.
My bar is somewhat further down the street.

(1959)

"More Light! More Light!"

Composed in the Tower before his execution
These moving verses, and being brought at that time
Painfully to the stake, submitted, declaring thus:
"I implore my God to witness that I have made no crime."

Nor was he forsaken of courage, but the death was horrible,
The sack of gunpowder failing to ignite.
His legs were blistered sticks on which the black sap
Bubbled and burst as he howled for the Kindly Light.

And that was but one, and by no means one of the worst;
Permitted at least his pitiful dignity;
And such as were by made prayers in the name of Christ,
That shall judge all men, for his soul's tranquility.

We move now to outside a German wood.
Three men are there commanded to dig a hole
In which the two Jews are ordered to lie down
And be buried alive by the third, who is a Pole.

Not light from the shrine at Weimar beyond the hill
Nor light from heaven appeared. But he did refuse.
A Lüger settled back deeply in its glove.
He was ordered to change places with the Jews.

Much casual death had drained away their souls.
The thick dirt mounted toward the quivering chin.
When only the head was exposed the order came
To dig him out again and to get back in.

No light, no light in the blue Polish eye.
When he finished a riding boot packed down the earth.
The Lüger hovered lightly in its glove.
He was shot in the belly and in three hours bled to death.

No prayers or incense rose up in those hours
Which grew to be years, and every day came mute
Ghosts from the ovens, sifting through crisp air,
And settled upon his eyes in a black soot.

(1961)

Tarantula or the Dance of Death

During the plague I came into my own.
It was a time of smoke-pots in the house
Against infection. The blind head of bone
          Grinned its abuse

Like a good democrat at everyone.
Runes were recited daily, charms were applied.
That was the time I came into my own.
          Half Europe died.

The symptoms are a fever and dark spots
First on the hands, then on the face and neck,
But even before the body, the mind rots.
          You can be sick

Only a day with it before you're dead.
But the most curious part of it is the dance.
The victim goes, in short, out of his head.
          A sort of trance

Glazes the eyes, and then the muscles take
His will away from him, the legs begin
Their funeral jig, the arms and belly shake
          Like souls in sin.

Some, caught in these convulsions, have been known
To fall from windows, fracturing the spine.
Others have drowned in streams. The smooth head-stone,
          The box of pine,

Are not for the likes of these. Moreover, flame
Is powerless against contagion.
That was the black winter when I came
          Into my own.

                             (1962)

A Hill

In Italy, where this sort of thing can occur,
I had a vision once—though you understand
It was nothing at all like Dante's, or the visions of saints,
And perhaps not a vision at all. I was with some friends,
Picking my way through a warm sunlit piazza
In the early morning. A clear fretwork of shadows

From huge umbrellas littered the pavement and made
A sort of lucent shallows in which was moored
A small navy of carts. Books, coins, old maps,
Cheap landscapes and ugly religious prints
Were all on sale. The colors and noise
Like the flying hands were gestures of exultation,
So that even the bargaining
Rose to the ear like a voluble godliness.
And then, when it happened, the noises suddenly stopped,
And it got darker; pushcarts and people dissolved
And even the great Farnese Palace itself
Was gone, for all its marble; in its place
Was a hill, mole-colored and bare. It was very cold,
Close to freezing, with a promise of snow.
The trees were like old ironwork gathered for scrap
Outside a factory wall. There was no wind,
And the only sound for a while was the little click
Of ice as it broke in the mud under my feet.
I saw a piece of ribbon snagged on a hedge,
But no other sign of life. And then I heard
What seemed the crack of a rifle. A hunter, I guessed;
At least I was not alone. But just after that
Came the soft and papery crash
Of a great branch somewhere unseen falling to earth.

And that was all, except for the cold and silence
That promised to last forever, like the hill.

Then prices came through, and fingers, and I was restored
To the sunlight and my friends. But for more than a week
I was scared by the plain bitterness of what I had seen.
All this happened about ten years ago,
And it hasn't troubled me since, but at last, today,
I remembered that hill; it lies just to the left
Of the road north of Poughkeepsie; and as a boy
I stood before it for hours in wintertime.

                                                        (1964)

"It Out-Herods Herod, Pray You Avoid It"

> Tonight my children hunch
> Toward their Western, and are glad
> As, with a Sunday punch,
> The Good casts out the Bad.

And in their fairy tales
The warty giant and witch
Get sealed in doorless jails
And the match-girl strikes it rich.

I've made myself a drink.
The giant and witch are set
To bust out of the clink
When my children have gone to bed.

For the wicked have grown strong,
Their numbers mock at death,
Their cow brings forth its young,
Their bull engendereth.

Their very fund of strength,
Satan, bestrides the globe;
He stalks its breadth and length
And finds out even Job.

Yet by quite other laws
My children make their case;
Half God, half Santa Claus,
But with my voice and face,

A hero comes to save
The poorman, beggarman, thief,
And make the world behave
And put an end to grief.

And that their sleep be sound
I say this childermas
Who could not, at one time,
Have saved them from the gas.

(1966)

DARYL HINE

Plain Fare

How slow they are awakening, these trees,
  This earth, how late they sleep
Naked. Past the window of the bus
Where wide and nameless rivers interrupt
The plain that divided us, they stretch
Like determined sluggards muttering, "Not Yet."

America, the work of a magic realist,
  Make of it what you will:
The vast and apparently pointless construction
By whom—when—for what purpose begun?
The little figures beside it to give an idea of scale;
And behind, before, about like a canvas the plain.
It is disquieting to think of anyone living here,
  And the lights one sees
Rare in the darkness to unbelievable lives belong.
We too flash on their incredulity and are gone,
Cowboy and farmer buried alive in their nest,
And me sitting up all night reading *Villette*.

Sometime before dawn another stop, for breakfast—
  Country ham
And eggs—where the unfledged travellers

135

Wait, their faces turned from one another
In a fine balance between friend and enemy, equally name-
    less,
For coffee, with weary contempt and despair.

The waitress is slow, friendly but inefficient,
        The boy is impressed,
He only knows why, with these sorry unwordly exiles.
Both smile, harried and shy. It is time,
There are miles to go before morning, but no hurry.
We have ceased to believe in arrival. I ask for tea
And must decide between milk and lemon. "Voyage"
        I used to think had
To derive from the French verb *voir* "to see,"
But blind as the best I stumbled to my seat
On the bus, take up *Villette*, switch on the overhead
Light and light yet one more cigarette.

—To be puzzled and a trifle disappointed.
        The eponymous heroine
Turns out to be a place called "little city"
—Why not just Brussels, which obviously it is?
This is the saddest book, I think, I ever read. On
The cover it says that Charlotte Brontë,
After the death of Emily, Anne and Branwell
And before her marriage and death a year after,
"Wrote this history of lost love."
        And when I look up
Mine is the only light still burning in the bus
Where my faceless fellow travellers and, outside, the
        country slumber.

. . . It is day, and the lights and roadside structures have
    vanished.
The novel is finished and the reasons no longer exist
        For my visit. From heaven
Out of sight an audible jet
Covers in a mere hour or so
The way that I could not afford to go.

                                              (1964)

The Trout

The water my prison shatters in a prism
As I leap alone the dying falls,
Cruel gasps of air, the musical chasm
Intrigue me with their broken intervals.

Deep in the noon of motionless canals
I dreamt away my pale reality
Till stirred by her immortal voice who calls
To the heights of the mountain and the depths of the sea.

I lean on air as prisoners on time
Not to let them down, my impetus
Only to the second hand sublime,
From every point of view ridiculous,

To climb the stair of stone where I was spawned,
Where ponds are oceans and the rapids give
Foretaste of the unbreathable beyond.
I try, I fall, I wriggle loose, I live

Drop by drop against the stream I am,
And in death's little cataract belong
Like Tristan to the torrent and the dam,
Liquid chamber music and still current song,

As I was laid upon the deep sea floor,
Part of the faded pattern of the carpet,
Or spilt like the sperm the kissing fish ignore
Held in each others' scales as in a net.

Yes I exist, a memory in man
And beast and bird, a universal wish
For the watery world where life began
And your angelic avatar the fish:

Ambitious, ghastly, with protuberant eyes
Or suspended like a living bathysphere,
I negotiate the steps of paradise
Leaping to measures that I cannot hear.

(1967)

DANIEL HOFFMAN

Exploration

I am who the trail took,
nose of whom I followed,
woodwit I confided in
through thorned-and-briared hallows;
favoring my right side for
clouds the sun had hemmed in.
Behind the North I sought daystar,
bore down highroads hidden
to undiscerning gaze.
My right, my right I turned to
on trails strangely unblazoned
where fistfive forkings burgeoned,
I took my right. Was destined
among deerdroppings on the ridge
or chipmunk stone astrain
or hoofmucks in the swampcabbage
to err? Landmarking birch
selfmultiplied in malice till
woods reared a whitebarred cage
around my spinning eye. The spool
of memory had run out my yarn
and lost the last hank. Found
I the maze I wander in
where my right, trusted hand,
leads round and round a certain copse,
a sudden mound of stone,
an anthill humming in the rocks
an expectant tune?

Lacklearning now my knowledge is
of how to coax recalcitrant
ignition from cold engines,
or mate a fugue in either hand
on spinet or converse
in any tongue but stonecrop signs.
Clouds hump like battling bulls. The firs
lash me with angry tines,
shred my clothes. A windwhipped will
uncompassed, lacking fur or fang,
strange to these parts, yet whom the anthill
anticipating, sang.

(1959)

Who Was It Came

Who was it came
Over the mountains bearing
Gifts we did not ask?

—Not the sapience of the thrush
Or the ant's perdurance,
Something a body might use—

Who was it brought
Cerements and a wrinkled skin,
A sour digestion

Over the mountains, offering
Crotchets and a rheumy gaze
And wits gone wandering?

Just when we thought to repossess
The taught frenzies of Chicago jazz
And bridal ardor

Here he comes,
Inexorable gaffer in an old hat
Croaking our names.

(1966)

JOHN HOLLANDER

Movie-Going

Drive-ins are out, to start with. One must always be
Able to see the over-painted Moorish ceiling
Whose pinchbeck jazz gleams even in the darkness, calling
The straying eye to feast on it, and glut, then fall
Back to the sterling screen again. One needs to feel
That the two empty, huddled, dark stage-boxes keep
Empty for kings. And having frequently to cope
With the abominable goodies, overflow
Bulk and (finally) exploring hands of flushed
Close neighbors gazing beadily out across glum
Distances is, after all, to keep the gleam
Alive of something rather serious, to keep
Faith, perhaps, with the City. When as children our cup
Of joys ran over the special section, and we clutched
Our ticket stubs and followed the bouncing ball, no clash
Of cymbals at the start of the stage-show could abash
Our third untiring time around. When we came back,
Older, to cop an endless series of feels, we sat
Unashamed beneath the bare art-nouveau bodies, set
High on the golden, after-glowing proscenium when
The break had come. And still, now as always, once
The show is over and we creep into the dull
Blaze of mid-afternoon sunshine, the hollow dole
Of the real descends on everything and we can know
That we have been in some place wholly elsewhere, a night
At noonday, not without dreams, whose portals shine
(Not ivory, not horn in ever-changing shapes)

But made of some weird, clear substance not often used for
  gates.

140

Stay for the second feature on a double bill
Always: it will teach you how to love, how not to live,
And how to leave the theater for that unlit, aloof
And empty world again. "B"-pictures showed us: shooting
More real than singing or making love; the shifting
Ashtray upon the mantel, moved by some idiot
Between takes, helping us learn beyond a trace of doubt
How fragile are imagined scenes; the dimming-out
Of all the brightness of the clear and highly lit
Interior of the hero's cockpit, when the stock shot
Of ancient dive-bombers peeling off cuts in, reshapes
Our sense of what is, finally, plausible; the grays
Of living rooms, the blacks of cars whose window glass
At night allows the strips of fake Time Square to pass
Jerkily by on the last ride; even the patch
Of sudden white, and inverted letters dashing
Up during the projectionist's daydream, dying
Quickly—these are the colors of our inner life.

Never ignore the stars, of course. But above all,
Follow the asteroids as well: though dark, they're more
Intense for never glittering; anyone can admire
Sparklings against a night sky, but against a bright
Background of prominence, to feel the Presences burnt
Into no fiery fame should be a more common virtue.
For, just as Vesta has no atmosphere, no verdure
Burgeons on barren Ceres, bit-players never surge
Into the rhythms of expansion and collapse, such
As all the flaming bodies live and move among.
But there, more steadfast than stars are, loved for their
    being,
Not for their burning, move the great Characters: see
Thin Donald Meek, that shuffling essence ever so
Affronting to Eros and to Pride; the pair of bloated
Capitalists, Walter Connolly and Eugene Pallette, seated
High in their offices above New York; the evil,
Blackening eyes of Sheldon Leonard, and the awful
Stare of Eduardo Cianelli. Remember those who have
    gone—
(Where's bat-squeaking Butterfly McQueen? Will we see
    again

That ever-anonymous drunk, waxed-moustached, rubber-
    legged
Caught in revolving doors?) and think of the light-years
    logged

Up in those humbly noble orbits, where no hot
Spotlight of solar grace consumes some blazing hearts,
Bestowing the flimsy immortality of stars
For some great distant instant. Out of the darkness stares
Venus, who seems to be what once we were, the fair
Form of emerging love, her nitrous atmosphere
Hiding her prizes. Into the black expanse peers
Mars, whom we in time will come to resemble: parched,
Xanthine desolations, dead Cimmerian seas, the far
Distant past preserved in the blood-colored crusts; fire
And water both remembered only. Having shined
Means having died. But having been real only, and shunned
Stardom, the planetoids are what we now are, humming
With us, above us, ever into the future, seeming
Ever to take the shapes of the world we wake to from
     dreams.

Always go in the morning if you can; it will
Be something more than habit if you do. Keep well
Away from most French farces. Try to see a set
Of old blue movies every so often, that the sight
Of animal doings out of the clothes of thirty-five
May remind you that even the natural act is phrased
In the terms and shapes of particular times and places.
Finally, remember always to honor the martyred dead.
The forces of darkness spread everywhere now, and the
     best
And brightest screens fade out, while many-antennaed
     beasts
Perch on the housetops, and along the grandest streets
Palaces crumble, one by one. The dimming starts
Slowly at first; the signs are few, as "Movies are
Better than Ever," "Get More out of Life. See a Movie" Or
Else there's no warning at all and, Whoosh! the theater
     falls,
Alas, transmogrified: no double-feature fills
A gleaming marquee with promises, now only lit
With "Pike and Whitefish Fresh Today" "Drano" and
     "Light
Or Dark Brown Sugar, Special." Try never to patronize
Such places (or pass them by one day a year). The noise
Of movie mansions changing form, caught in the toils
Of our lives' whithering, rumbles, resounds and tolls
The knell of neighborhoods. Do not forget the old
Places, for everyone's home has been a battlefield.

I remember: the RKO COLONIAL; the cheap
ARDEN and ALDEN both; LOEW'S LINCOLN SQUARE'S bright
   shape;
The NEWSREEL; the mandarin BEACON, resplendently ar-
   rayed;
The tiny SEVENTY-SEVENTH STREET, whose demise I rued
So long ago; the eighty-first street, sunrise-hued,
RKO; and then LOEW'S: at eighty-third, which had
The colder pinks of sunset on it; and then, back
Across Broadway again, and up, you disembarked
At the YORKTOWN and then the STODDARD, with their dark
Marquees; the SYMPHONY had a decorative disk
With elongated 'twenties nudes whirling in it;
(Around the corner the THALIA, daughter of memory! owed
Her life to Foreign Hits, in days when you piled your coat
High on your lap and sat, sweating and cramped, to catch
"La Kermesse Heroique" every third week, and watched
Fritz Lang from among an audience of refugees, bewitched
By the sense of Crisis on and off that tiny bit
Of screen) Then north again: the RIVERSIDE, the bright
RIVIERA rubbing elbows with it; and right
Smack on a hundredth street, the MIDTOWN; and the rest
Of them: the CARLTON, EDISON, LOEW'S OLYMPIA, and best
Because, of course, the last of all, its final burst
Anonymous, the NEMO! These were once the pearls
Of two-and-a-half miles of Broadway! How many have
   paled
Into a supermarket's failure of the imagination?

Honor them all. Remember how once their splendor blazed
In sparkling necklaces across America's blasted
Distances and deserts: think how, at night, the fastest
Train might stop for water somewhere, waiting, faced
Westward, in deepening dusk, till ruby illuminations
Of something different from Everything Here, Now, shine
Out from the local Bijou, truest gem, the most bright
Because the most believed in, staving off the night
Perhaps, for a while longer with its flickering light.

These fade. All fade. Let us honor them with our own fad-
   ing sight.

                                                    (1960)

The Ninth of July

In 1939 the skylark had nothing to say to me
As the June sunset splashed rose light on the broad side-
    walks
And prophesied no war after the end of that August;
Only, midway between playing ball in Manhattan and Po-
    land
I turned in my sleep on Long Island, groped in the dark of
    July,
And found my pillow at last down at the foot of my bed.
Through the window near her bed, brakes gasped on Ave-
    nue B
In 1952; her blonde crotch shadowed and silent
Astonished us both, and the iced gunpowder tea grew
    warm.
Till the last hollow crust of icecube cracked to its death in
    the glass.
The tea was hot on the cold hilltop in the moonlight
While a buck thrashed through the gray ghosts of burnt-out
    trees
And Thomas whispered of the S.S. from inside his sleeping-
    bag.
Someone else told a tale of the man who was cured of a
    hurt by the bears.
The bathtub drain in the Old Elberon house gucked and
    snorted
When the shadows of graying maples fell across the lawn:
The brown teddybear was a mild comfort because of his
    silence,
And I gazed at the porthole ring made by the windowshade
String, hanging silently, seeing a head and shoulders emerge
From the burning *Morro Castle* I'd seen that afternoon.
The rock cried out "I'm burning, too" as the drying heat
Entered its phase of noon over the steep concrete
Walls along Denver's excuse for a river: we read of remote
Bermudas, and gleaming Neal spat out over the parapet.
In the evening in Deal my b.b. rifle shattered a milkbottle
While the rhododendrons burned in the fading light. The
    tiny
Shot-sized hole in the bathhouse revealed the identical twats
Of the twins from over the hill. From over the hill on the
    other
Side of the lake a dark cloud turreted over the sunset;

Another lake sank to darkness on the other side of the hill,
Lake echoing lake in diminishing pools of reflection.
A trumpet blew Taps. While the drummer's foot boomed
    on the grandstand
The furriers' wives by the pool seemed to ignore the accor-
    dion
Playing "Long Ago and Far Away." None of the alewives
Rose to our nightcrawlers, wiggling on the other side of the
    mirror.
She was furrier under the darkness of all the blanketing
    heat
Than I'd thought to find her, and the bathroom mirror
    flashed
White with the gleam of a car on seventy-second street.
We lay there just having died; the two of us, vision and
    flesh,
Contraction and dream, came apart, while the fan on the
    windowsill
Blew a thin breeze of self between maker and muse, divid-
    ing
Fusing of firework, love's old explosion and outburst of
    voice.

This is the time most real: for unreeling time there are no
Moments, there are no points, but only the lines of memory
Streaking across the black film of the mind's night.
But here in the darkness between two great explosions of
    light,
Midway between the fourth of July and the fourteenth,
Suspended somewhere in summer between the ceremonies
Remembered from childhood and the historical confla-
    grations
Imagined in sad, learned youth—somewhere there always
    hangs
The American moment.
                    Burning, restless, between the deed
And the dream is the life remembered: the sparks of Con-
    cord were mine
As I lit a cherry-bomb once in a glow of myth
And hurled it over the hedge. The complexities of the
    Terror
Were mine as my poring eyes got burned in the fury of
    Europe
Discovered in nineteen forty-two. On the ninth of July
I have been most alive; world and I, in making each other
As always, make fewer mistakes.

The gibbous, historical moon
Records our nights with an eye neither narrowed against
the brightness
Of nature, nor widened with awe at the clouds of the life
of the mind.
Crescent and full, knowledge and touch commingled here
On this dark bed, window flung wide to the cry of the city
night,
We lie still, making the poem of the world that emerges
from shadows.

Doing and then having done is having ruled and com-
manded
A world, a self, a poem, a heartbeat in the moonlight.

To imagine a language means to imagine a form of life.

(1964)

Under Cancer

On the Memorial building's
Terrace the sun has been buzzing
Unbearably, all the while
The white baking happens
To the shadow of the table's
White-painted iron. It darkens,
Meaning that the sun is stronger,
That I am invisibly darkening
Too, the while I whiten.
And only after the stretching
And getting up, still sweating,
My shirt striped like an awning
Drawn on over airlessness;
After the cool shades
(As if of a long arcade
Where footsteps echo gravely)
Have devoured the light;
Only after the cold of
Plunge and shower, the pale
Scent of deodorant stick

Smelling like gin and limes,
And another stripy shirt
Can come, homing in at last,
The buzzing of having been burnt.
Only then, intimations
Of tossing, hot in the dark
Night, where all the long while
Silently, along edges,
There is flaking away.

In this short while of light
My shadow darkens without
Lengthening ever, ever.

(1965)

RICHARD HOWARD

Bonnard: A Novel

The tea party at Le Cannet. Just as we arrived it began,
        a downpour, and kept on.
        This might have been the time
before: Charles-Xavier playing Scriabin études, all the others
        at the open window.
        A landscape—lawn, garden,
strawberry patch, Japanese footbridge, barges moving on the river
        beyond—as in Verlaine
        behind a mist of rain,
and the regular noise of the rain on tens of thousands of leaves:
        such is the prose that wears
        the poem's guise at last.
White cats, one in almost every chair, pretend not to be watching
        young Jean worry the dog.
        Lucie, damp, dashes in
dishevelled from the forest, dumping out a great bag of morels
        on the table; the white
        cloth will surely be spoiled,
but the mushrooms look iridescent, like newly-opened oysters
        in the raindark air, blue
        by this light. Calling it
accidental is only declaring that it exists. Then tea
        downstairs, Jean opening
        the round pantry window,

the smell of wet soil and strawberries with our cinnamon toast. A

>perception is a kind
>of sorting out—one green

from another, parting leaf from leaf—but in the afternoon rain

>signs and shadows only,
>the separate life renounced,

until that resignation comes, in which all selfhood surrenders . . .

>Upstairs, more Scriabin
>and the perfect gestures

of Lucie and Jean playing ball with the dog. All the cats are deaf.

>Steady rain. The music
>continues, Charles-Xavier

shouting over the notes, ignoring them, "Beatitude teaches

>nothing. To live without
>happiness and not wither—

there is an occupation, almost a profession." Take the trees—

>we could "contrive to do
>without trees," but not leaves,

Charles-Xavier explains from the piano, still playing, "we require

>their decorum that is
>one of congestion, till

like Shelley we become lewd vegetarians." Apprehensive

>about the rain, I ask
>Jean to order a closed

carriage for Simone. The doctor frowns—a regular visitor

>these days?—and frightens her,
>eyeing Lucie's mushrooms;

his diagnosis: toadstools. Scriabin diminishes. Is the dog

>lost? Jean rushes outside.
>Punishment of the dog:

he is forbidden the strawberry patch. Darker now. One candle

>is found for the piano,
>and the music resumes

with Debussy, a little sphere of yellow in the sopping dusk.

>The river's surface looks—
>is it the rain?—like the sea

in shallows; this moment is an instance of the world be-
coming

             a mere convenience,
             more or less credible,
and the old questions rise to our lips—but have we spoken
a word?—

             before we remember,
             prompted by the weather
probably, or the time of day, that we already know some-
thing,

             we are not new-born, then.
             What is it that we know?
The carriage comes at last, but it is an open carriage, merely
             hooded. We crowd under,
             fending off the last drops
with a violet golf-umbrella Charles-Xavier has somehow
             managed for us. A slow
             cold drive under the trees,
Simone balancing the suspect mushrooms in her lap. I tell
her

             it is not dangerous;
             we cannot die, but are
in this light or lack of it—trees dripping, the green sky
fraudulent—

             much less individuals
             than we hope or fear to be.
Once home, we shall have a little supper of Lucie's fresh-
picked morels.

                                    (1966)

The Author of Christine

                      for Sanford Friedman

Often waking
before the sun decreed the kind of day
             this one would be
      or by its absence left
      the verdict up to him,
he gazed in doubt
at the blank slate and wondered, blue or gray,
             what *he* might leave
         scribbled against the time
         the darkness came for good;

that was his text.
The trouble was, he realized, to choose.
                       He roused the rooms,
               walking around the house
               that had to share the day

with his despair,
raising each blind as if it were the dead,
                    the morning light
             a record of his progress
             in sudden shafts of dust.

The trouble was
in trying so: imagining Christine
                    to be this way
             or that. Reality
             had to be happened on,

one had to *find*,
not create it. There is always life itself
                    beyond the prose
             that declares it to us,
             life being an absolute

we aspire to,
bliss, but surely cannot reach. Today
                    he would write more,
             creating in *Christine*
             his hopes of what was real,

knowing 'the real'
by what becomes of it and of ourselves.
                    Dust was his proof:
             the life we know we live
             is simply not enough:

the work dissolves,
leaches into the medium and is lost
                    there like water;
             the words sink into sand,
             dust dances in the sun.

Christine was chaos,
parcels of his own childhood where the past
                    appeared to be
             no more than behavior,
             merely authority.

Take the big scene
when Giorgio, leaving the attic, hobbles down
                    and asks Christine
             about the box, she pales
             and follows him back—why?

"The novelist
seldom penetrates character, the mystery
                            remains intact."
                    Thank you Thomas Hardy,
                    sighing over the mess
you made for her
yet asking "Where was Tess's guardian angel *then?*"
                            He much preferred
                    Hardy the poet now,
                    that doubting Thomas who
when Swinburne died
declared him "the sweet rival of the waves
                            and once their peer
                    in sad improvisations."
                    That was character.
To make Christine
out of what was not his choice, participate
                            in what would change
                    her, like the waves, and him . . .
                    Shoving his desk outside
into the sun,
he decided *Christine* could not be written from
                            his waking hopes:
                    by will to set himself
                    or the reader apart
from what the world
might be without the waves, bereft of wet
                            and wilderness.
                    No, he would have to let
                    the weeds of wavering
flourish, rehearse
to both of them, the reader and himself,
                            not ways that help
                    us on but that will help
                    acknowledge our defeat
in getting on—
that would be *Christine,* his novel, and
                            Christine be him.

                                        (1966)

BARBARA HOWES

A Letter from the Caribbean

Breezeways in the tropics winnow the air,
Are ajar to its least breath
But hold back, in a feint of architecture,
The boisterous sun
Pouring down upon

The island like a cloudburst. They
Slant to loft air, they curve, they screen
The wind's wild gaiety
Which tosses palm
Branches about like a marshal's plumes.

Within this filtered, latticed
World, where spools of shadow
Form, lift and change,
The triumph of incoming air
Is that it is there,

Cooling and salving us. Louvers,
Trellises, vines—music also—
Shape the arboreal wind, make skeins
Of it, and a maze
To catch shade. The days

Are all variety, blowing;
Aswirl in a perpetual current
Of wind, shadow, sun,
I marvel at the capacity
Of memory

Which, in some deep pocket
Of my mind, preserves you whole—
As wind is wind, as the lion-taming
Sun is sun, you are, you stay:
Nothing is lost, nothing has blown away.

(1966)

ROBERT HUFF

The Course

My father, gasping, in his white calked shoes . . .
I serving irons to professionals . . .
He stumbles on the fairway. If he falls
No part of him meets turf trod on by Jews.

This is the course that I keep dreaming up:
Armstrong, Miss Libbey, moneyed Legionnaires.
The eighteenth green slopes toward 5000 shares
Of blue-chipped Bourbon boiling in the cup.

Mole spirits rise. Around me in their clans
The human blind posture a stiff approach.
Ground gophers retch. Poison tilts mouse and roach.
Miss Libbey, dying slower than she tans,

Afraid of what accrues with each divorce,
Snickers as Dad swings, sweating, in the traps
He'd keep me out of. When his body snaps
My spine cracks into puddles of remorse.

I used to drop the bag and fight these dreams
Until I found I couldn't beat this part.
My ears and eyes are older than my heart.
They will not change red hazards into streams.

I come upon him cursing my first book
For sentimental gaping: "Lies, lies . . . lies—
Your mother, too, fawn-soft." Before he dies:
"Watch for the doglegs, son; learn how to hook.

"But give 'em hell," he gurgles, as the hand
That fed and gutted flails and flops about
And is at once his own and my first trout
Closing up finally on the wet trap sand.

I lift him in my arms and feel death quake
While, nine by nine, flags fall and geysers blow
The course to one black crater. Down we go,
Down, down together even as I wake.

(1966)

RICHARD HUGO

Degrees of Gray in Philipsburg

You might come here Sunday on a whim.
Say your life broke down. The last good kiss
you had was years ago. You walk these streets
laid out by the insane, past hotels
that didn't last, bars that did, the tortured try
of local drivers to accelerate their lives.
Only churches are kept up. The jail
turned seventy this year. The only prisoner
is always in, not knowing what he's done.

The principal supporting business now
is rage. Hatred of the various grays
the mountain sends, hatred of the mill,
the Silver Bill repeal, the best liked girls
who leave each year for Butte. One good
restaurant and bars can't wipe the boredom out.
The 1907 boom, eight going silver mines,
a dance floor built on springs—
all memory resolves itself in gaze,
in panoramic green you know the cattle eat
or two stacks high above the town,
two dead kilns, the huge mill in collapse
for fifty years that won't fall finally down.

Isn't this your life? That ancient kiss
still burning out your eyes? Isn't this defeat
so accurate, the church bell simply seems
a pure announcement: ring and no one comes?

Don't empty houses ring? Are magnesium
and scorn sufficient to support a town,
not just Philipsburg, but towns
of towering blondes, good jazz and booze
the world will never let you have
until the town you came from dies inside?

Say no to yourself. The old man, twenty
when the jail was built, still laughs
although his lips collapse. Someday soon,
he says, I'll go to sleep and not wake up.
You tell him no. You're talking to yourself.
The car that brought you here still runs.
The money you buy lunch with,
no matter where it's mined, is silver
and the girl who serves you food
is slender and her red hair lights the wall.

(1968)

The Lady in Kicking Horse Reservoir

Not my hands but green across you now.
Green tons hold you down, and ten bass curve
teasing in your hair. Summer slime
will pile deep on your breast. Four months of ice
will keep you firm. I hope each spring
to find you tangled in those pads
pulled not quite loose by the spillway pour,
stars in dead reflection off your teeth.

Lie there lily still. The spillway's closed.
Two feet down most lakes are common gray.
This lake is dark from the black blue Mission range
climbing sky like music dying Indians once wailed.
On ocean beaches, mystery fish
are offered to the moon. Your jaws go blue.
Your hands start waving every wind.
Wave to the ocean where we crushed a mile of foam.

We still love there in thundering foam
and love. Whales fall in love with gulls

and tide reclaims the Dolly skeletons
gone with a blast of aching horns to China.
Landlocked in Montana here
the end is limited by light, the final note
will trail off at the farthest point we see,
already faded, lover, where you bloat.

All girls should be nicer. Arrows rain
above us in the Indian wind. My future
should be full of windy gems, my past
will stop this roaring in my dreams.
Sorry. Sorry. Sorry. But the arrows sing:
no way to float her up. The dead sink
from dead weight. The Mission range
turns this water black late afternoons.

One boy slapped the other. Hard.
The slapped boy talked until his dignity
dissolved, screamed a single 'stop'
and went down sobbing in the company pond.
I swam for him all night. My only suit
got wet and factory hands went home.
No one cared the coward disappeared.
Morning then: cold music I had never heard.

Loners like work best on second shift.
No one liked our product and the factory closed.
Off south, the bison multiply so fast
a slaughter's mandatory every spring
and every spring the creeks get fat
and Kicking Horse fills up. My hope is vague.
The far blur of your bones in May
may be nourished by the snow.

The spillway's open and you spill out
into weather, lover down the bright canal
and mother, irrigating crops
dead Indians forgot to plant.
I'm sailing west with arrows to dissolving foam
where waves strand naked Dollys.
Their eyes are white as oriental mountains
and their tongues are teasing oil from whales.

(1968)

DAVID IGNATOW

The Dream

Someone approaches to say his life is ruined
and to fall down at your feet
and pound his head upon the sidewalk.
Blood spreads in a puddle.
And you, in a weak voice, plead
with those nearby for help;
your life takes on his desperation.
He keeps pounding his head.
It is you who are fated;
and you fall down beside him.
It is then you are awakened,
the body gone, the blood washed from the ground,
the stores lit up with their goods.

(1961)

RANDALL JARRELL

90 North

At home, in my flannel gown, like a bear to its floe,
I clambered to bed; up the globe's impossible sides
I sailed all night—till at last, with my black beard,
My furs and my dogs, I stood at the northern pole.

There in the childish night my companions lay frozen,
The stiff furs knocked at my starveling throat,
And I gave my great sigh: the flakes came huddling,
Were they really my end? In the darkness I turned to my
    rest.

—Here, the flag snaps in the glare and silence
Of the unbroken ice. I stand here,
The dogs bark, my beard is black, and I stare
At the North Pole . . .
                    And now what? Why, go back.

Turn as I please, my step is to the south.
The world—my world spins on this final point
Of cold and wretchedness: all lines, all winds
End in this whirlpool I at last discover.

And it is meaningless. In the child's bed
After the night's voyage, in that warm world
Where people work and suffer for the end
That crowns the pain—in that Cloud-Cuckoo-Land

I reached my North and it had meaning.
Here at the actual pole of my existence,
Where all that I have done is meaningless,
Where I die or live by accident alone—

Where, living or dying, I am still alone;
Here where North, the night, the berg of death
Crowd me out of the ignorant darkness,
I see at last that all the knowledge

I wrung from the darkness—that the darkness flung me—
Is worthless as ignorance: nothing comes from nothing,
The darkness from the darkness. Pain comes from the dark-
        ness
And we call it wisdom. It is pain.

                                                    (1941)

A Hunt in the Black Forest

After the door shuts and the footsteps die,
He calls out: "Mother?"
The wind roars in the leaves: his cold hands, curled
Within his curled, cold body, his blurred head
Are warmed and tremble; and the red leaves flow
Like cells across the spectral, veined,
Whorled darkness of his vision.
                                    The red dwarf
Whispers, "The leaves are turning"; and he reads
The dull, whorled notes, that tremble like a wish
Over the branched staves of the wood.

The stag is grazing in the wood.

A horn calls, over and over, its three notes.
The flat, gasped answer sounds and dies—
The geese call from a hidden sky.
The rain's sound grows into the roar
Of the flood below the falls; the rider calls
To the shape within the shades, a dwarf
Runs back into the brush. But smoke
Drifts to the gelding's nostrils, and he neighs.
From the wet starlight of the glade
A hut sends out its chink of fire.

The rider laughs out: in the branches, birds
Are troubled, stir.

He opens the door. A man looks up
And then slowly, with a kind of smile,
Acts out his own astonishment.
He points to his open mouth: the tongue
Is cut out. Bares his shoulder, points
To the crown branded there, and smiles. The hunter frowns.
The pot bubbles from the embers in the laugh
The mute laughs. With harsh habitual
Impatience, the hunter questions him
The man nods vacantly—
Shaken, he makes his gobbling sound
Over and over. The hunter ladles from the pot
Into a wooden bowl, the shining stew.
He eats silently. The mute
Counts spoonfuls on his fingers. Come to ten,
The last finger, he laughs out in joy
And scuttles like a mouse across the floor
To the door and the door's darkness. The king breathes
        hard,
Rises—and something catches at his heart,
Some patient senseless thing
Begins to squeeze his heart out in its hands.
His jerking body, bent into a bow,
Falls out of the hands onto the table,
Bends, bends further, till at last it breaks.
But, broken, it still breathes—a few whistling breaths
That slow, are intermittent, cease.

Now only the fire thinks, like a heart
Cut from its breast. Light leaps, the shadows fall
In the old alternation of the world . . .

Two sparks, at the dark horn of the window,
Look, as stars look, into the shadowy hut,
Turn slowly, searching:
Then a bubbled, gobbling sound begins,
The sound of the pot laughing on the fire.
—The pot, overturned among the ashes,
Is cold as death.

Something is scratching, panting. A little voice
Says, "Let *me!* Let *me!*" The mute
Puts his arms around the dwarf and raises him.

The pane is clouded with their soft slow breaths,
The mute's arms tire; but they gaze on and on,

Like children watching something wrong.
Their blurred faces, caught up in one wish,
Are blurred into one face: a child's set face.

(1948)

The Orient Express

One looks from the train
Almost as one looked as a child. In the sunlight
What I see still seems to me plain,
I am safe; but at evening
As the lands darken, a questioning
Precariousness comes over everything.

Once after a day of rain
I lay longing to be cold; and after a while
I was cold again, and hunched shivering
Under the quilt's many colors, gray
With the dull ending of the winter day.
Outside me there were a few shapes
Of chairs and tables, things from a primer;
Outside the window
There were the chairs and tables of the world. . . .
I saw that the world
That had seemed to me the plain
Gray mask of all that was strange
Behind it—of all that *was*—was all.

But it is beyond belief.
One thinks, "Behind everything
An unforced joy, an unwilling
Sadness (a willing sadness, a forced joy)
Moves changelessly"; one looks from the train
And there is something, the same thing
Behind everything: all these little villages,
A passing woman, a field of grain,
The man who says good-bye to his wife—
A path through a wood full of lives, and the train
Passing, after all unchangeable
And not now ever to stop, like a heart—

It is like any other work of art.
It is and never can be changed.
Behind everything there is always
The unknown unwanted life.

(1950)

The Woman at the Washington Zoo

The saris go by me from the embassies.

Cloth from the moon. Cloth from another planet.
They look back at the leopard like the leopard.

And I. . . .
         this print of mine, that has kept its color
Alive through so many cleanings; this dull null
Navy I wear to work, and wear from work, and so
To my bed, so to my grave, with no
Complaints, no comment: neither from my chief,
The Deputy Chief Assistant, nor his chief—
Only I complain. . . . this serviceable
Body that no sunlight dyes, no hand suffuses
But, dome-shadowed, withering among columns,
Wavy beneath fountains—small, far-off, shining
In the eyes of animals, these beings trapped
As I am trapped but not, themselves, the trap,
Aging, but without knowledge of their age,
Kept safe here, knowing not of death, for death—
Oh, bars of my own body, open, open!

The world goes by my cage and never sees me.
And there come not to me, as come to these,
The wild beasts, sparrows pecking the llamas' grain,
Pigeons settling on the bears' bread, buzzards
Tearing the meat the flies have clouded. . . .
                      Vulture,
When you come for the white rat that the foxes left,
Take off the red helmet of your head, the black
Wings that have shadowed me, and step to me as man:
The wild brothers at whose feet the white wolves fawn,
To whose hand of power the great lioness

Stalks, purring. . . .
                        You know what I was,
  You see what I am: change me, change me!

                                                    (1960)

In Montecito

In a fashionable suburb of Santa Barbara,
Montecito, there visited me one night at midnight
A scream with breasts. As it hung there in the sweet air
That was always the right temperature, the contractors
Who had undertaken to dismantle it, stripped off
The lips, let the air out of the breasts.
                              People disappear
Even in Montecito. Greenie Taliaferro,
In her white maillot, her good figure almost firm,
Her old pepper-and-salt hair stripped by the hairdresser
To nothing and dyed platinum—Greenie has left her Bent-
  ley.
They have thrown away her electric toothbrush, someone
  else slips
The key into the lock of her safety-deposit box
At the Crocker-Anglo Bank; her seat at the cricket matches
Is warmed by buttocks less delectable than hers.
Greenie's girdle is empty.
                              A scream hangs there in the night:
They strip off the lips, let the air out of the breasts,
And Greenie has gone into the Greater Montecito
That surrounds Montecito like the echo of a scream.

                                                    (1963)

The Lost Children

Two little girls, one fair, one dark,
One alive, one dead, are running hand in hand
Through a sunny house. The two are dressed
In red and white gingham, with puffed sleeves and sashes.

They run away from me . . . But I am happy;
When I wake I feel no sadness, only delight.
I've seen them again, and I am comforted
That, somewhere, they still are.

It is strange
To carry inside you someone else's body;
To know it before it's born;
To see at last that it's a boy or girl, and perfect;
To bathe it and dress it; to watch it
Nurse at your breast, till you almost know it
Better than you know yourself—better than it knows itself.
You own it as you made it.
You are the authority upon it.

But as the child learns
To take care of herself, you know her less.
Her accidents, adventures are her own,
You lose track of them. Still, you know more
About her than anyone *except* her.

Little by little the child in her dies.
You say, "I have lost a child, but gained a friend."
You feel yourself gradually discarded.
She argues with you or ignores you
Or is kind to you. She who begged to follow you
Anywhere, just so long as it was you,
Finds follow the leader no more fun.
She makes few demands; you are grateful for the few.

The young person who writes once a week
Is the authority upon herself.
She sits in my living room and shows her husband
My albums of her as a child. He enjoys them
And makes fun of them. I look too
And I realize the girl in the matching blue
Mother-and-daughter dress, the fair one carrying
The tin lunch box with the half-pint thermos bottle
Or training her pet duck to go down the slide
Is lost just as the dark one, who is dead, is lost.
But the world in which the two wear their flared coats
And the hats that match, exists so uncannily
That, after I've seen its pictures for an hour,
I believe in it: the bandage coming loose
One has in the picture of the other's birthday,
The castles they are building, at the beach for asthma.

I look at them and all the old sure knowledge
Floods over me, when I put the album down
I keep saying inside: "I *did* know those children.
I braided those braids. I was driving the car
The day that she stepped in the can of grease
We were taking to the butcher for our ration points.
I *know* those children. I know all about them.
Where are they?"

I stare at her and try to see some sign
Of the child she was. I can't believe there isn't any.
I tell her foolishly, pointing at the picture,
That I keep wondering where she is.
She tells me, "Here I am."
                   Yes, and the other
Isn't dead, but has everlasting life . . .

The girl from next door, the borrowed child,
Said to me the other day, "You like children so much,
Don't you want to have some of your own?"
I couldn't believe that she could say it.
I thought: "Surely you can look at me and see them."

When I see them in my dreams I feel such joy.
If I could dream of them every night!

When I think of my dream of the little girls
It's as if we were playing hide-and-seek.
The dark one
Looks at me longingly, and disappears;
The fair one stays in sight, just out of reach
No matter where I reach. I am tired
As a mother who's played all day, some rainy day.
I don't want to play it any more, I don't want to,
But the child keeps on playing, so I play.

                                    (1965)

LeROI JONES

Political Poem

for Basil

Luxury, then, is a way of
being ignorant, comfortably
an approach to the open market
of least information. Where theories
can thrive, under heavy tarpaulins
without being cracked by ideas.

(I have not seen the earth for years
and think now possibly "dirt" is
negative, positive, but clearly
social. I cannot plant a seed, cannot
recognize the root with clearer dent
than indifference. Though I eat
and shit as a natural man. (Getting up
from the desk to secure a turkey sandwich
and answer the phone: the poem undone
undone by my station, by my station,
and the bad words of Newark.) Raised up
to the breech, we seek to fill for this
crumbling century. The darkness of love,
in whose sweating memory all error is forced.

Undone by the logic of any specific oath. (Old gentlemen
who still follows fires, tho are quieter
and less punctual. It is a polite truth
we are left with. Who are you? What are you

saying? Something to be dealt with, as easily.
The noxious game of reason, saying, "No, No,
you cannot feel," like my dead lecturer
lamenting thru gipsies his fast suicide.

(1964)

DONALD JUSTICE

On a Painting by Patient B of the Independence State Hospital for the Insane

1

These seven houses have learned to face one another,
But not at the expected angles. Those silly brown lumps,
That are probably meant for hills and not other houses,
After ages of being themselves, though naturally slow,
Are learning to be exclusive without offending.
The arches and entrances (down to the right out of sight)
Have mastered the lesson of remaining closed.
And even the skies keep a certain understandable distance,
For these are the houses of the very rich.

2

One sees their children playing with leopards, tamed
At great cost, or perhaps it is only other children,
For none of these objects is anything more than a spot,
And perhaps there are not any children but only leopards
Playing with leopards, and perhaps there are only the spots.
And the little maids from the windows hanging like tongues,
Calling the children in, admiring the leopards,
Are the dashes a child might represent motion by means of,
Or dazzlement possibly, the brilliance of solid-gold houses.

3

The clouds resemble those empty balloons in cartoons
Which approximate silence. These clouds, if clouds they are

(And not the smoke from the seven aspiring chimneys),
The more one studies them the more it appears
They too have expressions. One might almost say
They have their habits, their wrong opinions, that their
Impassivity masks an essentially lovable foolishness,
And they will be given names by those who live under them
Not public like mountains' but private like companions'.

(1954

Here in Katmandu

We have climbed the mountain,
There's nothing more to do.
It is terrible to come down
To the valley
Where, amidst many flowers,
One thinks of snow,

As, formerly, amidst snow,
Climbing the mountain,
One thought of flowers,
Tremulous, ruddy with dew,
In the valley.
One caught their scent coming down.

It is difficult to adjust, once down,
To the absence of snow.
Clear days, from the valley,
One looks up at the mountain.
What else is there to do?
Prayerwheels, flowers!

Let the flowers
Fade, the prayerwheels run down.
What have these to do
With us who have stood atop the snow
Atop the mountain,
Flags seen from the valley?

It might be possible to live in the valley,
To bury oneself among flowers,
If one could forget the mountain,

How, setting out before dawn,
Blinded with snow,
One knew what to do.

Meanwhile it is not easy here in Katmandu,
Espe.ially when to the valley
That wind which means snow
Elsewhere, but here means flowers,
Comes down,
As soon it must, from the mountain.

(1956)

Anonymous Drawing

A delicate young Negro stands
With the reins of a horse clutched loosely in his hands;
So delicate, indeed, that we wonder if he can hold the spir-
    ited creature beside him
Until the master shall arrive to ride him.
Already the animal's nostrils widen with rage or fear.
But if we imagine him snorting, about to rear,
This boy, who should know about such things better than
    we,
Only stands smiling, passive and ornamental, in a fantastic
    livery
Of ruffles and puffed breeches,
Watching the artist, apparently, as he sketches.
Meanwhile the petty lord who must have paid
For the artist's trip up from Perugia, for the horse, for the
    boy, for everything here, in fact, has been delayed,
Kept too long by his steward, perhaps, discussing
Some business concerning the estate, or fussing
Over the details of his impeccable toilet
With a manservant whose opinion is that any alteration at
    all would spoil it.
However fast he should come hurrying now
Over this vast greensward, mopping his brow
Clear of the sweat of the fine Renaissance morning, it would
    be too late:
The artist will have had his revenge for being made to wait,
A revenge not only necessary but right and clever—
Simply to leave him out of the scene forever.

(1961)

But That Is Another Story

I do not think the ending can be right.
How can they marry and live happily
Forever, these who were so passionate
At chapter's end? Once they are settled in
The quiet country house, what will they do,
So many miles from anywhere?
Those blond ancestral ghosts crowding the stair,
Surely they disapprove? Ah me,
I fear love will catch cold and die
From pacing naked through those drafty halls
Night after night. Poor Frank. Poor Imogene.
Before them now their lives
Stretch empty as great Empire beds
After the lovers rise and the damp sheets
Are stripped by envious chambermaids.

And if the first night passes brightly enough,
What with the bonfires lit with old love letters,
That is no inexhaustible fuel, perhaps?
Time knows how it must end, not I.
Will Frank walk out one day
Alone through the ruined orchard with his stick,
Strewing the path with lissome heads
Of buttercups? Will Imogene
Conceal in the crotches of old trees
Love notes for grizzled gardeners and such?
Meanwhile they quarrel and make it up,
Only to quarrel again. A sudden storm
Pulls the last fences down. Now moonstruck sheep
Stray through the garden all night peering in
At the exhausted lovers where they sleep.

(1962)

The Man Closing Up

IMPROVISATIONS

ON THEMES FROM GUILLEVIC

1

Like a deserted beach,
The man closing up.

Broken glass on the rocks,
And seaweed coming in
To hang up on the rocks.

Walk with care,
It's slippery here.

Old pilings, rotted, broken like teeth,
Where a pier was,

A mouth,
And the tide coming in.

The man closing up
Is like this.

2

He has no hunger
For anything,
The man closing up.

He would even try stones,
If they were offered.

But he has no hunger
For stones.

3

He would make his bed,
If he could sleep on it.

He would make his bed with white sheets
And disappear into the white,

Like a man diving,
If he could be certain

That the light
Would not keep him awake,

The light that reaches
To the bottom.

4

The man closing up
Tries the doors.

But first
He closes the windows.

And before that even
He had looked out the windows.

There was no storm coming
That he could see.

There was no one out walking
At that hour.

Still,
He closes the windows
And tries the doors.

He knows about storms
And about people

And about hours
Like that one.

5

There is a word for it,
A simple word,
And the word goes around.

It curves like a staircase,
And it goes up like a staircase,
And it *is* a staircase,

An iron staircase
On the side of a lighthouse.
All in his head.

And it makes no sound at all
In his head,
Unless he says it.

Then the keeper
Steps on the rung,
The bottom rung,

And the ascent begins.
Clangorous,
Rung after rung.

He wants to keep the light going,
If he can.

But the man closing up
Does not say the word.

                                        (1966)

WELDON KEES

For My Daughter

Looking into my daughter's eyes I read
Beneath the innocence of morning flesh
Concealed, hintings of death she does not heed.
Coldest of winds have blown this hair, and mesh
Of seaweed snarled these miniatures of hands;
The night's slow poison, tolerant and bland,
Has moved her blood. Parched years that I have seen
That may be hers appear: foul, lingering
Death in certain war, the slim legs green.
Or, fed on hate, she relishes the sting
Of others' agony; perhaps the cruel
Bride of a syphilitic or a fool.
These speculations sour in the sun.
I have no daughter. I desire none.

(1943)

Aspects of Robinson

Robinson at cards at the Algonquin; a thin
Blue light comes down once more outside the blinds.
Gray men in overcoats are ghosts blown past the door.
The taxis streak the avenues with yellow, orange, and red.
This is Grand Central, Mr. Robinson.

Robinson on a roof above the Heights; the boats
Mourn like the lost. Water is slate, far down.
Through sounds of ice cubes dropped in glass, as osteopath,
Dressed for the links, describes an old Intourist tour.
—Here's where old Gibbons jumped from, Robinson.

Robinson walking in the Park, admiring the elephant.
Robinson buying the *Tribune,* Robinson buying the *Times.*
   Robinson
Saying, "Hello. Yes, this is Robinson. Sunday
At five? I'd love to. Pretty well. And you?"
Robinson alone at Longchamps, staring at the wall.

Robinson afraid, drunk, sobbing Robinson
In bed with a Mrs. Morse. Robinson at home;
Decisions: Toynbee or luminol? Where the sun
Shines, Robinson in flowered trunks, eyes toward
The breakers. Where the night ends, Robinson in East Side
   bars.

Robinson in Glen plaid jacket, Scotch-grain shoes,
Black four-in-hand and oxford button-down,
The jeweled and silent watch that winds itself, the brief-
Case, covert topcoat, clothes for spring, all covering
His sad and usual heart, dry as a winter leaf.

(1948)

Robinson at Home

Curtains draw back, the door ajar.
All winter long, it seemed, a darkening
Began. But now the moonlight and the odors of the street
Conspire and combine toward one community.

These are the rooms of Robinson.
Bleached, wan, and colorless this light, as though
All the blurred daybreaks of the spring
Found an asylum here, perhaps for Robinson alone,

Who sleeps. Were there more music sifted through the floors
And moonlight of a different kind,
He might awake to hear the news at ten,
Which will be shocking, moderately.

This sleep is from exhaustion, but his old desire
To die like this has known a lessening.
Now there is only this coldness that he has to wear.
But not in sleep.—Observant scholar, traveller,

Or uncouth bearded figure squatting in a cave,
A keen-eyed sniper on the barricades,
A heretic in catacombs, a famed roué,
A beggar on the street, the confidant of Popes—

All these are Robinson in sleep, who mumbles as he turns,
"There is something in this madhouse that I symbolize—
This city—nightmare—black—"

                            He wakes in sweat
To the terrible moonlight and what might be
Silence. It drones like wires far beyond the roofs,
And the long curtains blow into the room.

                                    (1948)

Round

"Wondrous life!" cried Marvell at Appleton House.
Renan admired Jesus Christ "wholeheartedly."
But here dried ferns keep falling to the floor,
And something inside my head
Flaps like a worn-out blind. Royal Cortissoz is dead,
A blow to the *Herald-Tribune*. A closet mouse
Rattles the wrapper on the breakfast food. Renan
Admired Jesus Christ "wholeheartedly."

Flaps like a worn-out blind. Cézanne
Would break out in the quiet streets of Aix
And shout, "Le monde, c'est terrible!" Royal
Cortissoz is dead. And something inside my head
Flaps like a worn-out blind. The soil
In which the ferns are dying needs more Vigoro.
There is no twilight on the moon, no mist or rain,
No hail or snow, no life. Here in this house

Dried ferns keep falling to the floor, a mouse
Rattles the wrapper on the breakfast food. Cézanne
Would break out in the quiet streets and scream. Renan
Admired Jesus Christ "wholeheartedly." And something in-
    side my head
Flaps like a worn-out blind. Royal Cortissoz is dead.
There is no twilight on the moon, no hail or snow.
One notes fresh desecrations of the portico.
"Wondrous life!" cried Marvell at Appleton House.

(1949)

January

Morning: blue, cold, and still.
Eyes that have stared too long
Stare at the wedge of light
At the end of the frozen room
Where snow on a windowsill,
Packed and cold as a life,
Winters the sense of wrong
And emptiness and loss
That is my awakening.
A lifetime drains away
Down a path of frost;
My face in the looking-glass
Turns again from the light
Toward fragments of the past
That break with the end of sleep.
This wakening, this breath
No longer real, this deep
Darkness where we toss,
Cover a life at the last.
Sleep is too short a death.

(1951)

1926

The porchlight coming on again,
Early November, the dead leaves
Raked in piles, the wicker swing

Creaking. Across the lots
A phonograph is playing *Ja-Da.*

An orange moon. I see the lives
Of neighbors, mapped and marred
Like all the wars ahead, and R.
Insane, B. with his throat cut,
Fifteen years from now, in Omaha.

I did not know them then.
My airedale scratches at the door.
And I am back from seeing Milton Sills
And Doris Kenyon. Twelve years old.
The porchlight coming on again.

(1954)

X. J. KENNEDY

Nude Descending a Staircase

Toe upon toe, a snowing flesh,
A gold of lemon, root and rind,
She sifts in sunlight down the stairs
With nothing on. Nor on her mind.

We spy beneath the banister
A constant thresh of thigh on thigh—
Her lips imprint the swinging air
That parts to let her parts go by.

One-woman waterfall, she wears
Her slow descent like a long cape
And pausing, on the final stair
Collects her motions into shape.

(1960)

Little Elegy

FOR A CHILD WHO SKIPPED ROPE

Here lies resting, out of breath,
Out of turns, Elizabeth
Whose quicksilver toes not quite
Cleared the whirring edge of night.

Earth whose circles round us skim
Till they catch the lightest limb,
Shelter now Elizabeth
And for her sake trip up Death.

(1960)

GALWAY KINNELL

Burning

He lives, who last night flopped from a log
Into the creek, and all night by an ankle
Lay pinned to the flood, dead as a nail
But for the skin of the teeth of his dog.

I brought him boiled eggs and broth.
He coughed and waved his spoon
And sat up saying he would dine alone,
Being fatigue itself after that bath.

I sat without in the sun with the dog.
Wearing a stocking on the ailing foot,
In monster crutches, he hobbled out,
And addressed the dog in bitter rage.

He told the yellow hound, his rescuer,
Its heart was bad, and it ought
Not wander by the creek at night;
If all his dogs got drowned he would be poor.

He stroked its head and disappeared in the shed
And came out with a stone mallet in his hands
And lifted that rocky weight of many pounds
And let it lapse on top of the dog's head.

I carted off the carcass, dug it deep.
Then he came too with what a thing to lug,
Or pour on a dog's grave, his thundermug,
And poured it out and went indoors to sleep.

I saw him sleepless in the pane of glass
Looking wild-eyed at sunset, then the glare
Blinded the glass—only a red square
Burning a house burning in the wilderness.

(1954)

Another Night
in the Ruins

1

In the evening
haze darkening on the hills,
purple
of the eternal, a last bird
crosses over, *'flop flop'*,
adoring
only the instant.

2

Nine years ago,
in a plane that rumbled all night
above the Atlantic,
I could see, lit up
by lightning bolts jumping out of it,
a thunderhead formed like the face
of my brother, looking nostalgically down
on blue,
lightning-flashed moments of the Atlantic.

3

He used to tell me,
"What good is the day?
On some hill of despair
the bonfire
you kindle can light the great sky—
though it's true, of course, to make it burn
you have to throw yourself in . . ."

4

Wind tears itself hollow
in the eaves of my ruins, ghost-flute
of snowdrifts
that build out there in the dark:
upside-down.
ravines into which night sweeps
our torn wings, our ink-spattered feathers.

5

I listen.
I hear nothing. Only
the cow, the cow
of nothingness, mooing
down the bones.

6

Is that a
rooster? He
thrashes in the snow
for a grain. Finds
it. Rips
it into
flames. Flaps. Crows.
Flames
bursting out of his brow.

7

How many nights must it take
one such as me to learn
that we aren't, after all, made
from that bird which flies out of its ashes,
that for a man
as he goes up in flames, his one work
is
to open himself, to *be*
the flames?

(1966)

The Bear

1

In late winter
I sometimes glimpse bits of steam
coming up from

some fault in the old snow
and bend close and see it is lung-colored
and put down my nose
and know
the chilly, enduring odor of bear.

2

I take a wolf's rib and whittle
it sharp at both ends
and coil it up
and freeze it in blubber and place it out
on the fairway of the bears.

And when it has vanished
I move out on the bear tracks,
roaming in circles
until I come to the first, tentative, dark
splash on the earth.

And I set out
running, following the splashes
of blood wandering over the world.
At the cut, gashed resting places
I stop and rest,
at the crawl-marks
where he lay out on his belly
to overpass some stretch of bauchy ice
I lie out
dragging myself forward with bear-knives in my fists.

3

On the third day I begin to starve,
at nightfall I bend down as I knew I would
at a turd sopped in blood,
and hesitate, and pick it up,
and thrust it in my mouth, and gnash it down,
and rise
and go on running.

4

On the seventh day,
living by now on bear blood alone,
I can see his upturned carcass far out ahead, a scraggled,
steamy hulk,
the heavy fur riffling in the wind.

I come up to him
and stare at the narrow-spaced, petty eyes,
the dismayed
face laid back on the shoulder, the nostrils
flared, catching
perhaps the first taint of me as he
died.

I hack
a ravine in his thigh, and eat and drink,
and tear him down his whole length
and open him and climb in
and close him up after me, against the wind,
and sleep.

5

And dream
of lumbering flatfooted
over the tundra,
stabbed twice from within,
splattering a trail behind me,
splattering it out no matter which way I lurch,
no matter which parabola of bear-transcendence,
which dance of solitude I attempt,
which gravity-clutched leap,
which trudge, which groan.

6

Until one day I totter and fall—
fall on this
stomach that has tried so hard to keep up,
to digest the blood as it leaked in,
to break up
and digest the bone itself: and now the breeze
blows over me, blows off
the hideous belches of ill-digested bear blood
and rotted stomach
and the ordinary, wretched odor of bear,

blows across
my sore, lolled tongue a song
or screech, until I think I must rise up
and dance. And I lie still.

7

I awaken I think. Marshlights
reappear, geese
come trailing again up the flyway.
In her ravine under old snow the dam-bear
lies, licking
lumps of smeared fur
and drizzly eyes into shapes
with her tongue. And one
hairy-soled trudge stuck out before me,
the next groaned out,
the next,
the next,
the rest of my days I spend
wandering: wondering
what, anyway,
was that sticky infusion, that rank flavor of blood, that
  poetry, by which I lived?

(1968)

CAROLYN KIZER

The Great Blue Heron

M.A.K., September, 1880-September, 1955

As I wandered on the beach
I saw the heron standing
Sunk in the tattered wings
He wore as a hunchback's coat.
Shadow without a shadow,
Hung on invisible wires
From the top of a canvas day,
What scissors cut him out?
Superimposed on a poster
Of summer by the strand
Of a long-decayed resort,
Poised in the dusty light
Some fifteen summers ago;
I wondered, an empty child,
"Heron, whose ghost are you?"

I stood on the beach alone,
In the sudden chill of the burned.
My thought raced up the path.
Pursuing it, I ran
To my mother in the house
And led her to the scene.
The spectral bird was gone.
But her quick eye saw him drifting
Over the highest pines
On vast, unmoving wings.
Could they be those ashen things,
So grounded, unwieldy, ragged,
A pair of broken arms

That were not made for flight?
In the middle of my loss
I realized she knew:
My mother knew what he was.

O great blue heron, now
That the summer house has burned
So many rockets ago,
So many smokes and fires
And beach-lights and water-glow
Reflecting pin-wheel and flare:
The old logs hauled away,
The pines and driftwood cleared
From that bare strip of shore
Where dozens of children play;
Now there is only you
Heavy upon my eye.
Why have you followed me here,
Heavy and far away?
You have stood there patiently
For fifteen summers and snows,
Denser than my repose,
Bleaker than any dream,
Waiting upon the day
When, like gray smoke, a vapor
Floating into the sky,
A handful of paper ashes,
My mother would drift away.

(1958)

Summer Near the River

from *The Book of Songs*

I have carried my pillow to the windowsill
And try to sleep, with my damp arms crossed upon it
But no breeze stirs the tepid morning.
Only I stir. . . . Come, tease me a little!
With such cold passion, so little teasing play,
How long can we endure our life together?

No use. I put on your long dressing-grown;
The untied sash trails over the dusty floor.
I kneel by the window, prop up your shaving mirror
And pluck my eyebrows.
I don't care if the robe slides open
Revealing a crescent of belly, a tan thigh.
I can accuse that non-existent breeze. . . .

I am as monogamous as the North Star
But I don't want you to know it. You'd only take advantage.
While you are as fickle as spring sunlight.
All right, sleep! The cat means more to you than I.
I can rouse you, but then you swagger out.
I glimpse you from the window, striding towards the river.

When you return, reeking of fish and beer,
There is salt dew in your hair. Where have you been?
Your clothes weren't that wrinkled hours ago, when you
   left.
You couldn't have loved someone else, after loving me!
I sulk and sigh, dawdling by the window.
Later, when you hold me in your arms,
It seems, for a moment, the river ceases flowing.

(1965)

KENNETH KOCH

Permanently

One day the Nouns were clustered in the street.
An Adjective walked by, with her dark beauty.
The Nouns were struck, moved, changed.
The next day a Verb drove up, and created the Sentence.

Each Sentence says one thing—for example, "Although it
   was a dark rainy day when the Adjective walked by, I
   shall remember the pure and sweet expression on her face
   until the day I perish from the green, effective earth."
Or, "Will you please close the window, Andrew?"
Or, for example, "Thank you, the pink pot of flowers on
   the window sill has changed color recently to a light
   yellow, due to the heat from the boiler factory which
   exists nearby."

In the springtime the Sentences and the Nouns lay silently
   on the grass.
A lonely Conjunction here and there would call, "And!
   But!"
But the Adjective did not emerge.

As the adjective is lost in the sentence,
So I am lost in your eyes, ears, nose, and throat—
You have enchanted me with a single kiss
Which can never be undone
Until the destruction of language.

(1956)

Locks

These locks on doors have brought me happiness:
The lock on the door of the sewing machine in the living
    room
Of a tiny hut in which I was living with a mad seamstress;
The lock on the filling station one night when I was drunk
And had the idea of enjoying a nip of petroleum;
The lock on the family of seals, which, when released,
    would have bitten;
The lock on the life raft when I was taking a bath instead
    of drowning;
The lock inside the nose of the contemporary composer
    who was playing the piano and would have ruined his
    concert by sneezing, while I was turning pages;
The lock on the second hump of a camel while I was not
    running out of water in the desert;
The lock on the fish hatchery the night we came up from
    the beach
And were trying to find a place to spend the night—it was
    full of contagious fish;
The lock on my new necktie when I was walking through
    a stiff wind
On my way to an appointment at which I had to look neat
    and simple;
The lock on the foghorn the night of the lipstick parade—
If the foghorn had sounded, everyone would have run
    inside before the most beautiful contestant appeared;
The lock in my hat when I saw her and which kept me from
    tipping it,
Which she would not have liked, because she believed that
    naturalness was the most friendly;
The lock on the city in which we would not have met any-
    one we knew;
The lock on the airplane which was flying without a pilot
Above Miami Beach on the night when I unlocked my bones
To the wind, and let the gales of sweetness blow through
    me till I shuddered and shook
Like a key in a freezing hand, and ran up into the Miami
    night air like a stone;
The lock on the hayfield, which kept me from getting out of
    bed
To meet the hayfield committee there; the lock on the barn,
    that kept the piled-up hay away from me;

The lock on the mailboat that kept it from becoming a
raincoat
On the night of the thunderstorm; the lock on the sailboat
That keeps it from taking me away from you when I am
asleep with you,
And, when I am not, the lock on my sleep, that keeps me
from waking and finding you are not there.

(1957)

You Were Wearing

You were wearing your Edgar Allan Poe printed cotton
blouse.
In each divided up square of the blouse was a picture of
Edgar Allan Poe.
Your hair was blonde and you were cute. You asked me,
"Do most boys think that most girls are bad?"
I smelled the mould of your seaside resort hotel bedroom
on your hair held in place by a John Greenleaf Whittier
clip.
"No," I said, "it's girls who think that boys are bad." Then
we read *Snowbound* together
And ran around in an attic, so that a little of the blue
enamel was scraped off my George Washington, Father
of His Country, shoes.

Mother was walking in the living room, her Strauss Waltzes
comb in her hair.
We waited for a time and then joined her, only to be served
tea in cups painted with pictures of Herman Melville
As well as with illustrations from his book *Moby Dick* and
from his novella, *Benito Cereno*.
Father came in wearing his Dick Tracy necktie: "How
about a drink, everyone?"
I said, "Let's go outside a while." Then we went onto the
porch and sat on the Abraham Lincoln swing.
You sat on the eyes, mouth, and beard part, and I sat on the
knees.
In the yard across the street we saw a snowman holding
a garbage can lid smashed into a likeness of the mad
English king, George the Third.

(1959)

AL LEE

The Far Side of Introspection

All night long into my sleeping bag's head pad the blood
drained through my ear from somewhere inside my head.
    I rested—the pulse thudding—
torporously but couldn't sleep. The bruised others said
    it was the pressure.
    But we were ready.

"How'll we know with such instruments when we get there?
Is Livingstone there or a flag? Why ought grown men
    crawl blind, damp, and hairless
like fishing worms?" the acid head asked us. "Would you
    rather be ascending?
    Too late now to do it,"

the esthetician said, "even should we wish
for picnic pastures, any muck but this rock,
    which scrapes us. No decision
can make you fatter or less famous." We'd been
    so long heroic, knocking
    at Hell or our own insides.

"All labors have led to this deepest lev-
el of our pushing through. No one has dug
    down so in our great home, ever,"
the psychoanalyst said. When we'd reached
    the ultimate stratum, lugging
    and setting our charges we breached it.

As it blasted up and down over
    and at us the wall wasn't molten

196

with brimstone nor cold like an iced moon;
it was all glare too bright to live in.
We lost our senses just to make man-
ageable the agony of light.

        Lean men with pigtails and pigtails
          shaved lifted us from our burden,
applied sedatives, and pulled out the rig
          we had drilled straight with. Around us
lay an unknown and mossy flatness fur-
ther than hopes until we slept, slept till now.

        This morning a horn woke us
          for the interrogator,
who sat smiling but made us squirm when he spoke.
          "Where from and what to find out?"
"Your inscape isn't," the esthetician said,
"the pinpoint to learn from we had in mind."

        "But from somewhere surely?"
          "Yes, of course, I guess so,"
the psychoanalyst continued, "but when you're
          getting down here, sullen,
you think about shaft-digging, not surfaces." "Yes,"
the tripper added, "just digging, man. Beautiful!"

        "But with what reason?"
          Forever northwards
sands of unexpected deserts dried. Eastward were seas
          which our tall Inspec-
tor said swept outward to lands he took to be all Earth.
Westward, rocks rose through mists with no sense of
direction.

                                      (1967)

DENISE LEVERTOV

The Springtime

The red eyes of rabbits
aren't sad. No one passes
the sad golden village in a barge
any more. The sunset
will leave it alone. If the
curtains hang askew
it is no one's fault.
Around and around and around
everywhere the same sound
of wheels going, and things
growing older, growing
silent. If the dogs
bark to each other
all night, and their eyes
flash red, that's
nobody's business. They have
a great space of dark to
bark across. The rabbits
will bare their teeth at
the spring moon.

(1957)

Partial Resemblance

A doll's hair concealing
an eggshell skull delicately
throbbing, within which
198

maggots in voluptuous unrest
jostle and shrug. Oh, Eileen, my
big doll, your gold hair was
not more sunny than this
human fur, but
your head was
radiant in its emptiness,
a small clean room.

Her warm and rosy mouth
is telling lies—she would
believe them if she could believe:
her pretty eyes
search out corruption. Oh, Eileen
how kindly your silence was, and
what virtue
shone in the opening and shutting of your
ingenious blindness.

(1961)

A Map of the Western Part of the County of Essex in England

Something forgotten for twenty years: though my fathers
and mothers came from Cordova and Vitepsk and Caernar-
    von,
and though I am a citizen of the United States and less a
stranger here than anywhere else, perhaps,
I am Essex-born:
Cranbrook Wash called me into its dark tunnel,
the little streams of Valentines heard my resolves,
Roding held my head above water when I thought it was
drowning me; in Hainault only a haze of thin trees
stood between the red doubledecker buses and the boar-
    hunt,
the spirit of merciful Phillipa glimmered there.
Pergo Park knew me, and Clavering, and Havering-atte-
    Bower,
Stanford Rivers lost me in osier beds, Stapleford Abbots
sent me safe home on the dark road after Simeon-quiet
    evensong,

Wanstead drew me over and over into its basic poetry,
in its serpentine lake I saw bass-viols among the golden
    dead leaves,
through its trees the ghost of a great house. In
Ilford High Road I saw the multitudes passing pale under
    the
light of flaring sundown, seven kings
in somber starry robes gathered at Seven Kings
the place of law
where my birth and marriage are recorded
and the death of my father. Woodford Wells
where an old house was called The Naked Beauty (a white
statue forlorn in its garden)
saw the meeting and parting of two sisters,
(forgotten? and further away
the hill before Thaxted? where peace befell us? not once
but many times?).
All the Ivans dreaming of their villages
all the Marias dreaming of their walled cities,
picking up fragments of New World slowly,
not knowing how to put them together nor how to join
image with image, now I know how it was with you, an
    old map
made long before I was born shows ancient
rights of way where I walked when I was ten burning with
    desire
for the world's great splendors, a child who traced voyages
indelibly all over the atlas, who now in a far country
remembers the first river, the first
field, bricks and lumber dumped in it ready for building,
that new smell, and remembers
the walls of the garden, the first light.

                                            (1961)

PHILIP LEVINE

On the Edge

My name is Edgar Poe and I was born
In 1928 in Michigan.
Nobody gave a damn. The gruel I ate
Kept me alive, nothing kept me warm,
But I grew up, almost to five foot ten,
And nothing in the world can change my weight.

I have been watching you these many years,
There in the office, pencil poised and ready,
Or on the highway when you went ahead.
I did not write; I watched you watch the stars
Believing that the wheel of fate was steady;
I saw you rise from love and go to bed;

I heard you lie, even to your daughter.
I did not write, for I am Edgar Poe,
Edgar the mad one, silly, drunk, unwise,
But Edgar waiting on the edge of laughter,
And there is nothing that he does not know
Whose page is blanker than the raining skies.

(1963)

The Horse

for Ichiro Kawamoto, humanitarian,
electrician, survivor of Hiroshima

They spoke of the horse alive
without skin, naked, hairless,

201

without eyes and ears, searching
for the stableboy's caress.
Shoot it, someone said, but they
let it go on colliding with
tattered walls, butting his long
skull to pulp, finding no path
where iron fences corkscrewed in
the street and bicycles turned
like question marks.
                          Some fled and
some sat down. The river burned
all that day and into the
night, the stones sighed a moment
and were still, and the shadow
of a man's hand entered
a leaf.
               The white horse never
returned, and later they found
the stableboy, his back crushed
by a hoof, his mouth opened
around a cry that no one heard.

They spoke of the horse again
and again; their mouths opened
like the gills of a fish caught
above water.
                     Mountain flowers
burst from the red clay walls, and
they said a new life was here.
Raw grass sprouted from the cobbles
like hair from a deafened ear.

The horse would never return.

There had been no horse. I could
tell from the way they walked
testing the ground for some cold
that the rage had gone out of
their bones in one mad dance.

                                        (1963)

Blasting from Heaven

The little girl won't eat her sandwich;
she lifts the bun and looks in, but the grey beef

coated with relish is always there.
Her mother says, "Do it for mother."
Milk and relish and a hard bun that comes off
like a hat—a kid's life is a cinch.

And a mother's life? "What can you do
with a man like that?" she asks the sleeping cook
and then the old Negro who won't sit.
"He's been out all night trying to get it.
I hope he gets it. What did he ever do
but get it?" The Negro doesn't look,

though he looks like he's been out all night
trying. Everyone's been out all night trying.
Why else would we be drinking beer
at attention? If she were younger
or if I were Prince Valiant, I would say that fate
brought me here to quiet the crying,

to sweeten the sandwich of the child,
to waken the cook, to stop the Negro from
bearing witness to the world. The dawn
still hasn't come, and now we hear
the 8 o'clock whistles blasting from heaven,
and with no morning the day is sold.

(1966)

Baby Villon

He tells me in Bangkok he's robbed
Because he's white; in London because he's black;
In Barcelona, Jew; in Paris, Arab:
Everywhere & at all times, & he fights back.

He holds up seven thick little fingers
To show me he's rated seventh in the world,
And there's no passion in his voice, no anger
In the flat brown eyes flecked with blood.

He asks me to tell all I can remember
Of my father, his uncle; he talks of the war

In North Africa and what came after,
The loss of his father, the loss of his brother,

The windows of the bakery smashed and the fresh bread
Dusted with glass, the warm smell of rye
So strong he ate till his mouth filled with blood.
"Here they live, here they live and not die,"

And he points down at his black head ridged
With black kinks of hair. He touches my hair,
Tells me I should never disparage
The stiff bristles that guard the head of the fighter.

Sadly his fingers wander over my face,
And he says how fair I am, how smooth.
We stand to end this first and last visit.
Stiff, 116 pounds, five feet two,

No bigger than a girl, he holds my shoulders,
Kisses my lips, his eyes still open,
My imaginary brother, my cousin,
Myself made otherwise by all his pain.

(1967)

Animals Are Passing from Our Lives

It's wonderful how I jog
on four honed-down ivory toes
my massive buttocks slipping
like oiled parts with each light step.

I'm to market. I can smell
the sour, grooved block, I can smell
the blade that opens the hole
and the pudgy white fingers

that shake out the intestines
like a hankie. In my dreams
the snouts drool on the marble,
suffering children, suffering flies,

suffering the consumers
who won't meet their steady eyes
for fear they could see. The boy
who drives me along believes

that any moment I'll fall
on my side and drum my toes
like a typewriter or squeal
and shit like a new housewife

discovering television,
or that I'll turn like a beast
cleverly to hook his teeth
with my teeth. No. Not this pig.

(1968)

LAURENCE LIEBERMAN

The Coral Reef

The sea is a circuit of holes:
mouths, bellies, cavities in coral-heads,
caves, deep cracks and wedges in the rock.
Brain coral stipple the bay meadows like toadstools,
each a community in siege. Shellfish, so frail,
secrete rock-skeletons,
rainbow-jeweled. These build. Rain, wind, the waves,
and boring animals corrode the sculptured lime,
dissolving the reefs to sand-deposits. The parrot
fish puckers his lips for love, and gnaws
death-kisses into coral.

Snorkelers hug the surface.
Divers scout gingerly among the poisonous
antlers, knowing the lightest brush with fire-coral
draws blood, and raises the flesh in welts: the pores
look out like portholes from the swellings. The sting
in each seems individual.
Coral-wounds are coated with slime, fish-slippery.
They are slow to heal. . . . In murky waters, sun blinds.
Sun trapped in snows of plankton glares like headlights
on wet asphalt, the white on the gray, light blocking out
sight. The scuba-diver

collides with a wall of fry,
so thick with silver-fish the luminous flanks
seem impervious, but his waving spear-end glances
not one fish on any side, the weightless flakes

dodging and veering, the larger movement of Overall
undeflected by internal
shifts. The school is running from gamefish: jack,
mackerel, gar, tarpon—they in turn pursued by predators:
shark, barracuda *no smile that curve of the jaws,*
an accidental twist of the gum-cartilage:
a chilling glance commands

    an instance that power needn't
be linked to size. grip speargun. if you shoot, don't miss
the head. spear in the tail. power mower gone berserk.
the handle cannot steer the blades. the head
a madly chopping bushel of teeth, wobbly.
weaving about the spear as axis.
as one who juggles a sixty-pound two-edged machete
under water. Trigger-finger shifts to the shutter.
Camera-shy fish and cuda-shy man, matched
for the moment, eye one another (neither advancing
to test the other's nerve),

    look away, look back. Cuda
turns! Barrel-length torpedos from sight!
Now, overhead, three Oldwife (Queen Triggerfish)
sail past, like kites. Wide and flat, they cannot
swim straight on, but turn spasmodically
from right to left, in squad
formation, cutting across their own paths,
and across his line of sight, narrowing to thumb's-
widths as they crisscross his axis, displaying one profile,
now another *(flash. discard bulb.):* triangular snouts
and trapezoidal posteriors,

    the graceful semi-parabolas
of dorsal and ventral fins, the axehead tail.
The man, tank on his back, descends. From seafloor
he peers under a shelf. In an inverted socket,
a lobster, the elusive female, her tail curled
on itself, conceals her treasure:
the orange bushel of eggs, blossom of caviar.
Her bubble-eyes on stalks (or stilts) look backward
behind her head, see around corners—they stare
and stare. The antennae, like a blindman's fingers
in the dark, must touch to tell.

    Dodging antennae, the diver
squirms into snapshot range. *large spiny forelegs.*

a male's. thrust over the lens. followed
by wide armored head. gloved hand traps leg—it drops
from body-joint. inert. like head of burnt match.
backwards lunge: muscular
tail contracts. scuffle of spear-jabs. pronged
back disengaged in a last rally of spasms.
drifts limp to the bottom. Halfway down,
the swarm are upon him, small nibblers lovingly
smooch and probe, their bites

     kiss-languish, entranced,
tenderly scooping flesh from shell, the carcass
suspended in skilled dismemberment, no part
touching bottom unemptied. Death-gyps! The dying
members, portioned into living guts, *survive,*
survive. Suddenly, the ledge
under his flipper sways, no footrest. Step off.
Move gently. The rock's alive, thousands of coraleyes,
feelers *busy busy,* tireless reef-toilers. Note
sponge, anemone, barnacle—lovely in their private
sleeps—malingerers these,

     parasites of the colony, taking
a free ride; the workers *the small,* drawing out of dun
selves mounds of iridescence: minuscule bodies
hatching, in fury of survival, gorgeous refuse, careless
towers of jewels, wreaths of rock-tissue, mouth's
masonry, flowers of fire . . .
At dawn, peering from a light-weight Cessna, cruising
low over the clear bay shallows, the water brutally
calm, the horseshoe-shaped reef entirely in view,
the beholder deciphers the expressions of an aging face,
chiseled by love. Dumbfounded,

     he is pierced with reverence.
The Saint-edge margin, Life/Death, fades, dissolves
in his eyes, *dreams: a boy's fishhook waiting,*
waiting to make wounds, to tug, to snap off in the big one
lost, to go deep, to die into life, to lie there in rich
corrosion; iron becoming
a part of the fish, the small hard thread of metal
breaking down and entering every canal and cell,
lastly into teeth, fins and scales. Intestines
are intelligence: such skill in distribution—equally—
to every pocket of life.

                                 (1966)

JOHN LOGAN

A Trip to Four or Five Towns

To James Wright

1

The gold-colored skin of my Lebanese friends.
Their deep, lightless eyes.
The serene, inner, careful
balance they share. The conjugal
smile of either for either.

2

This bellychilling, shoe soaking, factory-
dug-up-hill smothering Pittsburgh weather!
I wait for a cab in the smart mahogany
lobby of the seminary.
The marble *Pietà* is flanked around
with fake fern. She cherishes her dead son
stretched along her womb he triple crossed.
A small, slippered priest
pads up. Whom do you seek, my son?
Father, I've come in out of the rain.
I seek refuge from the elemental tears,
for my heavy, earthen body runs to grief
and I am apt to drown
in this small and underhanded rain
that drops its dross so delicately
on the hairs of the flowers, my father,
and follows down the veins of leaves
weeping quiet in the wood.
My yellow cab never came,

209

but I did not confess
beneath the painted Jesus Christ. I left
and never saved myself at all
that night in that late, winter rain.

3

In Washington, was it spring?
I took the plane.
I heard, on either side,
the soft executives, manicured and
fat, fucking this and fucking that.
My heavy second breakfast
lay across my lap.
At port, in the great concourse,
I could not walk to city bus
or cab? or limousine?
I sweat with shock, with havoc
of the hundred kinds of time,
trembling like a man away from home.

At the National Stripshow
where the girls wriggle right
and slow, I find I want to see in
under the sequin stepin.
And in my later dream of the negro girl's room
strong with ancient sweat and with her thick
aroma, I seem to play a melodrama
as her great, red dog barks twice
and I stab it with my pocket knife.

4

In Richmond the azalea banks
burst in rose and purple gullies by the car,
muted in the soft, wet
April twilight. The old estates
were pruned and rolled fresh
with spring, with splendor, touch-
ing the graceful stride of the boy who brings the paper.

5

My friend has a red-headed mother
capable of love in any kind
of weather. I am not sure
what she passes to her daughters
but from her brown eye and from her breast

she passes wit and spunk to her big sons.
And she is small and pleased when they put
their arms around her, having caught her.
They cut the grass naked to the waist.
They cure the handsome skins of chipmunks and of snakes.
And when they wake in their attic room
they climb down the ladder, half
asleep, feeling the rungs' pressure
on their bare feet, shirt tails out,
brown eyes shut. They eat
what she cooks. One shot a gorgeous colored hawk
and posed with it, proud, arms and full wings
spread. And one, at the beach,
balanced on his hands, posed
stripped, in the void of sand,
limbs a rudder in the wind,
amid the lonely, blasted wood.
And two sons run swift roans in the high, summer grass.
Now I would guess
her daughters had at least this same
grace and beauty as their mother,
though I have only seen their picture.
I know she is happy with her three
strong sons about her, for they are not clumsy
(one, calmed, so calmly,
bends a good ear to his guitar)
and they are not dull:
one built a small electric shaft topped with a glowing ball.

6

In New York I got drunk, to tell the truth,
and almost got locked up when a beat
friend with me took a leak in a telephone booth.
(E. E. Cummings on the Paris lawn.
"Reprieve pisseur Américain!")
At two o'clock he got knocked out
horning in with the girl in the room over him.
Her boy friend was still sober,
and too thin. I saw the blood of a poet
flow on the sidewalk. Oh, if I mock,
it is without heart, I thought
of the torn limbs of Orpheus
scattered in the grass on the hills of Thrace.
Do poets have to have such trouble with the female race?
I do not know. But if they bleed

I lose heart also.
When he reads, ah, when he reads, small but deep voiced,
he reads well: now weeps, now is cynical,
his large, horned eyes very black and tearful.

And when we visited a poet father
we rode to Jersey on a motor scooter.
My tie and tweeds looped in the winds.
I choked in the wake
of the Holland Pipe, and cops,
under glass like carps, eyed us.
That old father was so mellow and generous—
easy to pain,
white, open and at peace, and of good taste,
like his Rutherford house.
And he read, very loud and regal,
sixteen new poems based on paintings by Breughel!

7

The last night out,
before I climbed on the formal
Capital Viscount and was shot home
high, pure and clear,
seemed like the right time
to disappear.

(1959)

The Rescue

I doubt if you knew,
my two friends,
that day the tips
of the boats' white wings
trembled over the capped,
brilliant lake
and fireboats at the regatta
rocketed their giant streams
blue and white and green
in the sun just off the shore,
that I was dying there.

Young jets were play-
ing over the lake,
climbing and falling back
with a quick, metallic sheen
(weightless as I am
if I dream),
sound coming after the shine.
They rose and ran and
paused and almost touched,
except for one,
who seemed to hang back in the air
as if from fear.

I doubt if you know,
my two beloved friends—
you with the furious black beard,
your classical head
bobbing bodiless above the waves
like some just appearing god,
or you: brown, lean, your bright
face also of another kind,
disembodied
when you walked upon your hands—

That as you reached for me
(both) and helped my graying bulk
up out of the lake
after I wandered out too far
and battered weak along the pier,
it was my self you hauled
back from my despair.

(1966)

ROBERT LOWELL

Mr. Edwards and the Spider

I saw the spiders marching through the air,
Swimming from tree to tree that mildewed day
   In latter August when the hay
    Came creaking to the barn. But where
      The wind is westerly,
Where gnarled November makes the spiders fly
Into the apparitions of the sky,
They purpose nothing but their ease and die
Urgently beating east to sunrise and the sea;

What are we in the hands of the great God?
It was in vain you set up thorn and briar
   In battle array against the fire
    And treason crackling in your blood;
      For the wild thorns grow tame
And will do nothing to oppose the flame;
Your lacerations tell the losing game
You play against a sickness past your cure
How will the hands be strong? How will the heart endure?

A very little thing, a little worm,
Or hourglass-blazoned spider, it is said,
   Can kill a tiger. Will the dead
    Hold up his mirror and affirm
      To the four winds the smell
And flash of his authority? It's well
If God who holds you to the pit of hell,
Much as one holds a spider, will destroy,

Baffle and dissipate your soul. As a small boy
  On Windsor Marsh, I saw the spider die
When thrown into the bowels of fierce fire:
      There's no long struggle, no desire
        To get up on its feet and fly—
          It stretches out its feet
  And dies. This is the sinner's last retreat;
  Yes, and no strength exerted on the heat
Then sinews the abolished will, when sick
And full of burning, it will whistle on a brick.

  But who can plumb the sinking of that soul?
  Josiah Hawley, picture yourself cast
      Into a brick-kiln where the blast
        Fans your quick vitals to a coal—
          If measured by a glass,
  How long would it seem burning! Let there pass
  A minute, ten, ten trillion; but the blaze
  Is infinite, eternal: this is death,
To die and know it. This is the Black Widow, death.

(1946)

As a Plane Tree by the Water

      Darkness has called to darkness, and disgrace
      Elbows about our windows in this planned
      Babel of Boston where our money talks
      And multiplies the darkness of a land
      Of preparation where the Virgin walks
      And roses spiral her enamelled face
      Or fall to splinters on unwatered streets.
      Our Lady of Babylon, go by, go by,
      I was once the apple of your eye;
      Flies, flies are on the plane tree, on the streets.

      The flies, the flies, the flies of Babylon
      Buzz in my ear-drums while the devil's long
      Dirge of the people detonates the hour
      For floating cities where his golden tongue
      Enchants the masons of the Babel Tower
      To raise tomorrow's city to the sun

That never sets upon these hell-fire streets
Of Boston, where the sunlight is a sword
Striking at the withholder of the Lord:
Flies, flies are on the plane tree, on the streets.

Flies strike the miraculous waters of the iced
Atlantic and the eyes of Bernadette
Who saw Our Lady standing in the cave
At Massabielle, saw her so squarely that
Her vision put out reason's eyes. The grave
Is open-mouthed and swallowed up in Christ.
O walls of Jericho! And all the streets
To our Atlantic wall are singing: "Sing,
Sing for the resurrection of the King."
Flies, flies are on the plane tree, on the streets.

(1946)

Skunk Hour

For Elizabeth Bishop

Nautilus Island's hermit
heiress still lives through winter in her Spartan cottage;
her sheep still graze above the sea.
Her son's a bishop. Her farmer
is first selectman in our village;
she's in her dotage.

Thirsting for
the hierarchic privacy
of Queen Victoria's century,
she buys up all
the eyesores facing her shore,
and lets them fall.

The season's ill—
we've lost our summer millionaire,
who seemed to leap from an L. L. Bean
catalogue. His nine-knot yawl
was auctioned off to lobstermen.
A red fox stain covers Blue Hill.

And now our fairy
decorator brightens his shop for fall;
his fishnet's filled with orange cork,
orange, his cobbler's bench and awl;
there is no money in his work,
he'd rather marry.

One dark night,
my Tudor Ford climbed the hill's skull;
I watched for love-cars. Lights turned down,
they lay together, hull to hull,
where the graveyard shelves on the town. . . .
My mind's not right.

A car radio bleats,
"Love, O carless Love. . . ." I hear
my ill-spirit sob in each blood cell,
as if my hand were at its throat. . . .
I myself am hell;
nobody's here—

only skunks, that search
in the moonlight for a bite to eat.
They march on their soles up Main Street:
white stripes, moonstruck eyes' red fire
under the chalk-dry and spar spire
of the Trinitarian Church.

I stand on top
of our back steps and breathe the rich air—
a mother skunk with her column of kittens swills **the**
garbage pail.
She jabs her wedge-head in a cup
of sour cream, drops her ostrich tail,
and will not scare.

(1958)

Waking in the Blue

The night attendant, a B. U. sophomore,
rouses from the mare's-nest of his drowsy head
propped on *The Meaning of Meaning*.

He catwalks down our corridor.
Azure day
makes my agonized blue window bleaker.
Crows maunder on the petrified fairway.
Absence! My heart grows tense
as though a harpoon were sparring for the kill.
(This is the house for the "mentally ill.")

What use is my sense of humor?
I grin at Stanley, now sunk in his sixties,
once a Harvard all-American fullback,
(if such were possible!)
still hoarding the build of a boy in his twenties,
as he soaks, a ramrod
with the muscle of a seal
in his long tub,
vaguely urinous from the Victorian plumbing.
A kingly granite profile in a crimson golf-cap,
worn all day, all night,
he thinks only of his figure,
of slimming on sherbet and ginger ale—
more cut off from words than a seal.

This is the way day breaks in Bowditch Hall at McLean's;
the hooded night lights bring out "Bobbie,"
Porcellian '29,
a replica of Louis VXI
without the wig—
redolent and roly-poly as a sperm whale,
as he swashbuckles about in his birthday suit
and horses at chairs.

These victorious figures of bravado ossified young.

In between the limits of day,
hours and hours go by under the crew haircuts
and slightly too little nonsensical bachelor twinkle
of the Roman Catholic attendants.
(There are no Mayflower
screwballs in the Catholic Church.)

After a hearty New England breakfast,
I weigh two hundred pounds
this morning. Cock of the walk,
I strut in my turtle-necked French sailor's jersey
before the metal shaving mirrors,

nd see the shaky future grow familiar
n the pinched, indigenous faces
f these thoroughbred mental cases,
wice my age and half my weight.
Ve are all old-timers,
ach of us holds a locked razor.

(1959)

For the Union Dead

"RELINQUUNT OMNIA
SERVARE REM PUBLICAM."

The old South Boston Aquarium stands
n a Sahara of snow now. Its broken windows are boarded.
The bronze weathervane cod has lost half its scales.
The airy tanks are dry.

Once my nose crawled like a snail on the glass;
my hand tingled
to burst the bubbles
drifting from the noses of the cowed, compliant fish.

My hand draws back. I often sigh still
for the dark downward and vegetating kingdom
of the fish and reptile. One morning last March,
I pressed against the new barbed and galvanized

fence on the Boston Common. Behind their cage,
yellow dinosaur steamshovels were grunting
as they cropped up tons of mush and grass
to gouge their underworld garage.

Parking spaces luxuriate like civic
sandpiles in the heart of Boston.
A girdle of orange, Puritan-pumpkin colored girders
braces the tingling Statehouse,

shaking over the excavations, as it faces Colonel Shaw
and his bell-cheeked Negro infantry

on St. Gaudens' shaking Civil War relief,
propped by a plank splint against the garage's earthquake.

Two months after marching through Boston,
half the regiment was dead;
at the dedication,
William James could almost hear the bronze Negroes
    breathe.

Their monument sticks like a fishbone
in the city's throat.
Its Colonel is as lean
as a compass-needle.

He has an angry wrenlike vigilance,
a greyhound's gentle tautness;
he seems to wince at pleasure,
and suffocate for privacy.

He is out of bounds now. He rejoices in man's lovely,
peculiar power to choose life and death—
when he leads his black soldiers to death,
he cannot bend his back.

On a thousand small town New England greens,
the old white churches hold their air
of sparse, sincere rebellion; frayed flags
quilt the graveyards of the Grand Army of the Republic.

The stone statues of the abstract Union Soldier
grows slimmer and younger each year—
wasp-wasted, they doze over muskets
and muse through their sideburns . . .

Shaw's father wanted no monument
except the ditch,
where his son's body was thrown
and lost with his "niggers."

The ditch is nearer.
There are no statues for the last war here;
on Boyleston Street, a commercial photograph
shows Hiroshima boiling

over a Mosler Safe, the "Rock of Ages"
that survived the blast. Space is nearer.

When I crouch to my television set,
he drained faces of Negro school-children rise like
    balloons.

Colonel Shaw
s riding on his bubble,
he waits
or the blesséd break.

The Aquarium is gone. Everywhere,
giant finned cars nose forward like fish;
a savage servility
slides by on grease.

(1960)

WILLIAM H. MATCHETT

Water Ouzel

For Dora Willson

Follow back from the gull's bright arc and the osprey's
    plunge,
Past the silent heron, erect in the tidal marsh,
Up the mighty river, rolling in mud. Branch off
At the sign of the kingfisher poised on a twisted snag.
Not deceived when the surface grows calm, keep on,
Past the placidity of ducks, the delusive pastoral dreams
Drawn down by the effortless swallows that drink on the
    wing.
With the wheat fields behind you, do not neglect to choose
At every juncture the clearest and coldest path.
Push through the reeds where the redwing sways,
Climb through the warnings of hidden jays,
Climb, climb the jostling, narrowing stream
Through aspen sunlight into the evergreen darkness
Where chattering crossbills scatter the shreds of cones.
Here at last at the brink of the furthest fall,
With the water dissolving to mist as it shatters the pool
    below,
Pause beneath timber-line springs and the melting snow.
Here, where the shadows are deep in the crystal air,
So near a myriad beginnings, after so long a journey,
Expecting at least a golden cockatoo
Or a screaming eagle with wings of flame,
Stifle your disappointment, observe
The burgher of all this beauty, the drab
Citizen of the headwaters; struggle to love
The ridiculous ouzel, perched on his slippery stone
Like an awkward, overblown catbird deprived of its tail.

Not for him the limitless soaring above the storm,
Or the surface-skimming, or swimming, or plunging in.
He walks. In the midst of the turbulence, bathed in spray,
From a rock without foothold into the lunging current
He descends a deliberate step at a time till, submerged,
He has walked from sight and hope. The stream
Drives on, dashes, splashes, drops over the edge,
Too swift for ice in midwinter, too cold
For life in midsummer, depositing any debris,
Leaf, twig or carcass, along the way,
Wedging them in behind rocks to rot,
Such as these not reaching the ocean.

Yet, lo, the lost one emerges unharmed,
Hardly wet as he walks from the water.
Undisturbed by beauty or terror, pursuing
His own few needs with a nerveless will,
Nonchalant in the torrent, he bobs and nods
As though to acknowledge implicit applause.
This ceaseless tic, a trick of the muscles shared
With the solitary sandpiper, burlesqued
By the teeter-bob and the phoebe's tail,
Is not related to approbation. The dipper,
Denied the adventure of uncharted flight
Over vast waters to an unknown homeland, denied
Bodily beauty, slightly absurd and eccentric,
Will never attain acclaim as a popular hero.
No prize committee selects the clown
Whose only dangers are daily and domestic.

Yet he persists, and does not consider it persisting.
On a starless, sub-zero, northern night,
When all else has taken flight into sleep or the south,
He, on the edge of the stream, has been heard to repeat
The rippling notes of his song, which are clear and sweet.

(1953)

The Diver

Dressed in his clumsy, stiff, aquatic clothes,
His helmet screwed fast on so that he can
Do, say, see nothing in the world of man,
The diver shambles to the boatside, goes
Down the ladder, and the waters close
Over the steel that seals his sacred brain.
Over the boatside lean, his shadow scan
As it descends, shapeless and wavering.
It is no devilfish, is still a man—
But now it's gone.

         Creatures beyond our ken
He will describe in words on his return—
Pale words for objects seen—
The inhuman life that swirled before his sight,
Or fled, or fought. The treasure he seeks out
May yet be lifted up by creaking crane,
Splashing, out of the green, but in his brain
The jungles of the sea must flower still,
Whose hook has drawn the pale blood of the shark,
And when his streaming bulk climbs back aboard,
We'll mutter, say some contract has been signed
With what lies under, and that that occurred
Which has no human gesture and no word.

(1941)

WILLIAM MEREDITH

The Open Sea

We say the sea is lonely; better say
Ourselves are lonesome creatures whom the sea
Gives neither yes nor no for company.

Oh, there are people, all right, settled in the sea—
It is populous as Maine today—
But no one who will give you the time of day.

A man who asks there of his family
Or a friend or teacher gets a cold reply
Or finds him dead against that vast majority.

Nor does it signify that people who stay
Very long, bereaved or not, at the edge of the sea
Hear the drowned folk call: that is mere fancy,

They are speechless. And the famous noise of sea,
Which a poet has beautifully told us in our day,
Is hardly a sound to speak comfort to the lonely.

Although not yet a man given to prayer, I pray
For each creature lost since the start at sea,
And give thanks it was not I, nor yet one close to me.

(1953)

For Guillaume Apollinaire

The day is colorless like Swiss characters in a novel
And I sit at a desk in an old house left to the arts
Teaching your poems English.

I have read the French words in the dictionary starting
    with "W."
They are borrowings, too: *wesleyen, wigwam, wisigoth*
And *wattman*, an archaic electrical-tram driver.
If you were alive this summer you'd be 82.

The fourth floor of the mansion, just less than an acre,
Is servants' country. For years it was settled—
Chambermaids, kitchenmaids, footmen, a butler, a cook.
Somewhere there must be almost an acre of them now
Laid out in the Romanesque floor plan under the sod,
And the lady who rang for them.
The house is a good place to work. But these poems—
How quickly the strangeness would pass from things
    if it were not for them.

(1964)

JAMES MERRILL

The Octopus

There are many monsters that a glassen surface
Restrains. And none more sinister
Than vision asleep in the eye's tight translucence.
Rarely it seeks now to unloose
Its diamonds. Having divined how drab a prison
The purest mortal tissue is,
Rarely it wakes. Unless, coaxed out by lusters
Extraordinary, like the octopus
From the gloom of its tank half-swimming half-drifting
Toward anything fair, a handkerchief
Or child's face dreaming near the glass, the writher
Advances in a godlike wreath
Of its own wrath. Chilled by such fragile reeling
A hundred blows of a boot-heel
Shall not quell, the dreamer wakes and hungers.
Percussive pulses, drum or gong,
Build in his skull their loud entrancement,
Volutions of a Hindu dance.
His hands move clumsily in the first conventional
Gestures of assent.
He is willing to undergo the volition and fervor
Of many fleshlike arms, observe
These in their holiness of indirection
Destroy, adore, evolve, reject—
Till on glass rigid with his own seizure
At length the sucking jewels freeze.

(1951)

Mirror

I grow old under an intensity
Of questioning looks. *Nonsense,*
I try to say, *I cannot teach you children
How to live.—if not you, who will?*
Cries one of them aloud, grasping my gilded
Frame till the world sways. *If not you, who will?*
Between their visits the table, its arrangement
Of Bible, fern and Paisley, all past change,
Does very nicely. If ever I feel curious
As to what others endure,
Across the parlor *you* provide examples,
Wide open, sunny, of everything I am
Not. You embrace a whole world without once caring
To set it in order. That takes thought. Out there
Something is being picked. The red-and-white bandannas
Go to my heart. A fine young man
Rides by on horseback. Now the door shuts. Hester
Confides in me her first unhappiness.
This much, you see, would never have been fitted
Together, but for me. Why then is it
They more and more neglect me? Late one sleepless
Midsummer night I strained to keep
Five tapers from your breathing. *No,* the widowed
Cousin said, *let them go out.* I did.
The room brimmed with gray sound, all the instreaming
Muslin of your dream . . .

Years later now, two of the grown grandchildren
Sit with novels face-down on the sill,
Content to muse upon your tall transparence,
Your clouds, brown fields, persimmon far
And cypress near. One speaks. *How superficial
Appearances are!* Since then, as if a fish
Had broken the perfect silver of my reflectiveness,
I have lapses. I suspect
Looks from behind, where nothing is, cool gazes
Through the blind flaws of my mind. As days,
As decades lengthen, this vision
Spreads and blackens. I do not know whose it is,
But I think it watches for my last silver
To blister, flake, float leaf by life, each milling
Downward dumb conceit, to a standstill

From which not even you strike any brilliant
Chord in me, and to a faceless will,
Echo of mine, I am amenable.

(1958)

An Urban Convalescence

Out for a walk, after a week in bed,
I find them tearing up part of my block
And, chilled through, dazed and lonely, join the dozen
In meek attitudes, watching a huge crane
Fumble luxuriously in the filth of years.
Her jaws dribble rubble. An old man
Laughs and curses in her brain,
Bringing to mind the close of *The White Goddess.*

As usual in New York, everything is torn down
Before you have had time to care for it.
Head bowed, at the shrine of noise, let me try to recall
What building stood here. Was there a building at all?
I have lived on this same street for a decade.

Wait. Yes. Vaguely a presence rises
Some five floors high, of shabby stone
—Or am I confusing it with another one
In another part of town, or of the world?—
And over its lintel into focus vaguely
Misted with blood (my eyes are shut)
A single garland sways, stone fruit, stone leaves,
Which years of grit had etched until it thrust
Roots down, even into the poor soil of my seeing.
When did the garland become part of me?
I ask myself, amused almost,
Then shiver once from head to toe,

Transfixed by a particular cheap engraving of garlands
Bought for a few francs long ago,
All calligraphic tendril and cross-hatched rondure,
Ten years ago, and crumpled up to stanch
Boughs dripping, whose white gestures filled a cab,
And thought of neither then nor since.
Also, to clasp them, the small, red-nailed hand

Of no one I can place. Wait. No. Her name, her features
Lie toppled underneath that year's fashions.
The words she must have spoken, setting her face
To fluttering like a veil, I cannot hear now,
Let alone understand.

So that I am already on the stair,
As it were, of where I lived,
When the whole structure shudders at my tread
And soundlessly collapses, filling
The air with motes of stone.
Onto the still erect building next door
Are pressed levels and hues—
Pocked rose, streaked greens, brown whites.
Who drained the pousse-café?
Wires and pipes, snapped off at the roots, quiver.

Well, that is what life does. I stare
A moment longer, so. And presently
The massive volume of the world
Closes again.

Upon that book I swear
To abide by what it teaches:
Gospels of ugliness and waste,
Of towering voids, of soiled gusts,
Of a shrieking to be faced
Full into, eyes astream with cold—

With cold?
All right then. With self-knowledge.

Indoors at last, the pages of *Time* are apt
To open, and the illustrated mayor of New York,
Given a glimpse of how and where I work,
To note yet one more house that can be scrapped.

Unwillingly I picture
My walls weathering in the general view.

It is not even as though the new
Buildings did very much for architecture.

Suppose they did. The sickness of our time requires
That these as well be blasted in their prime.
You would think the simple fact of having lasted
Threatened our cities like mysterious fires.

There are certain phrases which to use in a poem
Is like rubbing silver with quicksilver. Bright
But facile, the glamour deadens overnight.
For instance, how 'the sickness of our time'

Enhances, then debases, what I feel.
At my desk I swallow in a glass of water
No longer cordial, scarcely wet, a pill
They had told me not to take until much later.

With the result that back into my imagination
The city glides, like cities seen from the air,
Mere smoke and sparkle to the passenger
Having in mind another destination

Which now is not that honey-slow descent
Of the Champs-Elysées, her hand in his,
But the dull need to make some kind of house
Out of the life lived, out of the love spent.

(1960)

Scenes of Childhood

for Claude Fredericks

My mother's lamp once out,
I press a different switch:
A field within the dim
White screen ignites,
Vibrating to the rapt
Mechanical racket
Of a real noon field's
Crickets and gnats.

And to its candid heart
I move with heart ajar,
With eyes that smart less
From pollen or heat
Than from the buried day

Now rising like a moon,
Shining, unwinding
Its taut white sheet.

Two or three bugs that lit
Earlier upon the blank
Sheen, all peaceable
Insensibility, drowse
As she and I cannot
Under the risen flood
Of thirty years ago—
A tree, a house

We had then, a late sun,
A door from which the primal
Figures jerky and blurred
As lightning bugs
From lanterns issue, next
To be taken for stars,
For fates. With knowing smiles
And beaded shrugs

My mother and two aunts
Loom on the screen. Their plucked
Brows pucker, their arms encircle
One another.
Their ashen lips move.
From the love seat's gloom
A quiet chuckle escapes
My white-haired mother

To see in that final light
A man's shadow mount
Her dress. And now she is
Advancing, sister-
less, but followed by
A fair child, or fury—
Myself at four, in tears.
I raise my fist,

Strike, she kneels down. The man's
Shadow afflicts us both.
Her voice behind me says
It might go slower.
I work dials, the film jams.
Our headstrong old projector

Glares at the scene which promptly
Catches fire.

Puzzled, we watch ourselves
Turn red and black, gone up
In a puff of smoke now coiling
Down fierce beams.
I switch them off. A silence.
Your father, she remarks,
Took those pictures; later
Says pleasant dreams,

Rises and goes. Alone
I gradually fade and cool.
Night scatters me with green
Rustlings, thin cries.
Out there between the pines
Have begun shining deeds,
Some low, inconstant (these
Would be fireflies),

Others as in high wind
Aflicker, staying lit.
There are nights we seem to ride
With cross and crown
Forth under them, through fumes,
Coils, the whole rattling epic—
Only to leap clear-eyed
From eiderdown,

Asleep to what we'd seen.
Father already fading—
Who focused your life long
Through little frames,
Whose microscope, now deep
In purple velvet, first
Showed me the skulls of flies,
The fur, the flames

Etching the jaws—father:
Shrunken to our true size.
Each morning, back of us,
Fields wail and shimmer.
To go out is to fall
Under fresh spells, cool web

And stinging song new-hatched
Each day, all summer.

A minute galaxy
About my head will easily
Needle me back. The day's
Inaugural *Damn*
Spoken, I start to run,
Inane, like them, but breathing
In and out the sun
And air I am.

The son and heir! In the dark
It makes me catch my breath
And hear, from upstairs, hers—
That faintest hiss
And slither, as of life
Escaping into space,
Having led its characters
To the abyss

Of night. Immensely still
The heavens glisten. One broad
Path of vague stars is floating
Off, a shed skin
Of all whose fine cold eyes
First told us, locked in ours:
You are the heroes without name
Or origin.

(1960)

The Mad Scene

Again last night I dreamed the dream called Laundry.
In it, the sheets and towels of a life we were going to share,
The milk-stiff bibs, the shroud, each rag to be ever
Trampled or soiled, bled on or groped for blindly,
Came swooning out of an enormous willow hamper
Onto moon-marbly boards. We had just met. I watched
From outer darkness. I had dressed myself in clothes
Of a new fiber that never stains or wrinkles, never

Wears thin. The opera house sparkled with tiers
And tiers of eyes, like mine enlarged by belladonna,
Trained inward. There I saw the cloud-clot, gust by gust,
Form, and the lightning bite, and roan mane unloosen.
Fingers were running in panic over the flute's nine gates.
Why did I flinch? I loved you. And in the downpour laughed
To have us wrung white, gnarled together, one
Topmost mordent of wisteria,
As the lean tree burst into grief.

(1962)

Days of 1964

Houses, an embassy, the hospital,
Our neighborhood sun-cured if trembling still
In pools of night's rain . . .
Across the street that led to the center of town
A steep hill kept one company part way
Or could be climbed in twenty minutes
For some literally breathtaking views,
Framed by umbrella pines, of city and sea.
Underfoot, cyclamen, autumn crocus grew
Spangled as with fine sweat among the relics
Of good times had by all. If not Olympus,
An out-of-earshot, year-round hillside revel.

I brought home flowers from my climbs.
Kyria Kleo who cleans for us
Put them in water, sighing *Virgin, Virgin.*
Her legs hurt. She wore brown, was fat, past fifty,
And looked like a Palmyra matron
Copied in lard and horsehair. How she loved
You, me, loved us all, the bird, the cat!
I think now she *was* love. She sighed and glistened
All day with it, or pain, or both.
(We did not notably communicate.)
She lived nearby with her pious mother
And wastrel son. She called me her real son.

I paid her generously, I dare say.
Love makes one generous. Look at us. We'd known
Each other so briefly that instead of sleeping
We lay whole nights, open, in the lamplight,
And gazed, or traded stories.

One hour comes back—you gasping in my arms
With love, or laughter, or both,
I having just remembered and told you
What I'd looked up to see on my way downtown at noon:
Poor old Kleo, her aching legs,
Trudging into the pines. I called,
Called three times before she turned.
Above a tight, skyblue sweater, her face
Was painted. Yes. Her face was painted
Clown-white, white of the moon by daylight,
Lidded with pearl, mouth a poinsettia leaf,
Eat me, pay me—the erotic mask
Worn the world over by illusion
To weddings of itself and simple need.

Startled mute, we had stared—was love illusion?—
And gone our ways. Next, I was crossing a square
In which a moveable outdoor market's
Vegetables, chickens, pottery kept materializing
Through a dream-press of hagglers each at heart
Leery lest he be taken, plucked,
The bird, the flower of that November mildness,
Self lost up soft clay paths, or found, foothold,
Where the bud throbs awake
The better to be nipped, self on its knees in mud—
Here I stopped cold, for both our sakes;

And calmer on my way home bought us fruit.

Forgive me if you read this. (And may Kyria Kleo,
Should someone ever put it into Greek
And read it aloud to her, forgive me, too.)
I had gone so long without loving,
I hardly knew what I was thinking.

Where I hid my face, your touch, quick, merciful,
Blindfolded me. A god breathed from my lips.
If that was illusion, I wanted it to last long;
To dwell, for its daily pittance, with us there,
Cleaning and watering, sighing with love or pain.

I hoped it would climb when it needed to the heights
Even of degradation, as I for one
Seemed, those days, to be always climbing
Into a world of wild
Flowers, feasting, tears—or was I falling, legs
Buckling, heights, depths,
Into a pool of each night's rain?
But you were everywhere beside me, masked,
As who was not, in laughter, pain, and love.

(1966)

W. S. MERWIN

Ballad of John Cable and Three Gentlemen

He that had come that morning,
One after the other,
Over seven hills,
Each of a new color,

Came now by the last tree,
By the red-colored valley,
To a gray river
Wide as the sea.

There at the shingle
A listing wherry
Awash with dark water;
What should it carry?

There on the shelving,
Three dark gentlemen.
Might they direct him?
Three gentlemen.

"Cable, friend John, John Cable,"
When they saw him they said,
"Come and be company
As far as the far side."

"Come follow the feet," they said,
"Of your family,
Of your old father
That came already this way."

But Cable said, "First I must go
Once to my sister again;
What will she do come spring
And no man on her garden?

She will say 'Weeds are alive
From here to the Stream of Friday;
I grieve for my brother's plowing,'
Then break and cry."

"Lose no sleep," they said, "for that fallow:
She will say before summer,
'I can get me a daylong man,
Do better than a brother.'"

Cable said, "I think of my wife:
Dearly she needs consoling;
I must go back for a little
For fear she die of grieving."

"Cable," they said, "John Cable,
Ask no such wild favor;
Still, if you fear she die soon,
The boat might wait for her."

But Cable said, "I remember:
Out of charity let me
Go shore up my poorly mother,
Cries all afternoon."

They said, "She is old and far,
Far and rheumy with years,
And, if you like, we shall take
No note of her tears."

But Cable said, "I am neither
Your hired man nor maid,
Your dog nor shadow
Nor your ape to be led."

He said, "I must go back:
Once I heard someone say
That the hollow Stream of Friday
Is a rank place to lie;

And this word, now I remember,
Makes me sorry: have you
Thought of my own body
I was always good to?

The frame that was my devotion
And my blessing was,
The straight bole whose limbs
Were long as stories—

Now, poor thing, left in the dirt
By the Stream of Friday
Might not remember me
Half tenderly."

They let him nurse no worry;
They said, "We give you our word:
Poor thing is made of patience;
Will not say a word."

"Cable, friend John, John Cable,"
After this they said,
"Come with no company
To the far side.

To a populous place,
A dense city
That shall not be changed
Before much sorrow dry."

Over shaking water
Toward the feet of his father,
Leaving the hills' color
And his poorly mother

And his wife at grieving
And his sister's fallow
And his body lying
In the rank hollow,

Now Cable is carried
On the dark river;
Not even a shadow
Followed him over.

On the wide river
Gray as the sea
Flags of white water
Are his company.

(1951)

Song of Three Smiles

Let me call a ghost,
Love, so it be little:
In December we took
No thought for the weather.

Whom now shall I thank
For this wealth of water?
Your heart loves harbors
Where I am a stranger.

Where was it we lay
Needing no other
Twelve days and twelve nights
In each other's eyes?

Or was it at Babel
'And the days too small
We spoke our own tongue
Needing no other?

If a seed grow green
Set a stone upon it
That it learn thereby
Holy charity.

If you must smile
Always on that other,
Cut me from ear to ear
And we all smile together.

(1953)

Small Woman on Swallow Street

Four feet up, under the bruise-blue
Fingered hat-felt, the eyes begin. The sly brim
Slips over the sky, street after street, and nobody
Knows, to stop it. It will cover
The whole world, if there is time. Fifty years'
Start in gray the eyes have; you will never
Catch up to where they are, too clever
And always walking, the legs not long but
The boots big with wide smiles of darkness
Going round and round at their tops, climbing.
They are almost to the knees already, where
There should have been ankles to stop them.
So must keep walking all the time, hurry, for
The black sea is down where the toes are
And swallows and swallows all. A big coat
Can help save you. But eyes push you down; never
Meet eyes. There are hands in hands, and love
Follows its furs into shut doors; who
Shall be killed first? Do not look up there:
The wind is blowing the building-tops, and a hand
Is sneaking the whole sky another way, but
It will not escape. Do not look up. God is
On High. He can see you. You will die.

(1957)

Sire

Here comes the shadow not looking where it is going,
And the whole night will fall; it is time.
Here comes the little wind which the hour
Drags with its everywhere like an empty wagon through
    leaves.
Here comes my ignorance shuffling after them
Asking them what they are doing.
Standing still, I can hear my footsteps
Come up behind me and go on

Ahead of me and come up behind me and
With different keys clinking in the pockets,
And still I do not move. Here comes
The white-haired thistle seed stumbling past through the
     branches
Like a paper lantern carried by a blind man.
I believe it is the lost wisdom of my grandfather
Whose ways were his own and who died before I could ask.

Forerunner, I would like to say, silent pilot,
Little dry death, future,
Your indirections are as strange to me
As my own. I know so little that anything
You might tell me would be a revelation.

Sir, I would like to say,
It is hard to think of the good woman
Presenting you with children, like cakes,
Granting you the eye of her needle,
Standing in doorways, flinging after you
Little endearments, like rocks, or her silence
Like a whole Sunday of bells. Instead, tell me:
Which of my many incomprehensions
Did you bequeath me, and where did they take you?
     Standing
In the shoes of indecision, I hear them
Come up behind me and go on ahead of me
Wearing boots, on crutches, barefoot, they could never
Get together on any door-sill or destination—
The one with the assortment of smiles, the one
Jailed in himself like a forest, the one who comes
Back at evening drunk with despair and turns
Into the wrong night as though he owned it—oh small
Deaf disappearance in the dusk, in which of their shoes
Will I find myself tomorrow?

                              (1962)

The Way to the River

The way to the river leads past the names of
Ash the sleeves the wreaths of hinges
Through the song of the bandage vendor

I lay your name by my voice
As I go

The way to the river leads past the late
Doors and the games of the children born looking backwards
They play that they are broken glass
The numbers wait in the halls and the clouds
Call
From windows
They play that they are old they are putting the horizon
Into baskets they are escaping they are
Hiding

I step over the sleepers the fires the calendars
My voice turns to you

I go past the juggler's condemned building the hollow
Windows gallery
Of invisible presidents the same motion in them all
In a parked cab by the sealed wall the hats are playing
Sort of poker with somebody's
Old snapshots game I don't understand they lose
The rivers one
After the other I begin to know where I am

I am home

Be here the flies from the house of the mapmaker
Walk on our letters I can tell
And the days hang medals between us
I have lit our room with a glove of yours be
Here I turn
To your name and the hour remembers
Its one word
Now
Be here what can we
Do for the dead the footsteps full of money
I offer you what I have my
Poverty

To the city of wires I have brought home a handful
Of water I walk slowly
In front of me they are building the empty
Ages I see them reflected not for long
Be here I am no longer ashamed of time it is too brief its
    hands

Have no names
I have passed it I know

> *Oh Necessity you with the face you with*
> *All the faces*

This is written on the back of everything

But we
Will read it together

(1962)

The Asians Dying

When the forests have been destroyed their darkness remains
The ash the great walker follows the possessors
Forever
Nothing they will come to is real
Nor for long
Over the watercourses
Like ducks in the time of the ducks
The ghosts of the villages trail in the sky
Making a new twilight

Rain falls into the open eyes of the dead
Again again with its pointless sound
When the moon finds them they are the color of everything

The nights disappear like bruises but nothing is healed
The dead go away like bruises
The blood vanishes into the poisoned farmlands
Pain the horizon
Remains
Overhead the seasons rock
They are paper bells
Calling to nothing living

The possessors move everywhere under Death their star
Like columns of smoke they advance into the shadows
Like thin flames with no light
They with no past
And fire their only future

(1966)

For the Anniversary of My Death

Every year without knowing it I have passed the day
When the last fires will wave to me
And the silence will set out
Tireless traveller
Like the beam of a lightless star

Then I will no longer
Find myself in life as in a strange garment
Surprised at the earth
And the love of one woman
And the shamelessness of men
As today writing after three days of rain
Hearing the wren sing and the falling cease
And bowing not knowing what to what

(1967)

HOWARD MOSS

Elegy for My Father

Father, whom I murdered every night but one,
That one, when your death murdered me,
Your body waits within the wasting sod.
Clutching at the straw-face of your God,
Do you remember me, your morbid son,
Curled in a death, all motive unbegun,
Continuum of flesh, who never thought to be
The mourning mirror of your potency?

All you had battled for the nightmare took
Away, as dropping from your eyes, the sea-
Salt tears, with messages that none could read,
Impotent, pellucid, were the final seeds
You sowed. Above you, the white night nurse shook
His head, and, moaning on the moods of luck,
We knew the double-dealing enemy:
From pain you suffered, pain had set you free.

Down from the ceiling, father, circles came:
Angels, perhaps, to bear your soul away.
But tasting the persisting salt of pain,
I think my tears created them, though, in vain,
Like yours, they fell. All losses link: the same
Creature marred us both to stake his claim.
Shutting my eyelids, barring night and day,
I saw, and see, your body borne away.

Two months dead, I wrestle with your name
Whose separate letters make a paltry sum

That is not you. If still you harbor mine,
Think of the house we had in summertime
When in the sea-light every early game
Was played with love and, if death's waters came,
You'd rescue me. How I would take you from,
Now, if I could, its whirling vacuum.

(1955)

King Midas

My food was pallid till I heard it ring
Against fine china. Every blessed thing
I touch becomes a work of art that baits
Its goldsmith's appetite: My bread's too rich,
My butter much too golden, and my meat
A nugget on my plate, as cold as ice;
Fresh water in my throat turns precious there,
Where every drop becomes a millionaire.

My hands leak gold into the flower's mouth,
Whose lips in tiers of rigid foliage
Make false what flowers are supposed to be.
I did not know I loved their warring thorns
Until they flowered into spikes so hard
My blood made obdurate the rose's stem.
My God was generous. But when I bleed,
It clogs the rosebed and cements the seed.

My dog was truly witty while he breathed.
I saw the tiny hairs upon his skin
Grow like a lion's into golden down.
I plucked them by the handfuls off of him,
And, now he is pure profit, my sculpturing
Might make a King go mad, for it was I
Who made those lively muscles stiffly pose—
This jaundice is relentless, and it grows.

I hate the glint of stars, the shine of wheat,
And when I walk, the tracings of my feet
Are affluent and litter where I go

With money that I sweat. I bank the slow
Gold-leaf of everything and, in my park,
A darkness shimmers that is not the dark,
A daylight glitters that is not the day—
All things are much less darling gilt this way.

Princess, come no closer; my tempered kiss,
Though it is royal still, will make you this
Or that kind of a statue. And my Queen,
Be armed against this gold paralysis,
Or you will starve and thinly bed alone,
And when you dream, a gold mine in your brain
Will have both eyes release their golden ore
And cry for tears they could not cry before.

I would be nothing but the dirt made loud,
A clay that ripples with the worm, decay
In ripeness of the weeds, a timid sun,
Or oppositely be entirely cloud,
Absolved of matter, dissolving in the rain.
Before gold kills me as it kills all men,
Dear Dionysus, give me back again
Ten fingertips that leave the world alone.

(1957)

Water Island

To the memory of a friend, drowned

off Water Island, April, 1960

Finally, from your house, there is no view;
The bay's blind mirror shattered over you
And Patchogue took your body like a log
The wind rolled up to shore. The senseless drowned
Have faces nobody would care to see,
But water loves those gradual erasures
Of flesh and shoreline, greenery and glass,
And you belonged to water, it to you,
Having built, on a hillock, above the bay,
Your house, the bay giving you reason to,
Where now, if seasons still are running straight,

The horseshoe crabs clank armor night and day,
Their couplings far more ancient than the eyes
That watched them from your porch. I saw one once
Whose back was a history of how we live;
Grown onto every inch of plate, except
Where the hinges let it move, were living things,
Barnacles, mussels, water weeds—and one
Blue bit of polished glass, glued there by time:
The origins of art. It carried them
With pride, it seemed, as if endurance only
Matters in the end. Or so I thought.

Skimming traffic lights, starboard and port,
Steer through planted poles that mark the way,
And other lights, across the bay, faint stars
Lining the border of Long Island's shore,
Come on at night, they still come on at night,
Though who can see them now I do not know.
Wild roses, at your back porch, break their blood,
And bud to test surprises of sea air,
And the birds fly over, gliding down to feed
At the two feeding stations you set out with seed,
Or splash themselves in a big bowl of rain
You used to fill with water. Going across
That night, too fast, too dark, no one will know,
Maybe you heard, the last you'll ever hear,
The cry of the savage and endemic gull
Which shakes the blood and always brings to mind
The thought that death, the scavenger, is blind,
Blunders and is stupid, and the end
Comes with ironies so fine the seed
Falters in the marsh and the heron stops
Hunting in the weeds below your landing stairs,
Standing in a stillness that now is yours.

(1960)

Finding Them Lost

Thinking of words that would save him, slanting
Off in the air, some cracked, some bent;
Finding them lost, he started saying
Some other words he never meant.

The green went back and forth in waves
As if his heart pumped out the lawn
In blood, not grass. A bench sailed down,
Becoming the bench he sat upon,

Staring out at the crazy garden,
With its women washed out to milky shades,
Or pressed through the trees' accordion,
While the past jerked past in lantern slides,

Badly lit, of images unbidden,
Faces, arms, and forgotten eyes
That, peeping through the leaves, half hidden,
Turned on and off like fireflies.

Fire and flies. *That* was it,
He thought, as the nurse bloomed, coming, coming
Straight through a tree to hold his hand.
Holding hers, he felt blood drumming

Through the twined bones of where they met.
It was three months the stubborn grass
Wouldn't rise up to meet his foot,
Or rising up, caught him unawares.

How to get back to pure imagination,
He asked the nerves of work and love,
And both networks of such importance,
He dreamed them. But what was he dreaming of?

Sleep, it was sleep, that found him napping
When the delicious dew of sweat
Brought forth the baby he'd been hiding
Wrapped in his skin, maybe his heart.

And what the mirror gave back was him
Finally, tired and very old.
"My life, begin . . ." But it didn't, wouldn't,
Though grass was grass and no bench sailed

Down to a garden to support him
And no one walked through a tree to hold
His hand. But a green lawn pulses in him.
Home, he still dreams of going home.

(1964)

Arsenic

I/THE FIRST LETTER

They will be telling you soon who you are,
The importunate, slovenly, younger thinkers—
But only because they are young. From afar,
You may hear certain familiar voices,
Romantic but growing increasingly dim,
Express themselves in some thirty sounds
Out of a possible twenty thousand;
The terraces will be swinging in place
With their few discordant violins, the lamps
Hissing with gas, the smell of an old
Shoebox suddenly tainting the wharf—
Or could the sky's incredible liquor
Be responsible for the odor of
A set of ancient mah-jongg tiles
You found in your mother's closet once?
What are they doing here on the coast?
They are lustreless now from disuse and the sun.

> *"I have taken a sufficient dose and still*
> *Feel nothing, a slight burning sensation,*
> *But no smell of garlic, the telltale sign.*
> *Strange. And several seconds have passed.*
> *No pain. But for those who follow, I note*
> *That the phone will appear farther away . . ."*

II/THE SECOND LETTER

Now they will tell you your favorite words,
Symbols gone sickly with use—such as
Gull   blue   ocean   house—
Are no longer possible. And they're right.
You *have* been a bit of a fool. You have
Been feeling your way
When you should have gone straight
To the heart of the matter. Which is what?
To have looked humiliation full
In the face instead of walking around
It, like a dog chained to a pole . . .

For instance, a letter arrived this week,
Saying

> *"You're not expressing yourself.*
> *It's hard to know who you are."*

These facts
Are relevant:
I have never killed.
I have loved three times—
Possibly four.
I have two suits
I will never wear.
The mornings are bad,
But by evening I'm
Myself again.

Do you know me now, Miss Mandarin?
You of the scented, mauve-lined page
Who tell me that you were once a nun
But now, when a sailor stalks the streets,
You feel the old magic welling up,
The thing most of all you're afraid to lose?
Don't tell me *you're* the one who wrote
Three hundred times on a warehouse wall
"Don't knock love!" If so, I shake
Your hand still blue from chalk . . .

III/THE THIRD LETTER

But there it is. One word
Used up already. Blue.
And here's another, thinly disguised:

Meanwhile the sea, a hundred yards away,
Already bored with its literary career,
Is beating itself up, again, again,
And, sick of the moon's attentions every night,
Is carving a sandbar farther out
Behind which it hopes to draw its skirts
And thus avoid the shore's vulgar display.
It's deluded, of course. It isn't very bright.
But it's beautiful. Which, around here, is right.

Now I am going back to the house
For a drink. From the upper porch, I see
A gull go by on the steadiest wings
You ever saw. If a scavenger's
That gorgeous, what will they say of me?
There's something to be said for everything,
For garbage, for instance, in this case.

"I've been meaning to write much sooner but
Something has kept me from saying just
What I wanted to . . . Are you well? Does J.
Still wake each night and need comforting?
I think, perhaps, that the lack of love,
Yes, love . . . I feel you no longer
Love, sincerely, with a thousand thoughts . . ."

Starlight, dear walk, when this view is
Nothing but emptied space and snow,
When no foot breaks its silences,
What faces, guests will then arrive
Frantic with their reasons to live?

(1967)

STANLEY MOSS

Two Fishermen

My father made a synagogue of a boat.
I fish in ghettos, cast toward the lilypads,
Strike rock and roil the unworried waters;
I in my father's image: rusty and off hinge,
The fishing box between us like a covenant.
I reel in, the old lure bangs against the boat.
As the sun shines I take his word for everything.
My father snarls his line, spends half an hour
Unsnarling mine. Eel, sunfish and bullhead
Are not for me. At seven I cut my name
For bait. The worm gnawed toward the mouth of my name.
"Why are the words for temple and school
The same," I asked, "And why a school of fish?"
My father does not answer. On a bad cast
My fish strikes, breaks water, takes the line.

Into a world of good and evil, I reel
A creature languished in the flood. I tear out
The lure, hooks cold. I catch myself,
Two hooks through the hand,
Blood on the floor of the synagogue. The wound
Is purple, shows a mouth of white birds;
Hook and gut dangle like a rosary,
Another religion in my hand.
I'm ashamed of this image of crucifixion.
A Jew's image is a reading man.
My father tears out the hooks, returns to his book,
A nineteenth-century history of France.
Our war is over:
Death hooks the corner of his lips.
The wrong angel takes over the lesson.

(1965)

Squall

I have not used my darkness well,
Nor the Baroque arm that hangs from my shoulder,
Nor the Baroque arm of my chair.
The rain moves out in a dark schedule.
Let the wind marry. I know the Creation
Continues through love. The rain's a wife.
I can not sleep or lie awake. Looking
At the dead I turn back, fling
My hat into their grandstands for relief.
How goes a life? Something like the ocean
Building dead coral.

(1966)

The Lonesome Dream

In the America of the dream,
the first rise of the moon
swings free of the ocean
as she reigns in her shining flesh
over a good, great valley
of plumed, untrampled grasses
and beasts with solemn eyes,
of lovers infallibly pitched
in their ascendant phase.

In this America, death
is virginal also, roaming
the good, great valley
in his huge boots, his shadow
steady and lean, his pistol
silver, his greeting clear
and courteous as a stranger's
who looks for another—a mind
to share his peaceable evenings.

Dreaming, we are another
race than the one which wakes
in the cold sweat of fear,
fires wild shots at death,
builds slippery towers of glass
to head him off, waylays him
with alcohol traps, rides him down
in the haunts of thought and thighs,
our teetering ghost towns.

Dreaming, we are the mad
who swear by the blood of trees
and speak with the tongues of streams
through props of steel and sawdust—
a colony of souls
ravaged by visions, bound
to some wild, secret cove
not yet possessed, a place
still innocent of us.

(1964)

Moon Fishing

When the moon was full they came to the water,
some with pitchforks, some with rakes,
some with sieves and ladles
and one with a silver cup.

And they fished till a traveler passed them and said,
"Fools,
to catch the moon you must let your women
spread their hair on the water—
even the wily moon will leap to that bobbing
net of shimmering threads,
gasp and flop till its silver scales
lie black and still at your feet."

And they fished with the hair of their women
till a traveler passed them and said,
"Fools,
do you think the moon is caught lightly,
with glitter and silk threads?
You must cut out your hearts and bait your hooks
with those dark animals;
what matter you lose your hearts to reel in your dream?"

And they fished with their tight, hot hearts
till a traveler passed them and said,
"Fools,
what good is the moon to a heartless man?

Put back your hearts and get on your knees
and drink as you never have,
until your throats are coated with silver
and your voices ring like bells."

And they fished with their lips and tongues
until the water was gone
and the moon had slipped away
in the soft, bottomless mud.

(1965)

HOWARD NEMEROV

I Only Am Escaped Alone to Tell Thee

I tell you that I see her still
At the dark entrance of the hall.
One gas lamp burning near her shoulder
Shone also from her other side
Where hung the long inaccurate glass
Whose pictures were as troubled water.
An immense shadow had its hand
Between us on the floor, and seemed
To hump the knuckles nervously,
A giant crab readying to walk,
Or a blanket moving in its sleep.

You will remember, with a smile
Instructed by movies to reminisce,
How strict her corsets must have been,
How the huge arrangements of her hair
Would certainly betray the least
Impassionate displacement there.
It was no rig for dallying,
And maybe only marriage could
Derange that queenly scaffolding—
As when a great ship, coming home,
Coasts in the harbor, dropping sail
And loosing all the tackle that had laced
Her in the long lanes . . .

                    I know
We need not draw this figure out
But all that whalebone came from whales

And all the whales lived in the sea,
In calm beneath the troubled glass,
Until the needle drew their blood.

I see her standing in the hall,
Where the mirror's lashed to blood and foam,
And the black flukes of agony
Beat at the air till the light blows out.

(1955)

The Murder of William Remington

It is true, that even in the best-run state
Such things will happen; it is true,
What's done is done. The law, whereby we hate
Our hatred, sees no fire in the flue,
But by the smoke, and not for thought alone
It punishes, but for the thing that's done.

And yet there is the horror of the fact,
Though we knew not the man. To die in jail,
To be beaten to death, to know the act
Of personal fury before the eyes can fail
And the man die against the cold last wall
Of the lonely world—and neither is that all:

There is the terror too of each man's thought,
That knows not, but must quietly suspect
His neighbor, friend, or self of being taught
To take an attitude merely correct;
Being frightened of his own cold image in
The glass of government, and his own sin,

Frightened lest senate house and prison wall
Be quarried of one stone, lest righteousness and high
Look faintly smiling down and seem to call
A crime the welcome chance of liberty,
And any man an outlaw who aggrieves
The patriotism of a pair of thieves.

(1958)

The View from an Attic Window

for Francis and Barbara

1

Among the high-branching, leafless boughs
Above the roof-peaks of the town,
Snowflakes unnumberably come down.

I watched out of the attic window
The laced sway of family trees,
Intricate genealogies

Whose strict, reserved gentility,
Trembling, impossible to bow,
Received the appalling fall of snow.

All during Sunday afternoon,
Not storming, but befittingly,
Out of a still, grey, devout sky,

The snowflakes fell, until all shapes
Went under, and thickening, drunken lines
Cobwebbed the sleep of solemn pines.

Up in the attic, among many things
Inherited and out of style,
I cried, then fell asleep awhile,

Waking at night now, as the snow-
flakes from darkness to darkness go
Past yellow lights in the street below.

2

I cried because life is hopeless and beautiful.
And like a child I cried myself to sleep
High in the head of the house, feeling the hull
Beneath me pitch and roll among the steep
Mountains and valleys of the many years
    Which brought me to tears.

Down in the cellar, furnace and washing machine,
Pump, fuse-box, water heater, work their hearts
Out at my life, which narrowly runs between

Them and this cemetery of spare parts
For discontinued men, whose hats and canes
    Are my rich remains.

And women, their portraits and wedding gowns
Stacked in the corners, brooding in wooden trunks;
And children's rattles, books about lions and clowns;
And headless, hanging dresses swayed like drunks
Whenever a living footstep shakes the floor;
    I mention no more;

But what I thought today, that made me cry,
Is this, that we live in two kinds of thing:
The powerful trees, thrusting into the sky
Their black patience, are one, and that branching
Relation teaches how we endure and grow;
    The other is the snow,

Falling in a white chaos from the sky,
As many as the sands of all the seas,
As all the men who died or who will die,
As stars in heaven, as leaves of all the trees;
As Abraham was promised of his seed;
    Generations bleed

Till I, high in the tower of my time
Among familiar ruins, began to cry
For accident, sickness, justice, war and crime,
Because all died, because I had to die.
The snow fell, the trees stood; the promise kept,
    And a child I slept.

                              (1960)

FRANK O'HARA

Chez Jane

The white chocolate jar full of petals
swills odds and ends around in a dizzying eye
of four o'clocks now and to come. The tiger,
marvellously striped and irritable, leaps
on the table and without disturbing a hair
of the flowers' breathless attention, pisses
into the pot, right down its delicate spout.
A whisper of steam goes up from that porcelain
eurythra. "Saint-Saëns!" it seems to be whispering,
curling unerringly around the furry nuts
of the terrible puss, who is mentally flexing.
Ah be with me always, spirit of noisy
contemplation in the studio, the Garden
of Zoos, the eternally fixed afternoons!
There, while music scratches its scrofulous
stomach, the brute beast emerges and stands,
clear and careful, knowing always the exact peril
at this moment caressing his fangs with
a tongue given wholly to luxurious usages;
which only a moment before dropped aspirin
in this sunset of roses, and now throws a chair
in the air to aggravate the truly menacing.

(1952)

To the Harbormaster

I wanted to be sure to reach you;
though my ship was on the way it got caught
in some moorings. I am always tying up

and then deciding to depart. In storms and
at sunset, with the metallic coils of the tide
around my fathomless arms, I am unable
to understand the forms of my vanity
or I am hard alee with my Polish rudder
in my hand and the sun sinking. To
you I offer my hull and the tattered cordage
of my will. The terrible channels where
the wind drives me against the brown lips
of the reeds are not all behind me. Yet
I trust the sanity of my vessel; and
if it sinks, it may well be in answer
to the reasoning of the eternal voices,
the waves which have kept me from reaching you.

(1954)

CHARLES OLSON

The Lordly and Isolate Satyrs

The lordly and isolate Satyrs—look at them come in
on the left side of the beach
like a motorcycle club! and the handsomest of them,
the one who has a woman, driving that snazzy
convertible
       Wow, did you ever see even in a museum
such a collection of boddisatvahs, the way
they come up to their stop, each of them
as though it was a rudder
the way they have to sit above it
and come to a stop on it, the monumental solidity
of themselves, the Easter Island
they make of the beach, the Red-headed Men

       These are the Androgynes,
the Fathers behind the father, the Great Halves

Or as that one was, inside his pants, the Yiddish poet
a vegetarian. Or another—all in his mouth—a snarl
of the Sources. Or the one I loved most, who once,
once only, let go the pain, the night he got drunk,
and I put him to bed, and he said, Bad blood.

       Or the one who cracks and doesn't know
that what he thinks are a thousand questions are suddenly
a thousand lumps thrown up where the cloaca
again has burst: one looks into the face and exactly as sud-
   denly
it isn't the large eyes and nose but the ridiculously small
   mouth
which you are looking down as one end of

                  —as the Snarled Man
is a monocyte.

Hail the ambiguous Fathers, and look closely
at them, they are the unadmitted, the club of Themselves,
weary riders, but who sit upon the landscape at the Great
Stones. And only have fun among themselves. They are
the lonely ones

Hail-them, and watch out. The rest of us,
on the beach as we had previously known it, did not know
there was this left side. As they came riding in from the sea
—we did not notice them until they were already creating
the beach we had not known was there—but we assume
they came in from the sea. We assume that. We don't know.

In any case the whole sea was now a hemi-
sphere,
and our eyes like half a fly's, we saw twice as much. Every-
thing opened, even if the newcomers just sat, didn't,
for an instant, pay us any attention. We were as we had
been, in that respect. We were as usual, the children were
being fed pop
and potato chips, and everyone was sprawled as people are
on a beach. Something had happened but the change
wasn't at all evident. A few drops of rain
would have made more of a disturbance.

There we were. They, in occupation of the
whole view
in front of us and off to the left where we were not used
to look.
And we, watching them pant from their exertions, and talk
to each other,
the one in the convertible the only one who seemed to be
circulating.
And he was dressed in magnificent clothes, and the woman
with him
a dazzling blond, the new dye making her hair a delicious
streaked ash. She was as distant as the others. She sat in her
flesh too.

These are our counterparts, the unknown ones.

They are here. We do not look upon them as invaders.
Dimensionally

they are larger than we—all but the woman. But we are not
suddenly
small. We are as we are. We don't even move, on the beach.

It is a stasis. Across nothing at all we stare at
them.

We can see what they are. They don't notice us. They have merely
and suddenly moved in. They occupy our view. They are between us
and the ocean. And they have given us a whole new half of beach.

As of this moment, there is nothing else to report.
It is Easter Island transplanted to us. With the sun, and a warm
summer day, and sails out on the harbor they're here, the Contemporaries. They have come in.

Except for the stirring of the leader, they are still
catching their breath. They are almost like scooters the way
they sit there, up a little, on their thing. It is as though
the extra effort of it tired them the most. Yet that just there
was where their weight and separateness—their immensities—
lay. Why they seem like boddisatvahs. The only thing one noticed
is the way their face breaks when they call across to each other.
Or actually speak quite quietly, not wasting breath. But the face
loses all containment, they are fifteen year old boys at the moment
they speak to each other. They are not gods. They are not even stone.
They are doubles. They are only Source. When they act like us
they go to pieces. One notices then that their skin
is only creased like red-neck farmers. And that they are all
freckled. The red-headed people have the hardest time
to possess themselves. Is it because they were over-
fired? Or why—even to their beautiful women—do the red
ones have only that half of the weight?

We look at them, and begin to know. We begin to see
who they are. We see why they are satyrs, and why one half
of the beach was unknown to us. And now that it is known,
now that the beach goes all the way to the headland we thought

we were huddling ourselves up against, it turns out it is the
same. It is beach. The Visitors—Resters—who, by being
there,
made manifest what we had not known—that the beach
    fronted wholly
to the sea—have only done that, completed the beach.

The difference is
we are more on it. The beauty of the white of the sun's
    light, the
blue the water is, and the sky, the movement on the painted
    lands-
cape, the boy-town the scene was, is now pierced with
    angels and
with fire. And winter's ice shall be as brilliant in its time as
life truly is, as Nature is only the offerer, and it is we
who look to see what the beauty is.

These visitors, now stirring
to advance, to go on wherever they do go restlessly never
    completing
their tour, going off on their motorcycles, each alone except
    for
the handsome one, isolate huge creatures wearing down
    nothing as
they go, their huge third leg like carborundum, only the
vault of their being taking rest, the awkward boddhas

We stay. And watch them
gather themselves up. We have no feeling except love. They
    are not
ours. They are of another name. These are what the gods
    are. They
look like us. They are only in all parts larger. But the size is
only different. The difference is, they are not here, they are
    not
on this beach in this sun which, tomorrow, when we come
    to swim,
will be another summer day. They can't talk to us. We have
    no desire
to stop them any more than, as they made their camp, only
    possibly
the woman in the convertible one might have wanted to be
    familiar
with. The Leader was too much as they.

They go. And the day

(1960)

The Boat

I dressed my father in his little clothes,
Blue sailor suit, brass buttons on his coat.
He asked me where the running water goes.

"Down to the sea," I said; "Set it afloat!"
Beside the stream he bent and raised the sail,
Uncurled the string and launched the painted boat.

White birds, flown like flags, wrenched his eyes pale.
He leaped on the tight deck and took the wind.
I watched the ship foam lurching in the gale,

And cried, "Come back, you don't know what you'll
    find!"
He steered. The ship grew, reddening the sky.
Water throbbed backward, blind stumbling after blind.

The rusty storm diminished in his eye,
And down he looked at me. A harbor rose.
I asked, "What happens, father, when you die?"

He told where all the running water goes,
And dressed me gently in my little clothes.

(1962)

DONALD PETERSEN

Walking Along the Hudson

The fat friar stroking golf balls
Has lost one of them in a bush.
We ask, may we look at the grounds?
"Oh, they come through here with cahs," says he,
And goes after the golf ball.

On the bluff's height stands the Friary,
Immaculate in yellow brick
And circled with a ribbon of asphalt, freshly laid.
If God is not here He is not anywhere.
(Yes, and the Holy Ghost is freshly laid.)

Beyond the tended lawn and the tennis courts,
Where does the spirit turn for exercise?
To the very edge of the bluff—
Down ruined steps and past a crumbling fountain
Where the old order stood, through trees
Older than any evidence of man,
The path of meditation winds through shade
To the knoll of prayer standing in full view
Of a field of water cabbage
And the many-prismed Hudson with its danger rock,
Its barges and their drones,
Reborn, made right, washed clean in the blows of the sun;
To the pool of stinks, effluvium of friars,
God's sluice, the putrid spring,
Where those who pass by
Feel drawn into Hell by their gut-strings,
Where the spirits of flatulence live out their lives
Wandering filmily through ferns and sumacs,

Inspiring stinkbugs and blowflies,
Where the traveler, reeling in fumes, stupid and lost,
Nevertheless clings to the narrowing path
And observes, from the undermined cliff, a graveyard of
    trees,
Huge trunks broken off like chalk,
Lying, elephant-colored, on the rocks;
And then the steep path upward, head swimming with heat,
And the thorns and creepers and branches
That snatch at your flesh as if to say,
"Don't go away! Don't go away!
You who pass by us to eternity,
Show us your pity!
If, as the breezes cry,
We have no being save in your consciousness,
Gaze on us, that we may exist—for see
(Ah, see), we truly die."

(1968)

SYLVIA PLATH

The Moon and the Yew Tree

This is the light of the mind, cold and planetary.
The trees of the mind are black. The light is blue.
The grasses unload their griefs on my feet as if I were God,
Prickling my ankles and murmuring of their humility.
Fumey, spiritous mists inhabit this place
Separated from my house by a row of headstones.
I simply cannot see where there is to get to.

The moon is no door. It is a face in its own right,
White as a knuckle and terribly upset.
It drags the sea after it like a dark crime; it is quiet
With the O-gape of complete despair. I live here.
Twice on Sunday, the bells startle the sky—
Eight great tongues affirming the Resurrection.
At the end, they soberly bong out their names.

The yew tree points up. It has a Gothic shape.
The eyes lift after it and find the moon.
The moon is my mother. She is not sweet like Mary.
Her blue garments unloose small bats and owls.
How I would like to believe in tenderness—
The face of the effigy, gentled by candles,
Bending, on me in particular, its mild eyes.

I have fallen a long way. Clouds are flowering
Blue and mystical over the face of the stars.
Inside the church, the saints will be all blue,
Floating on their delicate feet over the cold pews,
Their hands and faces stiff with holiness.

The moon sees nothing of this. She is bald and wild.
And the message of the yew tree is blackness—blackness
and silence.

(1963)

Daddy

You do not do, you do not do
Any more, black shoe
In which I have lived like a foot
For thirty years, poor and white,
Barely daring to breathe or Achoo.

Daddy, I have had to kill you.
You died before I had time—
Marble-heavy, a bag full of God,
Ghastly statue with one grey toe
Big as a Frisco seal

And a head in the freakish Atlantic
Where it pours bean green over blue
In the waters off beautiful Nauset.
I used to pray to recover you.
Ach, du.

In the German tongue, in the Polish town
Scraped flat by the roller
Of wars, wars, wars.
But the name of the town is common.
My Polack friend

Says there are a dozen or two.
So I never could tell where you
Put your foot, your root,
I never could talk to you.
The tongue stuck in my jaw.

It stuck in a barb wire snare.
Ich, ich, ich, ich,

I could hardly speak.
I thought every German was you.
And the language obscene

An engine, an engine
Chuffing me off like a Jew.
A Jew to Dachau, Auschwitz, Belsen.
I began to talk like a Jew.
I think I may well be a Jew.

The snows of the Tyrol, the clear beer of Vienna
Are not very pure or true.
With my gypsy ancestress and my weird luck
And my Taroc pack and my Taroc pack
I may be a bit of a Jew.

I have always been scared of *you*,
With your Luftwaffe, your gobbledygoo.
And your neat moustache
And your Aryan eye, bright blue.
Panzer-man, panzer-man, O You—

Not God but a swastika
So black no sky could squeak through.
Every woman adores a Fascist,
The boot in the face, the brute
Brute heart of a brute like you.

You stand at the blackboard, daddy,
In the picture I have of you,
A cleft in your chin instead of your foot
But no less a devil for that, no not
Any less the black man who

Bit my pretty red heart in two.
I was ten when they buried you.
At twenty I tried to die
And get back, back, back to you.
I thought even the bones would do.

But they pulled me out of the sack,
And they stuck me together with glue.
And then I knew what to do.
I made a model of you,
A man in black with a Meinkampf look

And a love of the rack and the screw.
And I said I do, I do.
So daddy, I'm finally through.
The black telephone's off at the root,
The voices just can't worm through.

If I've killed one man, I've killed two—
The vampire who said he was you
And drank my blood for a year,
Seven years, if you want to know.
Daddy, you can lie back now.

There's a stake in your fat black heart
And the villagers never liked you.
They are dancing and stamping on you.
They always *knew* it was you.
Daddy, daddy, you bastard, I'm through.

                                                    (1963)

Nick and the Candlestick

I am a miner. The light burns blue.
Waxy stalactites
Drip and thicken, tears

The earthen womb
Exudes from its dead boredom.
Black bat airs

Wrap me, raggy shawls,
Cold homicides.
They weld to me like plums.

Old cave of calcium
Icicles, old echoer.
Even the newts are white,

Those holy Joes.
And the fish, the fish—
Christ! they are panes of ice,

A vice of knives,
A piranha
Religion, drinking

Its first communion out of my live toes.
The candle
Gulps and recovers its small altitude,

Its yellows heaten.
O love, how did you get here?
O embryo

Remembering, even in sleep,
Your crossed position.
The blood blooms clean

In you, ruby.
The pain
You wake to is not yours.

Love, love,
I have hung our cave with roses,
With soft rugs—

The last of Victoriana.
Let the stars
Plummet to their dark address,

Let the mercuric
Atoms that cripple drip
Into the terrible well,

You are the one
Solid the spaces lean on, envious.
You are the baby in the barn.

(1963)

ADRIENNE RICH

The Roofwalker

for Denise Levertov

Over the half-finished houses
night comes. The builders
stand on the roof. It is
quiet after the hammers,
the pulleys hang slack.
Giants, the roofwalkers,
on a listing deck, the wave
of darkness about to break
on their heads. The sky
is a torn sail where figures
pass magnified, shadows
on a burning deck.

I feel like them up there:
exposed, larger than life,
and due to break my neck.

Was it worth while to lay—
with infinite exertion—
a roof I can't live under?
—All those blueprints,
closing of gaps,
measurings, calculations?
A life I didn't choose
chose me: even
my tools are the wrong ones
for what I have to do.

I'm naked, ignorant,
a naked man fleeing
across the roofs
who could with a shade of difference
be sitting in the lamplight
against the cream wallpaper
reading—not with indifference—
about a naked man
fleeing across the roofs.

(1961)

The Trees

The trees inside are moving out into the forest,
the forest that was empty all these days
where no bird could sit
no insect hide
no sun bury its feet in shadow
the forest that was empty all these nights
will be full of trees by morning.

All night the roots work
to disengage themselves from the cracks
in the veranda floor.
The leaves strain toward the glass
small twigs stiff with exertion
long-cramped boughs shuffling under the roof
like newly discharged patients
half-dazed, moving
to the clinic doors.

I sit inside, doors open to the veranda
writing long letters
in which I scarcely mention the departure
of the forest from the house.
The night is fresh, the whole moon shines
in a sky still open
the smell of leaves and lichen
still reaches like a voice into the rooms.
My head is full of whispers
which tomorrow will be silent.

Listen. The glass is breaking.
The trees are stumbling forward
into the night. Winds rush to meet them.
The moon is broken like a mirror,
its pieces flash now in the crown
of the tallest oak.

(1964)

Mourning Picture

(The Picture is by Edwin Romanzo Elmer, 1850–1923)

They have carried the mahogany chair and the cane rocker
out under the lilac bush,
and my father and mother darkly sit there, in black clothes.
Our clapboard house stands fast on its hill,
my doll lies in her wicker pram
gazing at western Massachusetts.
This was our world.
I could remake each shaft of grass
feeling its rasp on my fingers,
draw out the map of every lilac leaf
or the net of veins on my father's
grief-tranced hand.

Out of my head, half-bursting,
still filling, the dream condenses—
shadows, crystals, ceilings, meadows, globes of dew.
Under the dull green of the lilacs, out in the light
carving each spoke of the pram, the turned porch-pillars,
under high early-summer clouds,
I am Effie, visible and invisible,
remembering and remembered.

They will move from the house,
give the toys and pets away.
Mute and rigid with loss my mother
will ride the train to Baptist Corner,
the silk-spool will run bare.
I tell you, the thread that bound us lies

faint as a web in the dew.
Should I make you, world, again,
could I give back the leaf its skeleton, the air
its early-summer cloud, the house
its noonday presence, shadowless,
and leave *this* out? I am Effie, you were my dream.

(1965)

Charleston in the 1860s

(derived from the diaries of Mary Boykin Chestnut)

He seized me round the waist and kissed my throat . . .
Your eyes, dear, are they grey or blue,
eyes of an angel?
The carts have passed already with their heaped
night-soil, we breathe again.
Is this what war is? Nitrate . . .
But smell the pear,
the jasmine, the violets.
Why does this landscape always sadden you?
Now the freshet is up on every side,
the river comes to our doors,
limbs of primeval trees dip in the swamp.

So we fool on into the black
cloud ahead of us.
Everything human glitters fever-bright,
the thrill of waking up
out of a stagnant life?
There seems a spell upon
your lovers—all dead of wounds
or blown to pieces . . . Nitrate!
I'm writing blind with tears of rage.
In vain. Years, death, depopulation, fears,
bondage: these shall all be borne.
No imagination to forestall woe.

(1967)

THEODORE ROETHKE

Elegy for Jane

MY STUDENT, THROWN BY A HORSE

I remember the neckcurls, limp and damp as tendrils;
And her quick look, a sidelong pickerel smile;
And how, once startled into talk, the light syllables leaped
    for her,
And she balanced in the delight of her thought,
A wren, happy, tail into the wind,
Her song trembling the twigs and small branches.
The shade sang with her;
The leaves, their whispers turned to kissing;
And the mold sang in the bleached valleys under the rose.

Oh, when she was sad, she cast herself down into such a
    pure depth,
Even a father could not find her:
Scraping her cheek against straw;
Stirring the clearest water.

My sparrow, you are not here,
Waiting like a fern, making a spiny shadow.
The sides of wet stones cannot console me,
Nor the moss, wound with the last light.

If only I could nudge you from this sleep,
My maimed darling, my skittery pigeon.
Over this damp grave I speak the words of my love:
I, with no rights in this matter,
Neither father nor lover.

(1950)

Frau Bauman, Frau Schmidt, and Frau Schwartze

Gone the three ancient ladies
Who creaked on the greenhouse ladders,
Reaching up white strings
To wind, to wind
The sweet-pea tendrils, the smilax,
Nasturtiums, the climbing
Roses, to straighten
Carnations, red
Chrysanthemums; the stiff
Stems, jointed like corn,
They tied and tucked,—
These nurses of nobody else.
Quicker than birds, they dipped
Up and sifted the dirt;
They sprinkled and shook;
They stood astride pipes,
Their skirts billowing out wide into tents,
Their hands twinkling with wet;
Like witches they flew along rows
Keeping creation at ease;
With a tendril for needle
They sewed up the air with a stem;
They teased out the seed that the cold kept asleep,—
All the coils, loops, and whorls.
They trellised the sun; they plotted for more than themselves.

I remember how they picked me up, a spindly kid,
Pinching and poking my thin ribs
Till I lay in their laps, laughing,
Weak as a whiffet;
Now, when I'm alone and cold in my bed,
They still hover over me,
These ancient leathery crones,
With their bandannas stiffened with sweat,
And their thorn-bitten wrists,
And their snuff-laden breath blowing lightly over me in my
    first sleep.

(1952)

The Waking

I wake to sleep, and take my waking slow.
I feel my fate in what I cannot fear.
I learn by going where I have to go.

We think by feeling. What is there to know?
I hear my being dance from ear to ear.
I wake to sleep, and take my waking slow.

Of those so close beside me, which are you?
God bless the Ground! I shall walk softly there,
And learn by going where I have to go.

Light takes the Tree; but who can tell us how?
The lowly worm climbs up a winding stair;
I wake to sleep, and take my waking slow.

Great Nature has another thing to do
To you and me; so take the lively air,
And, lovely, learn by going where to go.

This shaking keeps me steady. I should know.
What falls away is always. And is near.
I wake to sleep, and take my waking slow.
I learn by going where I have to go.

(1953)

Words for the Wind

1

Love, love, a lily's my care,
She's sweeter than a tree.
Loving, I use the air
Most lovingly: I breathe;
Mad in the wind I wear
Myself as I should be,

All's even with the odd,
My brother the vine is glad.

Are flower and seed the same?
What do the great dead say?
Sweet Phoebe, she's my theme:
She sways whenever I sway.
"O love me while I am,
You green thing in my way!"
I cried, and the birds came down
And made my song their own.

Motion can keep me still:
She kissed me out of thought
As a lovely substance will;
She wandered; I did not:
I stayed, and light fell
Across her pulsing throat;
I stared, and a garden stone
Slowly became the moon.

The shallow stream runs slack;
The wind creaks slowly by;
Out of a nestling's beak
Comes a tremulous cry
I cannot answer back;
A shape from deep in the eye—
That woman I saw in a stone—
Keeps pace when I walk alone.

2

The sun declares the earth;
The stones leap in the stream;
On a wide plain, beyond
The far stretch of a dream,
A field breaks like the sea;
The wind's white with her name,
And I walk with the wind.

The dove's my will today.
She sways, half in the sun:
Rose, easy on a stem,
One with the sighing vine,
One to be merry with,
And pleased to meet the moon.
She likes wherever I am.

Passion's enough to give
Shape to a random joy:
I cry delight: I know
The root, the core of a cry.
Swan-heart, arbutus-calm,
She moves when time is shy:
Love has a thing to do.

A fair thing grows more fair;
The green, the springing green
Makes an intenser day
Under the rising moon;
I smile, no mineral man;
I bear, but not alone,
The burden of this joy.

3

Under a southern wind,
The birds and fishes move
North, in a single stream;
The sharp stars swing around;
I get a step beyond
The wind, and there I am,
I'm odd and full of love.

Wisdom, where is it found?—
Those who embrace, believe.
Whatever was, still is,
Says a song tied to a tree.
Below, on the ferny ground,
In rivery air, at ease,
I walk with my true love.

What time's my heart? I care.
I cherish what I have
Had of the temporal:
I am no longer young
But the winds and waters are;
What falls away will fall;
All things bring me to love.

4

The breath of a long root,
The shy perimeter
Of the unfolding rose,
The green, the altered leaf,

The oyster's weeping foot,
And the incipient star—
Are part of what she is.
She wakes the ends of life.

Being myself, I sing
The soul's immediate joy.
Light, light, where's my repose?
A wind wreathes round a tree.
A thing is done: a thing
Body and spirit know
When I do what she does:
Creaturely creature, she!—

I kiss her moving mouth,
Her swart hilarious skin;
She breaks my breath in half;
She frolicks like a beast;
And I dance round and round,
A fond and foolish man,
And see and suffer myself
In another being, at last.

(1955)

I'm Here

1

Is it enough?—
The sun loosening the frost on December windows,
The glitter of wet in the first of morning?
The sound of voices, young voices, mixed with sleighbells,
Coming across snow in early evening?

Outside, the same sparrows bicker in the eaves.
I'm tired of tiny noises:
The April cheeping, the vireo's insistence,
The prattle of the young no longer pleases.
Behind the child's archness
Lurks the bad animal.

—How needles and corners perplex me!
Dare I shrink to a hag,
The worst surprise a corner could have,
A witch who sleeps with her horse?
Some fates are worse.

2

I was queen of the vale—
For a short while,
Living all my heart's summer alone,
Ward of my spirit,
Running through high grasses,
My thighs brushing against flower-crowns;
Leaning, out of all breath,
Bracing my back against a sapling,
Making it quiver with my body;

At the stream's edge, trailing a vague finger;
Flesh-awkward, half-alive,
Fearful of high places, in love with horses;
In love with stuffs, silks,
Rubbing my nose in the wool of blankets;
Bemused; pleased to be;
Mindful of cries,
The meaningful whisper,
The wren, the catbird.

> So much of adolescence is an ill-defined dying,
> An intolerable waiting,
> A longing for another place and time,
> Another condition.

I stayed: a willow to the wind.
The bats twittered at noon.
The swallows flew in and out of the smokeless chimneys.
I sang to the edges of flame,
My skin whiter in the soft weather,
My voice softer.

3

I remember walking down a path,
Down wooden steps toward a weedy garden;
And my dress caught on a rose-brier.
When I bent to untangle myself,
The scent of the half-opened buds came up over me.
I thought I was going to smother.

In the slow coming-out of sleep,
On the sill of the eyes, something flutters,
A thing we feel at evening, and by doors,
Or when we stand at the edge of a thicket,
And the ground-chill comes closer to us,
From under the dry leaves,
A beachy wetness.

The body, delighting in thresholds,
Rocks in and out of itself.
A bird, small as a leaf,
Sings in the first
Sunlight.

And the time I was so sick—
The whole place shook whenever I got a chill—
I closed my eyes, and saw small figures dancing,
A congress of tree-shrews and rats,
Romping around a fire,
Jumping up and down on their hind feet,
Their forepaws joined together, like hands—
They seemed very happy.

In my grandmother's inner eye,
So she told me when I was little,
A bird always kept singing.
She was a serious woman.

4

My geranium is dying, for all I can do,
Still leaning toward the last place the sun was.
I've tried I don't know how many times to replant it.
But these roses: I can wear them by looking away.
The eyes rejoice in the act of seeing and the fresh after-
    image;
Without staring like a lout, or a moping adolescent;
Without commotion.
Look at the far trees at the end of the garden.
The flat branch of that hemlock holds the last of the sun,
Rocking it, like a sun-struck pond,
In a light wind.

I prefer the still joy:
The wasp drinking at the edge of my cup;
A snake lifting its head;
A snail's music.

5

What's weather to me? Even carp die in this river.
I need a pond with small eels. And a windy orchard.
I'm no midge of that and this. The dirt glitters like salt.
Birds are around. I've all the singing I would.
I'm not far from a stream.
It's not my first dying.
I can hold this valley,
Loose in my lap,
In my arms.

    If the wind means me,
    I'm here—
    Here.

                      (1956)

The Geranium

When I put her out, once, by the garbage pail,
She looked so limp and bedraggled,
So foolish and trusting, like a sick poodle,
Or a wizened aster in late September,
I brought her back in again
For a new routine—
Vitamins, water, and whatever
Sustenance seemed sensible
At the time: she'd lived
So long on gin, bobbie pins, half-smoked cigars, dead beer,
Her shriveled petals falling
On the faded carpet, the stale
Steak grease stuck to her fuzzy leaves.
(Dried-out, she creaked like a tulip.)

The things she endured!—
The dumb dames shrieking half the night
Or the two of us, alone, both seedy,
Me breathing booze at her,
She leaning out of her pot toward the window.

Near the end, she seemed almost to hear me—
And that was scary—
So when that snuffling cretin of a maid

Threw her, pot and all, into the trash-can,
I said nothing.

But I sacked the presumptious hag the next week,
I was that lonely.

(1963)

Infirmity

In purest song one plays the constant fool
As changes shimmer in the inner eye.
I stare and stare into a deepening pool
And tell myself my image cannot die.
I love myself: that's my one constancy.
Oh, to be something else, yet still to be!

Sweet Christ, rejoice in my infirmity;
There's little left I care to call my own.
Today they drained the fluid from a knee
And pumped a shoulder full of cortisone;
Thus I conform to my divinity
By dying inward, like an aging tree.

The instant ages on the living eye;
Light on its rounds, a pure extreme of light
Breaks on me as my meager flesh breaks down—
The soul delights in that extremity.
Blessed the meek; they shall inherit wrath;
I'm son and father of my only death.

A mind too active is no mind at all;
The deep eye sees the shimmer on the stone;
The eternal seeks, and finds, the temporal,
The change from dark to light of the slow moon,
Dead to myself, and all I hold most dear,
I move beyond the reach of wind and fire.

Deep in the greens of summer sing the lives
I've come to love. A vireo whets its bill.
The great day balances upon the leaves;

My ears still hear the bird when all is still;
My soul is still my soul, and still the Son,
And knowing this, I am not yet undone.

Things without hands take hands: there is no choice,—
Eternity's not easily come by.
When opposites come suddenly in place,
I teach my eyes to hear, my ears to see
How body from spirit slowly does unwind
Until we are pure spirit at the end.

(1963)

JAMES SCHUYLER

Buried at Springs

I

There is a hornet in the room
and one of us will have to go
out the window into the late
August mid-afternoon sun. I
won. There is a certain challenge
in being humane to hornets
but not much. A launch draws
two lines of wake behind it
on the bay like a delta
with a melted base. Sandy
billows, or so they look,
of feathery ripe heads of grass,
an acid-yellow kind of
goldenrod glowing or glowering
in shade. Rocks with rags
of shadow, washed dust clouts
that will never bleach.
It is not like this at all.
The rapid running of the
lapping water, a hollow knock
of someone shipping oars,
it's eleven years since
Frank sat at this desk and
saw and heard it all:
the incessant water the
immutable crickets only
not the same: new needles
on the spruce, new seaweed

293

on the lowtide rocks,
other grass and other water
even the great gold lichen
on a granite boulder
even the boulder quite
literally is not the same.

II

A day, subtle and suppressed
in mounds of juniper enfolding
scratchy pockets of shadow
while bigness—rocks, trees, a stump—
stand shadowless in an overcast
of ripe grass. There is nothing
but shade, like the boggy depths
of a stand of spruce, its resonance
just the thin scream
of mosquitoes ascending.
Boats are light lumps on the bay
stretching past erased islands
to ocean and the terrible tumble,
and London ("rain persisting")
and Paris ("changing to rain").
Delicate day, setting the bright
of a young spruce against the cold
of an old one hung with unripe cones
each exuding at its tip
gum, pungent, clear as a tear,
a day stained and fractured
as the quartz in ribbons in the rocks
of a dulled and distant point,
a day like a gull passing
slowly flapping its wings
in a kind of lope, a day without
breeze enough to shake loose
the last fireweed flowers,
a faintly clammy day, like wet silk,
stained by one dead branch
the harsh russet of dried blood.

(1967)

WINFIELD TOWNLEY SCOTT

Annual Legend

A million butterflies rose up from South America,
All together, and flew in a gold storm toward Spain:
Eastward, the annual legend, a shining amber cloud
Driven homeward as it had been and would be again
Since the conquerors searching the harder shining
Brought for the bargain a handful of wings of flame.

Balboa lies dead somewhere and Pizarro's helmet
Is a spider's kingdom; yet here was the arrogant breath
And the dangerous plume burning across the foreign air
That danced like an ancient Andalusian noon:
A blaze, it rose leaving the jungle dark and the leaves
Heavy with silence, and the wheeltracks folding to doom
Where majesty wandered:
                    A million butterflies,
Wheeling eastward from the soil where the nugget lies lost,
Turned homeward in vast diurnal fire that marched one day
Burning toward Spain; and after that, for a while,
Spread like a field of death, gold on the sea.

(1940)

ANNE SEXTON

Her Kind

I have gone out, a possessed witch,
haunting the black air, braver at night;
dreaming evil, I have done my hitch
over the plain houses, light by light:
lonely thing, twelve-fingered, out of mind.
A woman like that is not a woman, quite.
I have been her kind.

I have found the warm caves in the woods,
filled them with skillets, carvings, shelves,
closets, silks, innumerable goods;
fixed the suppers for the worms and the elves:
whining, rearranging the disaligned.
A woman like that is misunderstood.
I have been her kind.

I have ridden in your cart, driver,
waved my nude arms at villages going by,
learning the last bright routes, survivor
where your flames still bite my thigh
and my ribs crack where your wheels wind.
A woman like that is not ashamed to die.
I have been her kind.

(1959)

The Moss of His Skin

Young girls in old Arabia were often buried alive next to their
dead fathers, apparently as sacrifice to the goddesses of the
tribes . . .

HAROLD FELDMAN, *"Children of the Desert"*
Psychoanalysis and Psychoanalytic Review, Fall 1958

It was only important
to smile and hold still,
to lie down beside him
and to rest awhile,
to be folded up together
as if we were silk,
to sink from the eyes of mother
and not to talk.
The black room took us
like a cave or a mouth
or an indoor belly.
I held my breath
and daddy was there,
his thumbs, his fat skull,
his teeth, his hair growing
like a field or a shawl.
I lay by the moss
of his skin until
it grew strange. My sisters
will never know that I fall
out of myself and pretend
that Allah will not see
how I hold my daddy
like an old stone tree.

(1959)

Letter Written on a Ferry While Crossing Long Island Sound

I am surprised to see
that the ocean is still going on.
Now I am going back
and I have ripped my hand
from your hand as I said I would
and I have made it this far
as I said I would
and I am on the top deck now
holding my wallet, my cigarettes
and my car keys
at 2 o'clock on a Tuesday
in August of 1960.

Dearest,
although everything has happened,
nothing has happened.
The sea is very old.
The sea is the face of Mary,
without miracles or rage
or unusual hope,
grown rough and wrinkled
with incurable age.

Still,
I have eyes.
These are my eyes:
the orange letters that spell
ORIENT on the life preserver
that hangs by my knees;
the cement lifeboat that wears
its dirty canvas coat;
the faded sign that sits on its shelf
saying KEEP OFF.
Oh, all right, I say,
I'll save myself.

Over my right shoulder
I see four nuns
who sit like a bridge club,
their faces poked out
from under their habits,
as good as good babies who
have sunk into their carriages.
Without discrimination
the wind pulls the skirts
of their arms.
Almost undressed,
I see what remains:
that holy wrist,
that ankle,
that chain.

Oh God,
although I am very sad,
could you please
let these four nuns
loosen from their leather boots
and their wooden chairs
to rise out

over this greasy deck,
out over this iron rail,
nodding their pink heads to one side,
flying four abreast
in the old-fashioned side stroke;
each mouth open and round,
breathing together
as fish do,
singing without sound.

Dearest,
see how my dark girls sally forth,
over the passing lighthouse of Plum Gut,
its shell as rusty
as a camp dish,
as fragile as a pagoda
on a stone;
out over the little lighthouse
that warns me of drowning winds
that rub over its blind bottom
and its blue cover;
winds that will take the toes
and the ears of the rider
or the lover.

There go my dark girls,
their dresses puff
in the leeward air.
Oh, they are lighter than flying dogs
or the breath of dolphins;
each mouth opens gratefully,
wider than a milk cup.
My dark girls sing for this.
They are going up.
See them rise
on black wings, drinking
the sky, without smiles
or hands
or shoes.
They call back to us
from the gauzy edge of paradise,
good news, good news.

(1961)

KARL SHAPIRO

The Dome of Sunday

With focus sharp as Flemish-painted face
In film of varnish brightly fixed
And through a polished hand-lens deeply seen,
Sunday at noon through hyaline thin air
Sees down the street,
And in the camera of my eye depicts
Row-houses and row-lives:
Glass after glass, door after door the same,
Face after face the same, the same,
The brutal visibility the same;

As if one life emerging from one house
Would pause, a single image caught between
Two facing mirrors where vision multiplies
Beyond perspective,
A silent clatter in the high-speed eye
Spinning out photo-circulars of sight.

I see slip to the curb the long machines
Out of whose warm and windowed rooms pirouette
Shellacked with silk and light
The hard legs of our women.
Our women are one woman, dressed in black.
The carmine printed mouth
And cheeks as soft as muslin-glass belong
Outright to one dark dressy man,
Merely a swagger at her curvy side.
This is their visit to themselves:
All day from porch to porch they weave

300

A nonsense pattern through the even glare,
Stealing in surfaces
Cold vulgar glances at themselves.

And high up in the heated room all day
I wait behind the plate glass pane for one,
Hot as a voyeur for a glimpse of one,
The vision to blot out this woman's sheen;
All day my sight records expensively
Row-houses and row-lives.
But nothing happens; no diagonal
With melting shadow falls across the curb:
Neither the blinded negress lurching through fatigue,
Nor exiles bleeding from their pores,
Nor that bright bomb slipped lightly from its rack
To splinter every silvered glass and crystal prism,
Witch-bowl and perfume bottle
And billion candle-power dressing-bulb,
No direct hit to smash the shatter-proof
And lodge at last the quivering needle
Clean in the eye of one who stands transfixed
In fascination of her brightness.

(1941)

Nostalgia

My soul stands at the window of my room,
    And I ten thousand miles away;
My days are filled with Ocean's sound of doom,
    Salt and cloud and the bitter spray.
Let the wind blow, for many a man shall die.

My selfish youth, my books with gilded edge,
    Knowledge and all gaze down the street;
The potted plants upon the window ledge
    Gaze down with selfish lives and sweet.
Let the wind blow, for many a man shall die.

My night is now her day, my day her night,
    So I lie down, and so I rise;
The sun burns close, the star is losing height,
    The clock is hunted down the skies.
Let the wind blow, for many a man shall die.

Truly a pin can make the memory bleed,
    A word explode the inward mind
And turn the skulls and flowers never freed
    Into the air, no longer blind.
Let the wind blow, for many a man shall die.

Laughter and grief join hands. Always the heart
    Clumps in the breast with heavy stride;
The face grows lined and wrinkled like a chart,
    The eyes bloodshot with tears and tide.
Let the wind blow, for many a man shall die.

(1942)

The Dirty Word

The dirty word hops in the cage of the mind like the Pondi-
cherry vulture, stomping with its heavy left claw on the
sweet meat of the brain and tearing it with its vicious beak,
ripping and chopping the flesh. Terrified, the small boy
bears the big bird of the dirty word into the house, and
grunting, puffing, carries it up the stairs to his own room in
the skull. Bits of black feather cling to his clothes and his
hair as he locks the staring creature in the dark closet.

All day the small boy returns to the closet to examine
and feed the bird, to caress and kick the bird, that now
snaps and flaps its wings savagely whenever the door is
opened. How the boy trembles and delights at the sight of
the white excrement of the bird! How the bird leaps and
rushes against the walls of the skull, trying to escape from
the zoo of the vocabulary! How wildly snaps the sweet meat
of the brain in its rage.

And the bird outlives the man, being freed at the man's
death-funeral by a word from the rabbi.

But I one morning went upstairs and opened the door
and entered the closet and found in the cage of my mind
the great bird dead. Softly I wept it and softly removed it
and softly buried the body of the bird in the hollyhock
garden of the house I lived in twenty years before. And out
of the worn black feathers of the wing have I made pens to
write these elegies, for I have outlived the bird, and I have
murdered it in my early manhood.

(1947)

Love for a Hand

Two hands lie still, the hairy and the white,
And soon down ladders of reflected light
The sleepers climb in silence. Gradually
They separate on paths of long ago,
Each winding on his arm the unpleasant clew
That leads, live as a nerve, to memory.

But often when too steep her dream descends,
Perhaps to the grotto where her father bends
To pick her up, the husband wakes as though
He had forgotten something in the house.
Motionless he eyes the room that glows
With the little animals of light that prowl

This way and that. Soft are the beasts of light
But softer still her hand that drifts so white
Upon the whiteness. How like a water-plant
It floats upon the black canal of sleep,
Suspended upward from the distant deep
In pure achievement of its lovely want!

Quietly then he plucks it and it folds
And is again a hand, small as a child's.
He would revive it but it barely stirs
And so he carries it off a little way
And breaks it open gently. Now he can see
The sweetness of the fruit, his hand eats hers.

(1952)

CHARLES SIMIC

Sleep

The woodpecker goes beating a little drum.
The shadow of the hyena blackens my face.
In my legs which are to be judged harshly,
And my hands with their false fury,
The bones lull each other tenderly.
I am with all that shivers,
All that hangs limp and without life.

It rains toads. My blood runs
Past dark inner cities on fire.
I climb into deep wells,
Rock bottoms and bone bottoms
Where gall of my birth steams.

Things slip out of my grasp,
Other things come to a quiet end.
This is my song. Nothing of us remains.
Almost nothing. I am whatever beast inhabits me.

When the rain turns into snow
Every beast shall see its track and wonder.

(1966)

My Shoes

Shoes, secret face of my inner life:
Two gaping toothless mouths,
Two partly decomposed animal skins
Smelling of mice-nests.

304

My brother and sister who died at birth
Continuing their existence in you,
Guiding my life
Toward their incomprehensible innocence.

What use are books to me
When in you it is possible to read
The Gospel of my life on earth
And still beyond, of things to come?

I want to proclaim the religion
I have devised for your perfect humility
And the strange church I am building
With you as the altar.

Ascetic and maternal, you endure:
Kin to oxen, to Saints, to condemned men,
With your mute patience, forming
The only true likeness of myself.

(1967)

LOUIS SIMPSON

Carentan O Carentan

Trees in the old days used to stand
And shape a shady lane
Where lovers wandered hand in hand
Who came from Carentan.

This was the shining green canal
Where we came two by two
Walking at combat-interval.
Such trees we never knew.

The day was early June, the ground
Was soft and bright with dew.
Far away the guns did sound,
But here the sky was blue.

The sky was blue, but there a smoke
Hung still above the sea
Where the ships together spoke
To towns we could not see.

Could you have seen us through a glass
You would have said a walk
Of farmers out to turn the grass,
Each with his own hay-fork.

The watchers in their leopard suits
Waited till it was time,
And aimed between the belt and boot
And let the barrel climb.

I must lie down at once, there is
A hammer at my knee.
And call it death or cowardice,
Don't count again on me.

Everything's all right, Mother,
Everyone gets the same
At one time or another.
It's all in the game.

I never strolled, nor ever shall,
Down such a leafy lane.
I never drank in a canal,
Nor ever shall again.

There is a whistling in the leaves
And it is not the wind,
The twigs are falling from the knives
That cut men to the ground.

Tell me, Master-Sergeant,
The way to turn and shoot.
But the Sergeant's silent
That taught me how to do it.

O Captain, show us quickly
Our place upon the map.
But the Captain's sickly
And taking a long nap.

Lieutenant, what's my duty,
My place in the platoon?
He too's a sleeping beauty,
Charmed by that strange tune.

Carentan O Carentan
Before we met with you
We never yet had lost a man
Or known what death could do.

(1949)

I Dreamed That in a City Dark as Paris

I dreamed that in a city dark as Paris
I stood alone in a deserted square.
The night was trembling with a violet

Expectancy. At the far edge it moved
And rumbled; on that flickering horizon
The guns were pumping color in the sky.

There was the Front. But I was lonely here,
Left behind, abandoned by the army.
The empty city and the empty square
Was my inhabitation, my unrest.
The helmet with its vestige of a crest,
The rifle in my hands, long out of date,
The belt I wore, the trailing overcoat
And hobnail boots, were those of a *poilu*.
I was the man, as awkward as a bear.

Over the rooftops where cathedrals loomed
In speaking majesty, two aeroplanes,
Forlorn as birds, appeared. Then growing large,
The German *Taube* and the *Nieuport Scout*,
They chased each other tumbling through the sky,
Till one streamed down on fire to the earth.

These wars have been so great, they are forgotten
Like the Egyptian dynasts. My confrere
In whose thick boots I stood, were you amazed
To wander through my brain four decades later
As I have wandered in a dream through yours?

The violence of waking life disrupts
The order of our death. Strange dreams occur,
For dreams are licensed as they never were.

(1956)

To the Western World

A siren sang, and Europe turned away
From the high castle and the shepherd's crook.
Three caravels went sailing to Cathay
On the strange ocean, and the captains shook
Their banners out across the Mexique Bay.

And in our early days we did the same.
Remembering our fathers in their wreck
We crossed the sea from Palos where they came
And saw, enormous to the little deck,
A shore in silence waiting for a name.

The treasures of Cathay were never found.
In this America, this wilderness
Where the axe echoes with a lonely sound,
The generations labor to possess
And grave by grave we civilize the ground.

(1957)

The Redwoods

Mountains are moving, rivers
are hurrying. But we
are still.

We have the thoughts of giants—
clouds, and at night the stars.

And we have names—guttural, grotesque—
Hamet, Og—names with no syllables.

And perish, one by one, our roots
gnawed by the mice. And fall.

And are too slow for death, and change
to stone. Or else too quick,

like candles in a fire. Giants
are lonely. We have waited long

for someone. By our waiting, surely
there must be someone at whose touch

our boughs would bend; and hands
to gather us; a spirit

to whom we are light as the hawthorn tree.
O if there is a poet

let him come now! We stand at the Pacific
like great unmarried girls,

turning in our heads the stars and clouds,
considering whom to please.

(1961)

My Father in the Night Commanding No

My father in the night commanding No
Has work to do. Smoke issues from his lips;
    He reads in silence.
The frogs are croaking and the streetlamps glow.

And then my mother winds the gramophone;
The Bride of Lammermoor begins to shriek—
    Or reads a story
About a prince, a castle, and a dragon.

The moon is glittering above the hill.
I stand before the gateposts of the King—
    So runs the story—
Of Thule, at midnight when the mice are still.

And I have been in Thule! It has come true—
The journey and the danger of the world,
    All that there is
To bear and to enjoy, endure and do.

Landscapes, seascapes . . . where have I been led?
The names of cities—Paris, Venice, Rome—
    Held out their arms.
A feathered god, seductive, went ahead.

Here is my house. Under a red rose tree
A child is swinging; another gravely plays.
    They are not surprised
That I am here; they were expecting me.

And yet my father sits and reads in silence,
My mother sheds a tear, the moon is still,
    And the dark wind
Is murmuring that nothing ever happens.

Beyond his jurisdiction as I move
Do I not prove him wrong? And yet, it's true
    They will not change
There, on the stage of terror and of love.

The actors in that playhouse always sit
In fixed positions—father, mother, child
    With painted eyes.
How sad it is to be a little puppet!

Their heads are wooden. And you once pretended
To understand them! Shake them as you will,
    They cannot speak.
Do what you will, the comedy is ended.

Father, why did you work? Why did you weep,
Mother? Was the story so important?
    "Listen!" the wind
Said to the children, and they fell asleep.

                               (1961)

On the Lawn at the Villa

On the lawn at the villa—
That's the way to start, eh, reader?
We know where we stand—somewhere expensive—
You and I *imperturbes*, as Walt would say,
Before the diversions of wealth, you and I *engagés*.
On the lawn at the villa
Sat a manufacturer of explosives,
His wife from Paris,
And a young man named Bruno,

And myself, being American,
Willing to talk to these malefactors,
The manufacturer of explosives, and so on,
But somehow superior. By that I mean democratic.
It's complicated, being an American,
Having the money and the bad conscience, both at the same
    time.
Perhaps, after all, this is not the right subject for a poem.

We were all sitting there paralyzed
In the hot Tuscan afternoon,
And the bodies of the machine-gun crew were draped over
    the balcony.
So we sat there all afternoon.

                               (1963)

L. E. SISSMAN

The West Forties:

Morning, Noon, and Night

> But nothing whatever is by love debarred.
> —*Patrick Kavanagh*

I. WELCOME TO HOTEL MAJESTY
(SINGLES $4 UP)

On this hotel, their rumpled royalties
Descend from their cross-country busses, loyalties
Suspended, losses cut, loves left behind,
To strike it lucky in the state of mind
That manufactures marvels out of mud.
Ensanguined by a bar sign selling Bud,
The early-streamline lobby—in its shell
Of late-Edwardian ornament, with a bell-
Mouthed cupidon extolling every swag
On its tall, fruitful front (a stale sight gag
First uttered by the comic landsmen who
Compounded a Great White Way out of blue
Sky, gneiss, and schist a whole stone age ago,
Before time steeled the arteries we know)—
The lobby washes redly over guests
With rope-bound bags containing their one best
Suit, shirt, tie, Jockey shorts, and pair of socks,
Half-empty pint, electric-razor box,
Ex-wife's still-smiling picture, high-school ring,
Harmonica, discharge, and everything.
Amid the alien corn and ruthless tares,

312

I hear a royal cry of horseplayers
Winding their tin horns in a chant of brass,
Their voices claiming in the wilderness.

II. SAL'S ATOMIC SUBMARINES

The Puerto Rican busboy, Jesus, coughs
Above the cutting board where Sal compiles
An outbound order for the Abinger
Associates next door; then, carrying
A pantheon of heroes in a brown
Kraft-paper bag, he sidles by the chrome-
Formica-plastic dinette furniture
And gains the world, where anti-personnel
Gases from crosstown buses, vegetable
Soup simmering at Bickford's, and My Sin
Seeping from Walgreen's silently combine
To addle all outsiders. Only lithe,
Quick indigenes like Jesus (whose tan neck
Is thinner than my wrist) can long survive
And later even prosper in the air
Of these times' squares, these hexahedral hives
Where every worker drudges for his queen.

III. STAGE-DOOR JOHNNY'S

Silvana Casamassima, Vic Blad
(The talent agent), Lance Bartholomey,
Piretta Paul, Max Dove, A. Lincoln Brown,
Samarra Brown, Lil Yeovil, Beryl Cohn
(Theatrical attorney), Johnny Groen
(The owner), Merritt Praed, Morty Monroe,
Dame Phyllis Woolwich, Sir Jack Handel, Bart.,
Del Hector (the producer), Coquetel,
Fab Newcome, Temple Bell, Vanessa Vane,
Burt Wartman, C. R. Freedley, F.R.S.,
Alf Wandsworth (author of "Queer Street"), Mel Hess,
His Honor Judge Perutz, Merced McCall,
Tam Pierce, Jan Stewart, Tom Cobley, and all
The darlings, mirrored in their flourishing
Autographed caricatures on every wall,
Sail on, sealed in, important, bright, serene,
In league in Captain Nemo's submarine.

IV. PENNY ARCADIA

Like lava, rock erupts to fill the room
From each coäx-coäx-coäxial
Concentric speakers' throat, and rolls like doom
Over the unmoved pinball-playing boys
Whose jaws lightly reciprocate like long-
Stroke pistons coupled to the Tinguely loom
Of augmented electric music, strong
As sexuality and loud as noise,
Which keens across the dingy room at full
Gain and, its coin gone, as abruptly dies.

V. MEYER WAX LOANS

Clear and obscure, elbows of saxophones
Shine out like sink traps in an underworld
Of pledges unredeemed—a spectral band
Of brass and nickel marching in the dark
Toward the morning and redemption, where
Known lips will kiss their reeds, familiar hands
Resume their old and loving fingering.
Unlikely. In a hundred rented rooms
From here to Ybor City, pledgers plan
What next to pawn: the Rolleicord, the ring,
The eight-transistor Victor radio,
The travelling alarm. Alarm creeps in-
To all their calculations, now the bloom
Is off their promise, now the honeymoon
Is over with a cry, and time begins
To whittle expectations to a size
Convenient for their carrying to pawn.

VI. LOVEMOVIE

Before the glazed chrome case where Lovelies Swim
Au Natural, and under the sly lights,
Which wink and bump and wink and grind, except
For those that have burned out, the singing strings
Of Madame Violin essay "Caprice,"
Not missing many notes, considering
How cold it is outside the Lovemovie.
Stray pennies in her tin cup punctuate
The music like applause. Play, gypsies! Dance!

The thin strains of a Romany romance
Undaunt the ears of each peajacketed
Seaman on liberty, and of each old
Wanderer slowly losing to the cold,
And of each schoolboy who has come to see
Life in the flesh inside the Lovemovie.
Beneath her stiff green hair, an artist's grin
Knits up the ravelled cheek of Madame Violin.

VII. THE ARGO BUILDING:
NEW DELMAN'S GOOD NIGHT

The last bone button in the old tin tea
Box of the Argo Building lastly sees
ƆИIVAƎWƎЯ Ǝ⅃ᗺISIVИI   peeling off
His street-side window as he locks the door
Of 720 one more night and struts
His septuagenarian stuff down
The corridor, past Aabco Dental Labs,
Worldwide Investigations, Inc., Madame
Lillé, Corsetière, Star School of Tap,
Dr. O'Keefe, Franck Woodwind Institute,
Wink Publications, and Watch Hospital.
Up the wrought shaft, preceded by its wires
Ticking and twittering, the intrepid car
Rises like an old aeronaut to take
Its ballast-passenger aboard beneath
The pointed clear bulbs of its four flambeaux,
Sweetly attenuated Art Nouveau
Which was *vieux jeu* and is the rage, unknown
To old New Delman, whom it ferries down
In its black cage, funebrially slow,
To Stygian Forty-seventh Street below.

(1966)

WILLIAM JAY SMITH

The Park in Milan

The animals we have seen, all marvelous creatures,
The lion king, the pygmy antelope,
The zebra like a convict cutting corners,
Birds in cages, orioles and doves,
The sacred ibis with a beak like a gravy dish,
Tropical fish weaving a Persian carpet
For the dancing feet of sunlight, marvelous creatures,
Theirs is the kingdom of love.

               Love we have brought them
On a summer day, weary from walking;
Like children who cool their faces on piano keys,
We turn to the quiet park, the good, green trees,
And a wealth of animal being runs in our minds like music.

Like music all the miracles of being,
The flash and fire of sunlight and of sound,
The elephant in cage of muted thunder,
Zebras on the shaken, shaded ground.

Turning from them now like children turning,
We watch the city open like a wound,
With gutted church and bombed and broken buildings,
Girders like black bones that lace the void,
All we build through love through hate destroyed,
The world an aged animal that heaves and cries
Under the trees, the gay, green trees of summer.

Music fades; the streets are black with flies.

(1949)

Persian Miniature

Ah, all the sands of the earth lead unto heaven.
I have seen them rise on the wind, a golden thread,
The sands of the earth which enter the eye of heaven,
Over the graves, the poor, white bones of the dead.
Over the buckling ice, the swollen rivers,
Over the ravened plains, and the dry creek beds,
The sands are moving. I have seen them move,
And where the pines are bent, the orient
Grain awaits the passage of the wind.
Higher still the laden camels thread
Their way beyond the mountains, and the clouds
Are whiter than the ivory they bear
For Death's black eunuchs. Gold, silk, furs
Cut the blood-red morning. All is vain.
I have watched the caravans through the needle's eye
As they turn, on the threshing floor, the bones of the dead,
And green as a grasshopper's leg is the evening sky.

(1949)

W. D. SNODGRASS

April Inventory

The green catalpa tree has turned
All white; the cherry blooms once more.
In one whole year I haven't learned
A blessed thing they pay you for.
The blossoms snow down in my hair;
The trees and I will soon be bare.

The trees have more than I to spare.
The sleek, expensive girls I teach,
Younger and pinker every year,
Bloom gradually out of reach.
The pear tree lets its petals drop
Like dandruff on a tabletop.

The girls have grown so young by now
I have to nudge myself to stare.
This year they smile and mind me how
My teeth are falling with my hair.
In thirty years I may not get
Younger, shrewder, or out of debt.

The tenth time, just a year ago,
I made myself a little list
Of all the things I'd ought to know,
Then told my parents, analyst,
And everyone who's trusted me
I'd be substantial, presently.

I haven't read one book about
A book or memorized one plot.
Or found a mind I did not doubt.
I learned one date. And then forgot.
And one by one the solid scholars
Get the degrees, the jobs, the dollars.

And smile above their starchy collars.
I taught my classes Whitehead's notions;
One lovely girl, a song of Mahler's.
Lacking a source-book or promotions,
I showed one child the colors of
A luna moth and how to love.

I taught myself to name my name,
To bark back, loosen love and crying;
To ease my woman so she came,
To ease an old man who was dying.
I have not learned how often I
Can win, can love, but choose to die.

I have not learned there is a lie
Love shall be blonder, slimmer, younger;
That my equivocating eye
Loves only by my body's hunger;
That I have forces, true to feel,
Or that the lovely world is real.

While scholars speak authority
And wear their ulcers on their sleeves,
My eyes in spectacles shall see
These trees procure and spend their leaves.
There is a value underneath
The gold and silver in my teeth.

Though trees turn bare and girls turn wives,
We shall afford our costly seasons;
There is a gentleness survives
That will outspeak and has its reasons.
There is a loveliness exists,
Preserves us, not for specialists.

(1957)

Vuillard: *"The Mother and Sister of the Artist"*

(Instructions for the Visit)

Admire, when you come here, the glimmering hair
Of the girl; praise her pale
Complexion. Think well of her dress

Though that is somewhat out of fashion.
Don't try to take her hand, but smile for
Her hesitant gentleness.
Say the old woman is looking strong
Today; such hardiness. Remark,
Perhaps, how she has dressed herself black
Like a priest, and wears that sufficient air
That does become the righteous.
As you approach, she will push back
Her chair, shove away her plate
And wait,
Sitting squat and direct, before
The red mahogany chest
Massive as some great
Safe; will wait,
By the table and her greasy plate,
The bone half-chewed, her wine half-drained;
She will wait. And fix her steady
Eyes on you—the straight stare
Of an old politician.
Try once to meet her eyes. But fail.
Let your sight
Drift—yet never as if hunting for
The keys (you keep imagining) hung
By her belt. (They are not there.)
Watch, perhaps, that massive chest—the way
It tries to lean
Forward, toward her, till it seems to rest
Its whole household's weight
Of linens and clothing and provisions
All on her stiff back.
It might be strapped there like the monstrous pack
Of some enchanted pedlar. Dense, self-contained,
Like mercury in a ball,
She can support this without strain,
Yet she grows smaller, wrinkling
Like a potato, parched as dung;
It cramps her like a fist.
Ask no one why the chest
Has no knobs. Betray
No least suspicion
The necessities within
Could vanish at her
Will. Try not to think
That as she feeds, gains
Specific gravity,

She shrinks, light-
less as the world's
Hard core
And the per-
spective drains
In her.
Finally, above all,
You must not ever see,
Or let slip one hint you can see,
On the other side, the girl's
Cuffs, like cordovan restraints;
Forget her bony, tentative wrist,
The half-fed, worrying eyes, and how
She backs out, bows, and tries to bow
Out of the scene, grows too ethereal
To make a shape inside her dress
And the dress itself is beginning already
To sublime itself away like a vapor
That merges into the empty twinkling
Of the air and of the bright wallpaper.

(1961)

Monet: *"Les Nymphéas"*

The eyelids glowing, some chill morning.
O world half-known through opening, twilit lids
Before the vague face clenches into light;
O universal waters like a cloud,
Like those first clouds of half-created matter;
O all things rising, rising like the fumes
From waters falling, O forever falling;
Infinite, the skeletal shells that fall, relinquished,
The snowsoft sift of the diatoms, like selves
Downdrifting age upon age through milky oceans;
O slow downdrifting of the atoms;
O island nebulae and O the nebulous islands
Wandering these mists like falsefires, which are true,
Bobbing like milkweed, like warm lanterns bobbing
Through the snowfilled windless air, blinking and passing
As we pass into the memory of women
Who are passing. Within those depths
What ravening? What devouring rage?
How shall our living know its ends of yielding?

These things have taken me as the mouth an orange—
    That acrid sweet juice entering every cell;
And I am shared out. I become these things:
    These lilies, if these things are water lilies
Which are dancers growing dim across no floor;
    These mayflies; whirled dust orbiting in the sun;
This blossoming diffused as rushlights; galactic vapors;
    Fluorescence into which we pass and penetrate;
O soft as the thighs of women;
    O radiance, into which I go on dying . . .

                                                (1963)

"*After Experience Taught Me . . .*"

After experience taught me that all the ordinary
Surroundings of social life are futile and vain;

    I'm going to show you something very
    Ugly: someday, it might save your life.

Seeing that none of the things I feared contain
In themselves anything either good or bad

    What if you get caught without a knife;
    Nothing—even a loop of piano wire;

Excepting only in the effect they had
Upon my mind, I resolved to inquire

    Take the first two fingers of this hand;
    Fork them out—kind of a "V for Victory"—

Whether there might be something whose discovery
Would grant me supreme, unending happiness.

    And jam them into the eyes of your enemy.
    You have to do this hard. Very hard. Then press

No virtue can be thought to have priority
Over this endeavor to preserve one's being.

Both fingers down around the cheekbone
And setting your foot high into the chest

No man can desire to act rightly, to be blessed,
To live rightly, without simultaneously

    You must call up every strength you own
    And you can rip off the whole facial mask.

Wishing to be, to act, to live. He must ask
First, in other words, to actually exist.

      And you, whiner, who wastes your time
        Dawdling over the remorseless earth,
      What evil, what unspeakable crime
        Have you made your life worth?

(1964)

GARY SNYDER

Piute Creek

One granite ridge
A tree, would be enough
Or even a rock, a small creek,
A bark shred in a pool.
Hill beyond hill, folded and twisted
Tough trees crammed
In thin stone fractures
A huge moon on it all, is too much.
The mind wanders. A million
Summers, night air still and the rocks
Warm. Sky over endless mountains.
All the junk that goes with being human
Drops away, hard rock wavers
Even the heavy present seems to fail
This bubble of a heart.
Words and books
Like a small creek off a high ledge
Gone in the dry air.

A clear, attentive mind
Has no meaning but that
Which sees is truly seen.
No one loves rock, yet we are here.
Night chills. A flick
In the moonlight
Slips into Juniper shadow:
Back there unseen
Cold proud eyes
Of Cougar or Coyote
Watch me rise and go.

(1959)

Milton by Firelight

Piute Creek, August 1955

"Oh hell, what do mine eyes
    with grief behold?"
Working with an old
Singlejack miner, who can sense
The vein and cleavage
In the very guts of rock, can
Blast granite, build
Switchbacks that last for years
Under the beat of snow, thaw, mule-hooves.
What use, Milton, a silly story
Of our lost general parents,
        eaters of fruit?

The Indian, the chainsaw boy,
And a string of six mules
Came riding down to camp
Hungry for tomatoes and green apples.
Sleeping in saddle-blankets
Under a bright night-sky
Han River slantwise by morning.
Jays squall
Coffee boils

In ten thousand years the Sierras
Will be dry and dead, home of the scorpion.
Ice-scratched slabs and bent trees.
No paradise, no fall,
Only the weathering land
The wheeling sky,
Man, with his Satan
Scouring the chaos of the mind.
Oh Hell!
Fire down
Too dark to read, miles from a road
The bell-mare clangs in the meadow
That packed dirt for a fill-in
Scrambling through loose rocks
On an old trail
All of a summer's day.

(1959)

Above Pate Valley

We finished clearing the last
Section of trail by noon,
High on the ridge-side
Two thousand feet above the creek
Reached the pass, went on
Beyond the white pine groves,
Granite shoulders, to a small
Green meadow watered by the snow,
Edged with Aspen—sun
Straight high and blazing
But the air was cool.
Ate a cold fried trout in the
Trembling shadows. I spied
A glitter, and found a flake
Black volcanic glass—obsidian—
By a flower. Hands and knees
Pushing the Bear grass, thousands
Of arrowhead leavings over a
Hundred yards. No one good
Head, just razor flakes
On a hill snowed all but summer,
A land of fat summer deer,
They came to camp. On their
Own trails. I followed my own
Trail here. Picked up the cold-drill,
Pick, singlejack, and sack
Of dynamite.
Ten thousand years.

(1959)

WILLIAM STAFFORD

One Home

Mine was a Midwest home—you can keep your world.
Plain black hats rode the thoughts that made our code.
We sang hymns in the house; the roof was near God.

The light bulb that hung in the pantry made a wan light,
but we could read by it the names of preserves—
outside, the buffalo grass, and the wind in the night.

A wildcat sprang at Grandpa on the Fourth of July
when he was cutting plum bushes for fuel,
before Indians pulled the West over the edge of the sky.

To anyone who looked at us we said, "My friend";
liking the cut of a thought, we could say, "Hello."
(But plain black hats rode the thoughts that made our code.)

The sun was over our town; it was like a blade.
Kicking cottonwood leaves we ran toward storms.
Wherever we looked the land would hold us up.

(1955)

At the Bomb Testing Site

At noon in the desert a panting lizard
waited for history, its elbows tense,
watching the curve of a particular road
as if something might happen.

327

It was looking for something farther off
than people could see, an important scene
acted in stone for little selves
at the flute end of consequences.

There was just a continent without much on it
under a sky that never cared less.
Ready for a change, the elbows waited.
The hands gripped hard on the desert.

(1957)

Traveling Through the Dark

Traveling through the dark I found a deer
dead on the edge of the Wilson River road.
It is usually best to roll them into the canyon:
that road is narrow; to swerve might make more dead.

By glow of the tail-light I stumbled back of the car
and stood by the heap, a doe, a recent killing;
she had stiffened already, almost cold.
I dragged her off; she was large in the belly.

My fingers touching her side brought me the reason—
her side was warm; her fawn lay there waiting,
alive, still, never to be born.
Beside that mountain road I hesitated.

The car aimed ahead its lowered parking lights;
under the hood purred the steady engine.
I stood in the glare of the warm exhaust turning red;
around our group I could hear the wilderness listen.

I thought hard for us all—my only swerving—
then pushed her over the edge into the river.

(1960)

An Oregon Message

When we moved here, pulled
the trees in around us, curled
our backs to the wind, no one

had ever hit the moon—no one.
Now our trees are safer than the stars,
and only other people's neglect
is our precious and abiding shell,
pierced by meteors, radar, and the telephone.

From our snug place we shout
religiously for attention, in order to hide;
only silence or evasion will bring
dangerous notice, the hovering hawk
of the state, or the sudden quiet stare
and fatal estimate of an alerted neighbor.

This message we smuggle out in
its plain cover, to be opened
quietly: Friends everywhere—
we are alive! Those moon rockets
have missed millions of secret
places! Best wishes.

Burn this.

(1968)

MARK STRAND

Keeping Things Whole

In a field
I am the absence
of field.
This is
always the case.
Wherever I am
I am what is missing.

When I walk
I part the air
and always
the air moves in
to fill the spaces
where my body's been.

We all have reasons
for moving.
I move
to keep things whole.

(1963)

ROBERT SWARD

Uncle Dog: The Poet at 9

I did not want to be old Mr.
Garbage man, but uncle dog
Who rode sitting beside him.

Uncle dog had always looked
To me to be truck-strong
Wise-eyed, a cur-like Ford

Of a dog. I did not want
To be Mr. Garbage man because
All he had was cans to do.

Uncle dog sat there me-beside-him
Emptying nothing. Barely even
Looking from garbage side to side:

Like rich people in the backseats
Of chauffeur-cars, only shaggy
In an unwagging tall-scrawny way.

Uncle dog belonged any just where
He sat, but old Mr. Garbage man
Had to stop at everysingle can.

I thought. I did not want to be Mr.
Everybody calls them that first.
A dog is said, Dog! Or by name.

I would rather be called Rover
Than Mr. And sit like a tough
Smart mongrel beside a garbage man.

Uncle dog always went to places
Unconcerned, without no hurry.
Independent like some leashless

Toot. Honorable among scavenger
Can-picking dogs. And with a bitch
At every other can. And meat:

His for the barking. Oh, I wanted
To be uncle dog—sharp, high fox-
Eared, cur-Ford truck-faced

With his pick of the bones.
A doing, truckman's dog
And not a simple child-dog

Nor friend to man, but an uncle
Traveling, and to himself—
And a bitch at every second can.

(1957)

MAY SWENSON

Frontispiece

In this book I see your face and in your face
your eyes holding the world and all else besides
as a cat's pupils rayed and wide
to what is before them and what more alive
ticks in the shadows flickers in the waves

Your hair in a slow stream curves
from your listening brow
to your ear shaped like a sea-thing found
in that water-haunted house where murmurs
your chase-fierce name   The vow

that corners your mouth
compelled you to that deep between words and acts
where they cross as sand with salt
There spills the layered light
your sockets lips and nostrils drank

before they sank
On stages of the sea the years tall
tableaus build   The lighthouse you commanded
the room the oak and mutable Orlando
reoccur as the sea's pages to land's mind   The wall

the steep and empty slate
your cane indented until you laid it as a mark
above where the tide would darken

is written in weed and shell how you were sane
when walking you wrapped your face
in the green scarf
the gray
and then the black
The waves carve your hearse and tomb
and toll your voyage out again again

                                                        (1956)

Notes Made in the Piazza San Marco

The wingéd lion on top of that column
(his paws have been patched, he appears to wear boots)
is bronze but has a white eye—
his tail sails out long . . . Could it help him fly?

On the other column St. Theodore
standing on an alligator,
he and it as white as salt,
wears an iron halo and an iron sword.

San Marco is crusty and curly with many crowns,
or is it a growth of golden thrones?
The five domes
covered, it looks like, with stiff crinkly parachute silk

have gold balls on twigs on turnip-tips,
sharp turrets in between with metal flags that cannot wave.
On all their perches statues gay and grave:
Erect somewhere among the towers a tall-necked woman

wearing an of-course-gold coronet
is helping a beast with baboon's head and lion's body to stand
on hindlegs. She's placing her hand
in his mouth . . . I wonder why.

In recesses of arches half in shade
are robed Venetians made
of red, blue, gold, green mosaics small as caramels,
fishermen encumbered by their robes launching a boat,

their faces all pricked out with those square
skin-colored pores . . .
Above them in a gold sky angels fly standing up.
About to step off the balcony

in the center of the main façade, four
horses exactly as big as horses but consciously more
handsome—gold running in rivulets
from their shoulders to under their bellies, their necks'

curt blade-shaped manes sloping like Roman helmets—
have a pair of heads front
and a pair to the side,
the lips tugged back into wide

loops. The bits are absent.
A pink and white checkered palace relatively plain
with a pleasant loggia half way up
puts a rectangle out to the quay of the Grand Canal:

On one of its corners Adam and Eve look rueful, the Tree
between them—its low branches with leaves attached
happen to cover their genitals. Three
times hugged around the trunk, the serpent laughs.

There's often a rush of pigeons in the Piazza,
a leather scarf swept past your eyes
as if snatched from the ground,
when from the campanile great tongues let loose

and flog you, and flog you with gouts of iron sound.
The air must always burn deep blue here—
a velvet box for all that gold and white.
It turns thin and clear

toward the water. The Canal is a green vase lying down.
Gondolas knock their tethered necks on the quay:
Black, saddled with red, riderless, restless, they
are touching hips and shifting on the single-footing waves.

(1963)

Motherhood

> She sat on a shelf,
> her breasts two bellies
> on her poked-out belly,

on which the navel looked
like a sucked-in mouth—
her knees bent and apart,
her long left arm raised,
with the large hand knuckled
to a bar in the ceiling—
her right hand clamping
the skinny infant to her chest—
its round, pale, new,
soft muzzle hunting
in the brown hair for a nipple,
its splayed, tiny hand picking
at her naked, dirty ear.
Twisting its little neck,
with tortured, ecstatic eyes
the size of lentils, it looked
into her severe, close-set,
solemn eyes, that beneath bald
eyelids glared—dull lights
in sockets of leather.

She twitched some chin-hairs,
with pain or pleasure,
as the baby-mouth found and
yanked at her nipple;
its pink-nailed, jointless
fingers, wandering her face,
tangled in the tufts
of her cliffy brows.
She brought her big
hand down from the bar—
with pretended exasperation
unfastened the little hand,
and locked it within her palm—
while her right hand,
with snag-nailed forefinger
and short, sharp thumb, raked
the new orange hair
of the infant's skinny flank—
and found a louse,
which she lipped, and
thoughtfully crisped
between broad teeth.
She wrinkled appreciative
nostrils, which, without a nose,

stood open—damp, holes
above the poke of her mouth.

She licked her lips, flicked
her leather eyelids—
then, suddenly flung
up both arms and grabbed
the bars overhead.
The baby's scrabbly fingers
instantly caught the hair—
as if there were metal rings there—
in her long, stretched armpits.
And, as she stately swung,
and then proudly, more swiftly
slung herself from corner
to corner of her cell—
arms longer than her round
body, short knees bent—
her little wild-haired,
poke-mouthed infant hung,
like some sort of trophy,
or decoration, or shaggy medal—
shaped like herself—but new,
clean, soft and shining
on her chest.

(1963)

JAMES TATE

The Lost Pilot

for my father, 1922–1944

Your face did not rot
like the others—the co-pilot,
for example, I saw him

yesterday. His face is corn-
mush: his wife and daughter,
the poor ignorant people, stare

as if he will compose soon.
He was more wronged than Job.
But your face did not rot

like the others—it grew dark,
and hard like ebony;
the features progressed in their

distinction. If I could cajole
you to come back for an evening,
down from your compulsive

orbiting, I would touch you,
read your face as Dallas,
your hoodlum gunner, now,

with the blistered eyes, reads
his braille editions. I would
touch your face as a disinterested

scholar touches an original page.
However frightening, I would
discover you, and I would not

turn you in; I would not make
you face your wife, or Dallas,
or the co-pilot, Jim. You

could return to your crazy
orbiting, and I would not try
to fully understand what

it means to you. All I know
is this: when I see you,
as I have seen you at least

once every year of my life,
spin across the wilds of the sky
like a tiny, African god,

I feel dead. I feel as if I were
the residue of a stranger's life,
that I should pursue you.

My head cocked toward the sky,
I cannot get off the ground,
and, you, passing over again,

fast, perfect, and unwilling
to tell me that you are doing
well, or that it was mistake

that placed you in that world,
and me in this; or that misfortune
placed these worlds in us.

(1966)

CONSTANCE URDANG

The Children

What have I made
children
with voices like bull-calves bellowing
tall like the legendary children of the tribes
of the California
earth-children
to make friends with the burrowing moles
grass—
children sprouting everywhere (seeded
on impossible wings) wild
weed-children
                    wood—
children
saplings all bark and twigs
air-children flying
children in the spring
where it bubbles up without let-up
slow sleepy children
heavy-lidded
nodding
in sun in shade
hot cold wet dry soft hard
tadpoles with see-through tails
naked nestlings
blind nurslings
sly
greedy
Oh, bite, teeth!

Kick, feet!
Pinch! Punch! (Pow!
Bam!! Blam!! Zap!!) aLL
           O
            V
             E
              R

made
love made
children

(1968)

PETER VIERECK

Homecoming

*(a charade on hedonistic "civilized" materialism and
its eventual purgatory through moral isolation)*

My seven sons came back from Indonesia.
Each had ruled an atoll twenty years alone.
Twenty years of loneliness, twenty years of craziness,
Of hell's and Eden's silence on an exiled coral throne.
My six grunting sons had forgotten what a language is;
My seventh was a warlock, chanting every language known.

My seven sunburnt sons arrived at the airport.
The airport had a banner up. Its words were "WELCOME
    HOME."
The mayor made a speech, and the virgins rainbowed over
    them
The many-tongued hooray of confetti's polychrome.
But, though seven new Rolls-Royces sped them richly to
    my parlor,
They only filed their long sharp teeth; the warlock's were
    afoam.

The day before my seven sons returned from atoll-lone-
    liness,
The butler starched his livery to welcome them in style;
"*Thé dansant* for the young masters?" gushed the house-
    maid, strewing doilies;
I bought my sons a set of Proust to titillate their guile.
My seven Dresden China cups were waiting, hot with tea;
And all was ready as my sons tramped in. They didn't smile.

342

"You homesick boys from far-off Indonesia,
Relax and romp," I said, "and know you're loved.
It's true that twenty years alone with coral
Is not God's hand at its most velvet-gloved.
But let's test your sense of humor; don't be morbid;
I'll get tantrums if my welcome is rebuffed."

Did they listen? No, they only watched the seventh . . .
Till he made a kind of signal. Then they roared and went
    amok.
Two swung from chandeliers and pounced on the butler.
Two held the maid down, and clawed off her smock.
Two ate the Proust set. "Be careful, kids," I wheedled;
"Romp all you like but spare my teacups any shock.

"I can buy you chubby housemaids by the dozen.
You can eat a butler, even eat a book.
But whoever chips—no matter who—my china,
He'll get magicked back to nature's loneliest nook."
"No matter who?" the warlock asked—and tripped me
Right across my magic teacups. I awoke

On this hellish, Eden-beautied reef of coral
In a perfect climate full of perfect food,
Where my sense of humor's tested by the silence
And I've nothing else to do but fish and brood.
"Sons, come back and get me out of Indonesia!"
But, of course, they couldn't hear me. No one could.

(1950)

DAVID WAGONER

Leaving Something Behind

A fox at your neck and snakeskin on your feet,
You have gone to the city behind an ivory brooch,
Wearing your charms for and against desire, bearing your
  beauty
Past all the gaping doorways, amazing women on edge
And leading men's eyes astray while skirting mayhem,
And I, for a day, must wish you safe in your skin.

The diggers named her the Minnesota Girl. She was fifteen,
Eight thousand years ago, when she drowned in a glacial
  lake,
Curling to sleep like her sea-snail amulet, holding a turtle-
  shell,
A wolf's tooth, the tine of an antler, carrying somehow
A dozen bones from the feet of water birds. She believed in
  her charms,
But something found her and kept her. She became what she
  wore.

She loved her bones and her own husk of creatures
But left them piecemeal on the branching shore.
Without you, fox paws, elephant haunches, all rattling tails,
Snail's feet, turtles' remote hearts, muzzles of wolves,
Stags' ears, and the tongues of water birds are only them-
  selves.
Come safely back. There was nothing in her arms.

(1964)

Diary

At Monday dawn, I climbed into my skin
And went to see the money. There were the shills:
I conned them—oh, the coins fell out of their mouths,
And paint peeled from the walls like dollar bills.
Below their money-belts, I did them in.

All day Tuesday, grand in my underwear,
I shopped for the world, bought basements and airplanes,
Bargained for corners and pedestrians
And, when I'd marketed the elms away,
Swiped from the water, stole down to the stones.

Suddenly Wednesday offered me my shirt,
Trousers, and shoes. I put them on to dream
Of the one-way stairway and the skittering cloud,
Of the dangerous, footsore crossing at the heart
Where trees, rivers, and stones reach for the dead.

And the next day meant the encircling overcoat
Wherein I sweltered, woolly as a ram:
From butt to swivel, I hoofed it on the loam,
Exacting tribute from the flock in the grass.
My look passed through the werewolf to the lamb.

Friday shied backwards, pulling off my clothes:
The overcoat fell open like a throat;
Shirt-tail and shoe went spidery as a thought,
And covetous drawers whipped knee-deep in a knot.
My skin in a spiral tapered into gold.

And it was naked Saturday for love
Again: the graft grew milky at a kiss.
I lay on the week with money, lust, and vapor,
Megalomania, fear, the tearing-off,
And love in a coil. On Sunday, I wrote this.

(1964)

The Poets Agree to Be Quiet by the Swamp

They hold their hands over their mouths
And stare at the stretch of water.
What can be said has been said before:

Strokes of light like herons' legs in the cattails,
Mud underneath, frogs lying even deeper.
Therefore, the poets may keep quiet.
But the corners of their mouths grin past their hands.
They stick their elbows out into the evening,
Stoop, and begin the ancient croaking.

(1964

Staying Alive

Staying alive in the woods is a matter of calming down
At first and deciding whether to wait for rescue,
Trusting to others,
Or simply to start walking and walking in one direction
Till you come out—or something happens to stop you.
By far the safer choice
Is to settle down where you are, and try to make a living
Off the land, camping near water, away from shadows.
Eat no white berries;
Spit out all bitterness. Shooting at anything
Means hiking further and further every day
To hunt survivors;
It may be best to learn what you have to learn without a gun
Not killing but watching birds and animals go
In and out of shelter
At will. Following their example, build for a whole season:
Facing across the wind in your lean-to,
You may feel wilder,
But nothing, not even you, will have to stay in hiding.
If you have no matches, a stick and a fire-bow
Will keep you warmer,
Or the crystal of your watch, filled with water, held up to
the sun
Will do the same in time. In case of snow
Drifting toward winter,
Don't try to stay awake through the night, afraid of freez-
ing—
The bottom of your mind knows all about zero;
It will turn you over
And shake you till you waken. If you have trouble sleeping

Even in the best of weather, jumping to follow
With eyes strained to their corners
The unidentifiable noises of the night and feeling
Bears and packs of wolves nuzzling your elbow,
Remember the trappers
Who treated them indifferently and were left alone.
If you hurt yourself, no one will comfort you
Or take your temperature,
So stumbling, wading, and climbing are as dangerous as
  flying.
But if you decide, at last, you must break through
In spite of all danger,
Think of yourself by time and not by distance, counting
Wherever you're going by how long it takes you;
No other measure
Will bring you safe to nightfall. Follow no streams: they run
Under the ground or fall into wilder country.
Remember the stars
And moss when your mind runs into circles. If it should rain
Or the fog should roll the horizon in around you,
Hold still for hours
Or days if you must, or weeks, for seeing is believing
In the wilderness. And if you find a pathway,
Wheel-rut, or fence-wire,
Retrace it left or right: someone knew where he was going
Once upon a time, and you can follow
Hopefully, somewhere,
Just in case. There may even come, on some uncanny eve-
  ning,
A time when you're warm and dry, well fed, not thirsty,
Uninjured, without fear,
When nothing, either good or bad, is happening.
This is called staying alive. It's temporary.
What occurs after
Is doubtful. You must always be ready for something to
  come bursting
Through the far edge of a clearing, running toward you,
Grinning from ear to ear
And hoarse with welcome. Or something crossing and hover-
  ing
Overhead, as light as air, like a break in the sky,
Wondering what you are.
Here you are face to face with the problem of recognition.
Having no time to make smoke, too much to say,
You should have a mirror
With a tiny hole in the back for better aiming, for reflecting

Whatever disaster you can think of, to show
The way you suffer.
These body signals have universal meaning: If you are lying
Flat on your back with arms outstretched behind you,
You say you require
Emergency treatment; if you are standing erect and holding
Arms horizontal, you mean you are not ready;
If you hold them over
Your head, you want to be picked up. Three of anything
Is a sign of distress. Afterward, if you see
No ropes, no ladders,
No maps or messages falling, no searchlights or trails blaz-
    ing,
Then, chances are, you should be prepared to burrow
Deep for a deep winter.

                                                    (1965)

The Shooting of John Dillinger Outside the
Biograph Theater, July 22, 1934

Chicago ran a fever of a hundred and one that groggy
    Sunday.
A reporter fried an egg on a sidewalk; the air looked shaky.
And a hundred thousand people were in the lake like shirts
    in a laundry.
Why was Johnny lonely?
Not because two dozen solid citizens, heat-struck, had keeled
    over backward.
Not because those lawful souls had fallen out of their sockets
    and melted.
But because the sun went down like a lump in a furnace or a
    bull in the Stockyards.
Where was Johnny headed?
Under the Biograph Theater sign that said, "Our Air is
    Refrigerated,"
Past seventeen FBI men and four policemen who stood in
    doorways and sweated.
Johnny sat down in a cold seat to watch Clark Gable get
    electrocuted.

Had Johnny been mistreated?

Yes, but Gable told the D. A. he'd rather fry than be shut up
forever.

Two women sat by Johnny. One looked sweet, one looked
like J. Edgar Hoover.

Polly Hamilton made him feel hot, but Anna Sage made him
shiver.

Was Johnny a good lover?

Yes, but he passed out his share of squeezes and pokes like
a jittery masher

While Agent Purvis sneaked up and down the aisle like an
extra usher,

Trying to make sure they wouldn't slip out till the show was
over.

Was Johnny a fourflusher?

No, not if he knew the game. He got it up or got it back.

But he liked to take snapshots of policemen with his own
Kodak,

And once in a while he liked to take them with an automatic.

Why was Johnny frantic?

Because he couldn't take a walk or sit down in a movie

Without being afraid he'd run smack into somebody

Who'd point at his rearranged face and holler,"Johnny!"

Was Johnny ugly?

Yes, because Dr. Wilhelm Loeser had given him a new
profile

With a baggy jawline and squint eyes and an erased dimple,

With kangaroo-tendon cheekbones and a gigolo's mustache
that should've been illegal.

Did Johnny love a girl?

Yes, a good-looking, hard-headed Indian named Billie
Frechette.

He wanted to marry her and lie down and try to get over it,

But she was locked in jail for giving him first-aid and com-
fort.

Did Johnny feel hurt?

He felt like breaking a bank or jumping over a railing

Into some panicky teller's cage to shout, "Reach for the
ceiling!"

Or like kicking some vice president in the bum checks and
smiling.

What was he really doing?

Going up the aisle with the crowd and into the lobby

With Polly saying, "Would *you* do what Clark done?" And
Johnny saying, "Maybe."

And Anna saying, "If he'd been smart, he'd of acted lik
   Bing Crosby."
Did Johnny look flashy?
Yes, his white-on-white shirt and tie were luminous.
His trousers were creased like knives to the tops of his shoes
And his yellow straw hat came down to his dark glasses.
Was Johnny suspicious?
Yes, and when Agent Purvis signalled with a tremblin
   cigar,
Johnny ducked left and ran out of the theater,
And innocent Polly and squealing Anna were left nowhere
Was Johnny a fast runner?
No, but he crouched and scurried past a friendly liquor stor
Under the coupled arms of double-daters, under awnings
   under stars,
To the curb at the mouth of an alley. He hunched there.
Was Johnny a thinker?
No, but he was thinking more or less of Billie Frechette
Who was lost in prison for longer than he could possibl
   wait,
And then it was suddenly too hard to think around a bullet
Did anyone shoot straight?
Yes, but Mrs. Etta Natalsky fell out from under her pictur
   hat.
Theresa Paulus sprawled on the sidewalk, clutching her lef
   foot.
And both of them groaned loud and long under the street
   light.
Did Johnny like that?
No, but he lay down with those strange women, his face in
   the alley,
One shoe off, cinders in his mouth, his eyelids heavy.
When they shouted questions at him, he talked back to
   nobody.
Did Johnny lie easy?
Yes, holding his gun and holding his breath as a last trick
He waited, but when the Agents came close, his breath
   wouldn't work.
Clark Gable walked his last mile; Johnny ran half a block
Did he run out of luck?
Yes, before he was cool, they had him spread out on dished-
   in marble
In the Cook County Morgue, surrounded by babbling people
With a crime reporter presiding over the head of the table.
Did Johnny have a soul?

Yes, and it was climbing his slippery wind-pipe like a trapped
    burglar.
It was beating the inside of his ribcage, hollering, "Let me
    out of here!"
Maybe it got out, and maybe it just stayed there.
Was Johnny a money-maker?
Yes, and thousands paid 25¢ to see him, mostly women,
And one said, "I wouldn't have come, except he's a moral
    lesson,"
And another, "I'm disappointed. He feels like a dead man."
Did Johnny have a brain?
Yes, and it always worked best through the worst of dangers,
Through flat-footed hammerlocks, through guarded doors,
    around corners,
But it got taken out in the morgue and sold to some doctors.
Could Johnny take orders?
No, but he stayed in the wicker basket carried by six men
Through the bulging crowd to the hearse and let himself be
    locked in,
And he stayed put as it went driving south in a driving rain.
And he didn't get stolen?
No, not even after his old hard-nosed dad refused to sell
The quick-drawing corpse for $10,000 to somebody in a
    carnival.
He figured he'd let *Johnny* decide how to get to Hell.
Did anyone wish him well?
Yes, half of Indiana camped in the family pasture,
And the minister said, "With luck, he could have been
    a minister."
And up the sleeve of his oversized gray suit, Johnny twitched
    a finger.
Does anyone remember?
Everyone still alive. And some dead ones. It was a new kind
    of holiday
With hot and cold drinks and hot and cold tears. They
    planted him in a cemetery
With three unknown vice presidents, Benjamin Harrison,
    and James Whitcomb Riley,
Who never held up anybody.

(1966)

DIANE WAKOSK

Inside Out

I walk the purple carpet into your eye
carrying the silver butter server
but a truck rumbles by,
        leaving its black tire prints on my foot
and old images   the sound of banging screen doors o
                        hot afternoon
    and a fly buzzing over the Kool-Aid spilled on the sin
flicker, as reflections on the metal surface.

Come in, you said,
inside your paintings, inside the blood factory, inside th
old songs that line your hands, inside
eyes that change like a snowflake every second,
inside spinach leaves holding that one piece of gravel,
inside the whiskers of a cat,
inside your old hat, and most of all inside your mouth wher
                                yo
grind the pigments with your teeth, painting
with a broken bottle on the floor, and painting
with an ostrich feather on the moon that rolls out of m
                                mouth

You cannot let me walk inside you too long inside
the veins where my small feet touch
bottom.
You must reach inside and pull me
like a silver bullet
from your arm.

                                   (1965

THEODORE WEISS

Barracks Apt. 14

All must be used:

this clay whisky jug, bearing
a lamp-shade; the four brown pears,
lying ruggedly among each other
in the wicker basket; the cactus
in its pot; and the orange berries,
old now as they dangle from their twigs
as though badly hung there.

These as well as the silence,
the young woman reading Aristotle
with difficulty, and the little girl
in the next room, voluble in bed:
"I'm talking in my sleep . . . laughing
in my sleep . . . waking in my sleep"

all are parts hopeful, possible,
expecting their place in the song;
more appealing because parts
that must harmonize into something
that rewards them for being, rewards
with what they are.

       Do this and do,
till suddenly the scampering field
you would catch, the shiny crows
just out of reach, the pears
through which a brown tide breaks,
and the cactus you cannot cling to

long like that thorny Aristotle
suddenly, turning, turn on you

as meaning, the ultimate greenness
they have all the time been seeking
in the very flight they held
before you. No matter what you do,
at last you will be overwhelmed,
the distance will be broken,

the music will confound you.

(1957)

To Forget Me

Now when I have thrust my body
from me far as doubt is, almost far
as death who recently thrived in me,
who, hands throbbing with fulfilment,
warmed in the lesson I nearly learned,

when I have refused and choked
the voices staunch in me, have spurned
them, racing through my hands like gifts,
like water clearest over pebbles lifted
as they lift, a ripple as of sunlight

in the folds filling the body,
now when I plant me, a surly rock
against me, mouth locked that no voices,
inside or out, be heard, and birds
like the morning light but scorings

over and under of the dark,
and when I, turned my back on me,
have sought the starkest future that must
in every way forget me, yearning to be
cleansed of me, to shadow, shade,

least murmur in me of the memory
of my name and time, still the world
is practicing its round of pleasures,
more plentiful than ever for my absence:
as though this place had nobody to say

them nay, presences stride: birds
clamber through, an open top azure:
spices speak like genius on the emptied
mouth. And when you stoop, the massy-
hummed administerings of evening,

its stirring silks, a precision
on the lips, kiss ransacks every corner
of my body where I have not been. I am
flooded to that realm the lightnings
coil, I inmost far out in the world.

(1959)

The Web

for Hannah Arendt

High summer's sheen upon all things
that dust is glazed and I am lost
within the florid scene, I think
of someone stitched into a complex
tapestry; and sitting in a niche—
five glittering crows a crown
about her head, held there no doubt
by thread run through their feet,
but held as well, or so it seems,
by what she does and what she sings—
she stitches too,

            as one should sing,
absorbed by what she hears, so sing
the more, her glance, entwining
in her work, lit up, that radiance,
high summer's sheen, be visible
and piling in a telltale foam
from her shy skill, that all things

eagerly like stars around the moon
attain their story, listen to it,
from her lip and hand, her settled
will; and still, as she is nested
in her craft, like dolphins leaped
above their element, she spins.

Ah, let this be a lasting omen:
the world a moment takes its blessing
from the sleight-of-hand of woman,
and by our passion held in common,
as we when we were young, our limbs
air-borne, bore leaves and ballads
of the birds, the clouds and storms
and all the world beside mere flower-
ing of our singled sigh;
                              thought
nothing of the skulking, not yet
lowering gloom such opulence must
shed; nor thought a wind, until now
banked or spent among our breath
with our consent, a gleaming shade
in our design, would, blowing,
blast the web—torn also by the tatter
crows, fled far beyond their thread-
bare wings—and, last, its instruments.

(1962)

REED WHITTEMORE

A Day with the Foreign Legion

On one of those days with the Legion
When everyone sticks to sofas
And itches and bitches—a day
For gin and bitters and the plague—
Down by Mount Tessala, under the plane trees,
Seated at iron tables, cursing the country,
Cursing the times and the natives, cursing the drinks,
Cursing the food and the bugs, cursing the Legion,
Were Kim and Bim and all those brave
Heroes of all those books and plays and movies
The remorseless desert serves.
And as they sat at the iron tables cursing the country,
Cursing the food and the bugs, cursing the Legion,
Some Sergeant or other rushed in from The Fort
Gallantly bearing the news
From which all those the remorseless desert serves
Take their cues:
"Sir!"
     "What is it, Sergeant?"
               "Sir, the hordes
March e'en now across the desert swards."

Just like the movies.

Now in the movies
The Sergenat's arrival touches off bugles and bells,
Emptying bunks and showers, frightening horses,
Pushing up flags and standards, hardening lines
Of unsoldierly softness, and putting farewells

Hastily in the post so two weeks hence
A perfectly lovely lovely in far-off Canada
Will go pale and bite buttons and stare at the air in Canada.
And in the movies,
Almost before the audience spills its popcorn,
The company's formed and away, with Bim or Kim
Solemnly leading them out into a sandstorm,
Getting them into what is quite clearly a trap,
Posting a double guard,
Sending messengers frantic to Marrakech,
Inadvertently pouring the water away,
Losing the ammunition, horses and food,
And generally carrying on in the great tradition
By making speeches
Which bring back to mind the glorious name of the Legion,
And serve as the turning point,
After which the Arabs seem doped and perfectly helpless,
Water springs up from the ground, the horses come back,
Plenty of food is discovered in some old cave,
And reinforcements arrive led by the girl
From Canada.

But in this instance nothing from *Beau Geste*
Or the Paramount lot was attempted,
It being too hot, too terribly hot, for dramatics
Even from Kim and Bim
Aging under the plane trees,
Cursing the food and the bugs, cursing the Sergeant
Who gallantly bore the news because he was young,
Full of oats and ignorance, so damned young
In his pretty khaki; nothing at all,
So late in the day, with everyone crocked
And bitten to death and sweaty and all,
Was attempted despite the Sergeant,
Who whirled on his heel, his mission accomplished, and
    marched,
Hip hip,
Out of the bar, a true trooper, as if to the wars.

So the lights went on and the audience,
Pleasantly stupid, whistled and clapped at the rarity
Of a film breaking down in this late year of Our Lord.
But of course it was not the film; it was not the projector;
Nor was it the man in the booth, who hastened away
As soon as the feature was over, leaving the heroes
Cursing the food and the bugs, cursing the Legion

As heathendom marched and the Sergeant whirled, hip hip;
But some other, darker cause having to do
With the script perhaps, or the art.
Or not art—
None of these but still deeper, deeper and darker,
Rooted in Culture or . . . Culture, or . . .

Or none of these things. Or all.

What was it?

None of these things, or all. It was the time,
The time and the place, and how could one blame them,
Seated at iron tables cursing the country?
What could they do,
Seated under the plane trees watching the Sergeant
Whirl on his heel, hip hip, in his pretty khaki?
What could they say,
Drinking their gin and bitters by Mount Tessala,
What could they say?

For what after all *could* be said,
After all was said,
But that the feature had merely run out, and the lights had
    gone on
Because it was time for the lights to go on, and time
For them not to dash out in the desert,
But to rage
As befitted their age
At the drinks and the country, letting their audience
Clamp, stamp, whistle and hoot as darkness
Settled on Mount Tessala, the lights went on,
The enemy roamed the desert, and everyone itched.

                                                        (1950)

Still Life

I must explain why it is that at night, in my own house,
Even when no one's asleep, I feel I must whisper.
Thoreau and Wordsworth would call it an act of devotion,
I think; others would call it fright; it is probably

Something of both. In my living room there are matters I'd
    rather not meddle with
Late at night.

I prefer to sit very still on the couch, watching
All the inanimate things of my daytime life—
The furniture and the curtains, the pictures and books—
Come alive,
Not as in some childish fantasy, the chairs dancing
And Disney prancing backstage, but with dignity,
The big old rocker presiding over a silent
And solemn assembly of all my craftsmen,
From Picasso and other dignities gracing my walls
To the local carpenter benched at my slippered feet.

I find these proceedings
Remarkable for their clarity and intelligence, and I wish I
    might somehow
Bring into daylight the eloquence, say, of a doorknob.
But always the gathering breaks up; everyone there
Shrinks from the tossing turbulence
Of living,
A cough, a creaking stair.

                                                  (1956)

The Party

They served tea in the sandpile, together with
Mudpies baked on the sidewalk.
After tea
The youngest said that he had had a good dinner,
The oldest dressed for a dance,
And they sallied forth together with watering pots
To moisten a rusted fire truck on account of it
Might rain.

I watched from my study,
Thought of my part in these contributions to world
Gaiety, and resolved
That the very least acknowledgment I could make

Would be to join them;
        so we
All took our watering pots (filled with pies)
And poured tea on our dog. Then I kissed the children
And told them that when they grew up we would have
Real tea parties.
"That did be fun!" the youngest shouted, and ate pies
With wild surmise.

                           (1959)

The Tarantula

Everyone thinks I am poisonous. I am not.
Look up and read the authorities on me, especially
One Alexander Petrunkevitch, of Yale, now retired,
Who was said of me (and I quote): my "bite is dangerous
Only
To insects and small mammals such as mice."
I would have you notice that "only"; that is important,
As you who are neither insect nor mouse can appreciate.
I have to live as you do,
And how would you like it if someone construed your relations
With the chicken, say, as proof of your propensities?
Furthermore,
Petrunkevitch has observed, and I can vouch for it,
That I am myopic, lonely and retiring. When I am born
I dig a burrow for me, and me alone,
And live in it all my life except when I come
Up for food and love (in my case the latter
Is not really satisfactory: I
"Wander about after dark in search of females,
And occasionally stray into houses," after which I
Die). How does that sound?
Furthermore,
I have to cope with the digger wasp of the genus
Pepsis; and despite my renown as a killer (nonsense, of
    course),
I can't. Petrunkevitch says so.
Read him. He's good on the subject. He's helped *me*.

Which brings me to my point here. You carry
This image about of me that is at once libelous
And discouraging, all because you, who should know bette
Find me ugly. So I am ugly. Does that mean that you
Should persecute me as you do? Read William Blake.
Read William Wordsworth.
Read Williams in general, I'd say. There was a book
By a William Tarantula once, a work of some consequenc
In my world on the subject of beauty,
Beauty that's skin deep only, beauty that some
Charles (note the "Charles") of the Ritz can apply and tak
    off
At will, beauty that—
                        but I digress.
What I am getting at
Is that you who are blessed (I have read) with under
    standing
Should understand me, little me. My name is William
Too.

                                                    (1959

RICHARD WILBUR

The Beautiful Changes

One wading a Fall meadow finds on all sides
The Queen Anne's Lace lying like lilies
On water; it glides
So from the walker, it turns
Dry grass to a lake, as the slightest shade of you
Valleys my mind in fabulous blue Lucernes.

The beautiful changes as a forest is changed
by a chameleon's tuning his skin to it;
As a mantis, arranged
On a green leaf, grows
Into it, makes the leaf leafier, and proves
Any greenness is deeper than anyone knows.

Your hands hold roses always in a way that says
They are not only yours; the beautiful changes
In such kind ways,
Wishing ever to sunder
Things and things' selves for a second finding, to lose
For a moment all that it touches back to wonder.

(1947)

Ceremony

A striped blouse in a clearing by Bazille
Is, you may say, a patroness of boughs
Too queenly kind toward nature to be kin.

363

But ceremony never did conceal,
Save to the silly eye, which all allows,
How much we are the woods we wander in.

Let her be some Sabrina fresh from stream,
Lucent as shallows slowed by wading sun,
Bedded on fern, the flowers' cynosure:
Then nymph and wood must nod and strive to dream
That she is airy earth, the trees, undone,
Must ape her languor natural and pure.

Ho-hum. I am for wit and wakefulness,
And love this feigning lady by Bazille.
What's lightly hid is deepest understood,
And when with social smile and formal dress
She teaches leaves to curtsy and quadrille,
I think there are most tigers in the wood.

(1948)

Year's-End

Now winter downs the dying of the year,
And night is all a settlement of snow;
From the soft street the rooms of houses show
A gathered light, a shapen atmosphere,
Like frozen-over lakes whose ice is thin
And still allows some stirring down within.

I've known the wind by water banks to shake
The late leaves down, which frozen where they fell
And held in ice as dancers in a spell
Fluttered all winter long into a lake;
Graved on the dark in gestures of descent,
They seemed their own most perfect monument.

There was perfection in the death of ferns
Which laid their fragile cheeks against the stone
A million years. Great mammoths overthrown
Composedly have made their long sojourns,
Like palaces of patience, in the grey
and changeless lands of ice. And at Pompeii

The little dog lay curled and did not rise
But slept the deeper as the ashes rose
And found the people incomplete, and froze
The random hands, the loose unready eyes
Of men expecting yet another sun
To do the shapely thing they had not done.

These sudden ends of time must give us pause.
We fray into the future, rarely wrought
Save in the tapestries of afterthought.
More time, more time. Barrages of applause
Come muffled from a buried radio.
The New-year bells are wrangling with the snow.

(1949)

After the Last Bulletins

After the last bulletins the windows darken
And the whole city founders readily and deep,
Sliding on all its pillows
To the thronged Atlantis of personal sleep,

And the wind rises. The wind rises and bowls
The day's litter of news in the alleys. Trash
Tears itself on the railings,
Soars and falls with a soft crash,

Tumbles and soars again. Unruly flights
Scamper the park, and taking a statue for dead
Strike at the positive eyes,
Batter and flap the stolid head

And scratch the noble name. In empty lots
Our journals spiral in a fierce noyade
Of all we thought to think,
Or caught in corners cramp and wad

And twist our words. And some from gutters flail
Their tatters at the tired patrolman's feet,
Like all that fisted snow
That cried beside his long retreat

Damn you! damn you! to the emperor's horse's heels.
Oh none too soon through the air white and dry
Will the clear announcer's voice
Beat like a dove, and you and I

From the heart's anarch and responsible town
Return by subway-mouth to life again,
Bearing the morning papers,
And cross the park where saintlike men

White and absorbed with stick and bag remove
The litter of the night, and footsteps rouse
with confident morning sound
The songbirds in the public boughs.

(1953)

The Undead

Even as children they were late sleepers,
Preferring their dreams, even when quick with monsters,
To the world with all its breakable toys,
Its compacts with the dying;

From the stretched arms of withered trees
They turned, fearing contagion of the mortal,
And even under the plums of summer
Drifted like winter moons.

Secret, unfriendly, pale, possessed
Of the one wish, the thirst for mere survival,
They came, as all extremists do
In time, to a sort of grandeur:

Now, to their Balkan battlements
Above the vulgar town of their first lives,
They rise at the moon's rising. Strange
That their utter self-concern

Should, in the end, have left them selfless:
Mirrors fail to perceive them as they float
Through the great hall and up the staircase;
Nor are the cobwebs broken.

Into the pallid night emerging,
Wrapped in their flapping capes, routinely maddened
   By a wolf's cry, they stand for a moment
     Stoking the mind's eye

With lewd thoughts of the pressed flowers
And bric-a-brac of rooms with something to lose,—
   Of love-dismembered dolls, and children
     Buried in quilted sleep.

Then they are off in a negative frenzy,
Their black shapes cropped into sudden bats
   That swarm, burst, and are gone. Thinking
     Of a thrush cold in the leaves

Who has sung his few summers truly,
Or an old scholar resting his eyes at last,
   We cannot be much impressed with vampires,
     Colorful though they are;

Nevertheless their pain is real,
And requires our pity. Think how sad it must be
   To thirst always for a scorned elixir,
     The salt quotidian blood

Which, if mistrusted, has no savor;
To prey on life forever and not possess it,
   As rock-hollows, tide after tide,
     Glassily strand the sea.

                  (1961)

On the Marginal Way

Another cove of shale,
But the beach here is rubbled with strange rock
   That is sleek, fluent, and taffy-pale.
I stare, reminded with a little shock
How, by a shore in Spain, George Borrow saw
A hundred women basking in the raw.

They must have looked like this,
That catch of bodies on the sand, that strew
   Of rondure, crease, and orifice,

Lap, flank, and knee—a too abundant view
Which, though he'd had the lenses of a fly,
Could not have waked desire in Borrow's eye.

        Has the light altered now?
The rocks flush rose and have the melting shape
    Of bodies fallen anyhow.
It is a Géricault of blood and rape,
Some desert town despoiled, some caravan
Pillaged, its people murdered to a man,

        And those who murdered them
Galloping off, a rumpling line of dust
    Like the wave's white, withdrawing hem.
But now the vision of a colder lust
Clears, as the wind goes chill and all is greyed
By a swift cloud that drags a carrion shade.

        If these are bodies still,
Theirs is a death too dead to look asleep,
    Like that of Auschwitz' final kill,
Poor slaty flesh abandoned in a heap
And then, like sea-rocks buried by a wave,
Bulldozed at last into a common grave.

        It is not tricks of sense
But the time's fright within me which distracts
    Least fancies into violence
And makes my thought take cover in the facts,
As now it does, remembering how the bed
Of layered rock two miles above my head

        Hove ages up and broke
Soundless asunder, when the shrinking skin
    Of Earth, blacked out by steam and smoke,
Gave passage to the muddled fire within,
Its crannies flooding with a sweat of quartz,
And lathered magmas out of deep retorts

        Welled up, as here, to fill
With tumbled rockmeal, stone-fume, lithic spray,
    The dike's brief chasm and the sill.
Weathered until the sixth and human day
By sanding winds and water, scuffed and brayed
By the slow glacier's heel, these forms were made

That now recline and burn
Comely as Eve and Adam, near a sea
   Transfigured by the sun's return.
And now three girls lie golden in the lee
Of a great arm or thigh, and are as young
As the bright boulders that they lie among.

   Though, high above the shore
On someone's porch, spread wings of newsprint flap
   The tidings of some dirty war,
It is a perfect day: the waters clap
Their hands and kindle, and the gull in flight
Loses himself at moments, white in white,

   And like a breaking thought
Joy for a moment floods into the mind,
   Blurting that all things shall be brought
To the full state and stature of their kind,
By what has found the manhood of this stone.
May that vast motive wash and wash our own.

                      (1965)

Running

1   1933

What were we playing? Was it prisoner's base?
I ran with whacking keds
Down the cart-road past Rickard's place,
And where it dropped beside the tractor-sheds

Leapt out into the air above a blurred
Terrain, through jolted light,
Took two hard lopes, and at the third
Spanked off a hummock-side exactly right,

And made the turn, and with delighted strain
Sprinted across the flat
By the bull-pen, and up the lane.
Thinking of happiness, I think of that.

II   PATRIOT'S DAY

Restless that noble day, appeased by soft
Drinks and tobacco, littering the grass
While the flag snapped and brightened far aloft,
We waited for the marathon to pass,

We fathers and our little sons, let out
Of school and office to be put to shame.
Now from the street-side someone raised a shout,
And into view the first small runners came.

Dark in the glare, they seemed to thresh in place
Like preening flies upon a window-sill,
Yet gained and grew, and at a cruel pace
Swept by us on their way to Heartbreak Hill—

Legs driving, fists at port, clenched faces, men,
And in amongst them, stamping on the sun,
Our champion Kelly, who would win again,
Rocked in his will, at rest within his run.

III   DODWELLS HILL ROAD

I jog up out of the woods
To the crown of the road, and slow to a swagger there,
The wind harsh and cool to my throat,
A good ache in my rib-cage.

Loud burden of streams at run-off,
And the sun's rocket frazzled in blown tree-heads:
Still I am part of that great going,
Though I stroll now, and am watchful.

Where the road turns and debouches,
The land sinks westward into exhausted pasture.
From fields which yield to aspen now
And pine at last will shadow,

Boy-shouts reach me, and barking.
What is the thing which men will not surrender?
It is what they have never had, I think,
Or missed in its true season,

So that their thoughts turn in
At the same roadhouse nightly, the same cloister,
The wild mouth of the same brave river
Never now to be charted.

You, whoever you are,
If you want to walk with me you must step lively.
I run, too, when the mood offers,
Though the god of that has left me.

But why in the hell spoil it?
I make a clean gift of my young running
To the two boys who break into view,
Hurdling the rocks and racing,

Their dog dodging before them
This way and that, his yaps flushing a pheasant
Who lifts now from the blustery grass,
Flying full tilt already.

(1967)

CHARLES WRIGHT

The Daughters of Blum

The daughters of Blum
Are growing older.
These chill winter days,
Locking their rooms, they
Seem to pause, checking,

Perhaps, for the lights,
The window curtain,
Or something they want
To remember that
Keeps slipping their minds.

You have seen them, how
They stand there, perplexed,
—And a little shocked—
As though they had spied,
Unexpectedly,

From one corner of
One eye, the lives they
Must have left somewhere
Once on a dresser—
Gloves waiting for hands.

(1967)

JAMES WRIGHT

American Twilights, 1957

to Caryl Chessman

1

The buckles glitter, billies lean
Supple and cold as men on walls.
The trusties' faces, yawning green,
Summon up heart, as someone calls
For light, for light! and evening falls.

Checking the cells, the warden piles
Shadow on shadow where he goes
Beyond the catwalk, down the files,
Sneering at one who thumbs his nose.
One weeps, and stumbles on his toes.

Tear and tormented snicker and heart
Click in the darkness; close, and fade.
Clean locks together mesh and part,
And lonely lifers, foot and head,
Huddle against the bed they made.

2

Lie dark, beloved country, now
Trouble no dream, so still you lie.
Citizens drawl their dreams away;
Stupored, they hid their agony
Deep in the rock; but men must die.

Tall on the earth I would have sung
Heroes of hell, could I have learned
Their names to marvel on my tongue;

373

The land is dark where they have turned,
And now their very names are burned.

But buried under trestled rock
The broken thief and killer quake:
Tower by tower and clock by clock
Citizens wind the towns asleep.
God, God have pity when they wake.

Haunted by gallows, peering in dark,
I conjure prisons out of wet
And strangling pillows where I mark
The misery man must not forget,
Though I have found no prison yet.

Lo now, the desolation man
Has tossed away like a gnawed bone
Will hunt him where the sea began,
Summon him out of tree and stone,
Damn him, before his dream be gone:—

Seek him behind his bars, to crack
Out the dried kernel of his heart.
God, God have pity if he wake,
Have mercy on man who dreamed apart.
God, God have pity on man apart.

(1959)

Having Lost My Sons, I Confront the Wreckage of the Moon: Christmas, 1960

After dark
Near the South Dakota border,
The moon is out hunting, everywhere,
Delivering fire,
And walking down hallways
Of a diamond.

Behind a tree,
It lights on the ruins
Of a white city:
Frost, frost.

Where are they gone,
Who lived there?

Bundled away under wings
And dark faces.

I am sick
Of it, and I go on,
Living, alone, alone,
Past the charred silos, past the hidden graves
Of Chippewas and Norwegians.

This cold winter
Moon spills the inhuman fire
Of jewels
Into my hands.

Dead riches, dead hands, the moon
Darkens,
And I am lost in the beautiful white ruins
Of America.

(1961)

The Jewel

There is this cave
In the air behind my body
That nobody is going to touch:
A cloister, a silence
Closing around a blossom of fire.
When I stand upright in the wind,
My bones turn to dark emeralds.

(1962)

Two Poems About President Harding

1 HIS DEATH

In Marion, the honey locust trees are falling.
Everybody in town remembers the white hair,

The campaign of a lost summer, the front porch
Open to the public, and the vaguely stunned smile
Of a lucky man.

"Neighbor, I want to be helpful," he said once.
Later, "You think I'm honest, don't you?"
Weeping drunk.

I am drunk this evening in 1961,
In a jag for my countryman,
Who died of crab meat on the way back from Alaska.
Everyone knows that joke.

How many honey locusts have fallen,
Pitched rootlong into the open graves of strip mines,
Since the First World War ended
And Wilson the gaunt deacon jogged sullenly
Into silence?
Tonight,
The cancerous ghosts of old con men
Shed their leaves.
For a proud man,
Lost between the turnpike near Cleveland
And the chiropractors' signs looming among dead mulberry
    trees,
There is no place left to go
But home.

"Warren lacks mentality," one of his friends said.
Yet he was beautiful, he was the snowfall
Turned to white stallions standing still
Under dark elm trees.

He died in public. He claimed the secret right
To be ashamed.

2 HIS TOMB IN OHIO

> "... he died of a busted gut."
> —MENCKEN ON BRYAN.

A hundred slag piles north of us,
At the mercy of the moon and rain,
He lies in his ridiculous
Tomb, our fellow citizen.
No, I have never seen that place,

Where many shadows of faceless thieves
Chuckle and stumble and embrace
On beer cans, stogie butts, and graves.

One holiday, one rainy week
After the country fell apart,
Hoover and Coolidge came to speak
And snivel about his broken heart.
His grave, a huge absurdity,
Embarrassed cops and visitors.
Hoover and Coolidge crept away
By night, and women closed their doors.

Now junkmen call their children in
Before they catch their death of cold;
Young lovers let the moon begin
Its quick spring; and the day grows old;
The mean one-legger who rakes up leaves
Has chased the loafers out of the park;
Minnegan Leonard half-believes
In God, and the poolroom goes dark;

America goes on, goes on
Laughing, and Harding was a fool.
Even his big pretentious stone
Lays him bare to ridicule.
I know it. But don't look at me.
By God, I didn't start this mess.
Whatever moon and rain may be,
The hearts of men are merciless.

(1961 & 1962)

Before the Cashier's Window in a Department Store

1

The beautiful cashier's white face has risen once more
Behind a young manager's shoulder.
They whisper together, and stare

Straight into my face.
I feel like grabbing a stray child
Or a skinny old woman
And diving into a cellar, crouching
Under a stone bridge, praying myself sick,
Till the troops pass.

2

Why should he care? He goes.
I slump deeper.
In my frayed coat, I am pinned down
By debt. He nods,
Commending my flesh to the pity of the daws of God.

3

Am I dead? And, if not, why not?
For she sails there, alone, looming in the heaven of the
    beautiful.
She knows
The bulldozers will scrape me up
After dark, behind
The officers' club.
Beneath her terrible blaze, my skeleton
Glitters out. I am the dark. I am the dark
Bone I was born to be.

4

Tu Fu woke shuddering on a battlefield
Once, in the dead of night, and made out
The mangled women, sorting
The haggard slant-eyes
The moon was up.

5

I am hungry. In two more days
It will be Spring. So: this
Is what it feels like.

(1965)

In Response to a Rumor That the Oldest Whorehouse in Wheeling, West Virginia, Has Been Condemned

I will grieve alone,
As I strolled alone, years ago, down along
The Ohio shore.
I hid in the hobo jungle weeds
Upstream from the sewer main,
Pondering, gazing.

I saw, down river,
At Twenty-third and Water Streets
By the vinegar works,
The doors open in early evening.
Swinging their purses, the women
Poured down the long street to the river
And into the river.

I do not know how it was
They could drown every evening.
What time near dawn did they climb up the other shore,
Drying their wings?

For the river at Wheeling, West Virginia
Has only two shores:
The one in hell, the other
In Bridgeport, Ohio.

And nobody would commit suicide, only
To find beyond death
Bridgeport, Ohio.

(1968)

Biographies

A. R. AMMONS (b. 1926, Whiteville, North Carolina) is, at present, assistant professor of English at Cornell University. His numerous books of poetry include *Ommateum, Expressions of Sea Level, Corsons Inlet, Tape for the Turn of the Year, Northfield Poems,* and *Selected Poems.* He has been awarded a Guggenheim Fellowship as well as a traveling fellowship of the American Academy of Arts and Letters.

ALAN ANSEN (b. 1922, Brooklyn, New York) received his B.A. and M.A. from Harvard University. His books of poems include *The Old Religion, Disorderly Houses,* and the privately published volumes, *Believe and Tremble, Field Report,* and *Day by Day.* Mr. Ansen resides in Athens, Greece.

JOHN ASHBERY (b. 1927, Rochester, New York), a graduate of Harvard and Columbia, is executive editor of *Art News* as well as art critic for the *New York Herald Tribune* (Paris edition). He won the Yale Series of Younger Poets Prize in 1956 for his first volume of poetry, *Some Trees.* His other volumes of poetry include *The Tennis Court Oath, Rivers and Mountains,* and *Selected Poems.*

MARVIN BELL (b. 1937, New York City) is presently teaching in the Writers Workshop at The University of Iowa. In addition to being poetry editor of *The North American Review,* he is co-editor of *Midland II* and the author of *Things We Dreamt We Died For, Poems for Nathan and Saul,* and *A Probable Volume of Dreams.*

MICHAEL BENEDIKT (b. 1937, New York City), a frequent contributor to *Art News* and *Art International,* is the author of *The Body.* He has also edited and translated *Ring Around the World,* selected poems of Jean L'Anselme, and is the editor of five anthologies of modern drama.

JOHN BERRYMAN (b. 1914, McAlester, Oklahoma), a graduate of Columbia College and the University of Cambridge, has taught at Harvard, Princeton, and the University of Minnesota. His critical biography, *Stephen Crane,* was published in the "American Men of Letters" series, and one of his stories, "The Imaginary Jew," won the Kenyon-Doubleday Award. His collections of poems include *The Dispossessed, Homage to Mistress Bradstreet, Berryman's Sonnets,* and *His Toy, His Dream, His Rest.* He is the recipient of numerous awards and prizes, including the Bollingen Prize and the Pulitzer Prize for Poetry in 1965 for *77 Dream Songs.*

ELIZABETH BISHOP (b. 1911, Worcester, Massachusetts), a 1934 Vassar graduate, served as consultant in poetry to the Library of Congress, 1949–1950. She has won many prizes and fellowships, including the Pulitzer Prize in 1956 for *Poems.* Her other volumes of poetry include *North and South* and *Questions of Travel.* Miss Bishop is a member of the National Institute of Arts and Letters.

ROBERT BLY (b. 1926, Madison, Minnesota) received his B.A. from Harvard. He is the author of two books of poetry, *Silence in the Snowy Fields* and *A Light Around the Body.* He has edited two books: *The Sea and the Honeycomb,* a collection of brief poems from various languages, and *Forty Poems Touching on Recent American History.* He has received several awards, among them a Guggenheim Fellowship and an award from the National Institute of Arts and Letters.

PHILIP BOOTH (b. 1925, Hanover, New Hampshire) is currently professor of English and poet-in-residence at Syracuse University. His books of poetry include *Letter from a Distant Land, The Islanders,* and *Weathers and Edges.* His recent awards include a National Institute of Arts and Letters Grant and a Rockefeller Foundation Fellowship.

EDGAR BOWERS (b. 1924, Rome, Georgia) received his B.A. from the University of North Carolina and his Ph.D. from Stanford. He is presently professor of English at the University of California in Santa Barbara. The author of *The Form of Loss* and *The Astronomers,* he has also had poems published in *Paris Review, Sewanee Review, Poetry,* and *The New York Times,* as well as in various anthologies.

TOM CLARK (b. 1941, Chicago, Illinois) has been poetry editor of *The Paris Review* since 1963. His books of poetry include *The Sand Burg, Airplanes, The Emperor of the Animals,* and *Stones.* Mr. Clark is currently residing in California.

GREGORY CORSO (b. 1930, New York City) is well known, along with Allen Ginsberg and Jack Kerouac, for his association with the rise of the "Beat" movement in New York and San Francisco. He is the author of such books of poetry as *The*

Vestal Lady on Brattle, Gasoline, The Happy Birthday of Death, and *Long Live Man.* His first novel, *The American Express,* was published by Olympia Press in 1961. He is also the author of a short play, *In This Hung-up Age.*

HENRI COULETTE (b. 1927, Los Angeles) received his B.A. from California State College in Los Angeles and his M.F.A. and Ph.D. from the University of Iowa. His poems have appeared in *Hudson Review, Paris Review,* and *The New Yorker.* In 1965, his first book of poems, *The War of the Secret Agents and Other Poems,* won the Lamont Poetry Selection. He is currently a professor in the English department of California State College.

ROBERT CREELEY (b. 1926, Arlington, Massachusetts) is currently teaching at the State University of New York. Author of numerous books of poetry, the last of which, *Words,* was published by Scribner's in 1967, he is also a winner of the Levinson Prize as well as a Rockefeller Grant and a Guggenheim Fellowship.

J. V. CUNNINGHAM (b. 1911, Cumberland, Maryland) is currently professor of English at Brandeis University. His many books include *The Helmsman, The Judge's Fury, Doctor Drink, Exclusions of a Rhyme,* and *To What Strangers, What Welcome.* He has just finished a new volume of poetry entitled *Some Salt.*

JAMES DICKEY (b. 1923, Atlanta), formerly consultant in poetry in English to the Library of Congress (1966–1968), is the author of *Poems, Buckdancer's Choice, Helmets, Poems of the Air, Drowning with Others,* and *Into the Stone,* as well as *The Suspect in Poetry,* a collection of critical essays. In 1966 he won the National Book Award for *Buckdancer's Choice.*

WILLIAM DICKEY (b. 1928, Bellingham, Washington) is currently associate professor of English at San Francisco State College. His poetry has appeared in such periodicals as *The New Yorker, Atlantic,* and *Harper's,* and his published books of poetry include *Of the Festivity* and *Interpreter's House.* He is the recipient of the Yale Series of Younger Poets Prize and the Urban League Prize of *Poetry* magazine.

ALAN DUGAN (b. 1923, Brooklyn, New York) is the author of *Poems (1961), Poems Two (1963),* and *Poems Three (1967),* all published by the Yale University Press. A winner of the National Book Award and the Pulitzer Prize, he is currently living in New York City.

ALVIN FEINMAN (b. 1929, Brooklyn, New York) received his B.A. from Brooklyn College and his M.A. in philosophy from Yale. He is the author of *Preambles and Other Poems.*

EDWARD FIELD (b. 1924, Brooklyn, New York) is the author of the award-winning documentary *To Be Alive,* commissioned by Johnson's Wax for the New York World's Fair. He is the author of *Stand Up, Friend, with Me; Variety Photoplays; Songs and Stories of the Netsilik Eskimos;* and *Sex Stories.* His poetry has also appeared in *The Nation, Partisan Review, Harper's, New York Review of Books, Evergreen,* and *Paris Review,* as well as in many other periodicals. In 1962 he received the Lamont Award.

DONALD FINKEL (b. 1929, New York City) is currently poet-in-residence at Washington University in St. Louis. His books of poetry include *The Clothing's New Emperor, Simeon, A Joyful Noise,* and *Answer Back.* His poems have appeared in such periodicals as *Accent, Atlantic Monthly, Hudson Review, Paris Review, Poetry* and *The New Yorker,* as well as in numerous anthologies. He was awarded the annual Helen Bullis Prize in 1964 and a Guggenheim Fellowship in 1967–1968.

ISABELLA GARDNER (b. 1915, Newton, Massachusetts), a former editor of *Poetry,* is the author of *Birthdays From the Ocean, The Looking Glass, Un Altra Infanzia,* translations by Alfredo Rizzardi, and *West of Childhood.* Her poems have appeared in *Kenyon Review, Sewanee Review, The New Yorker,* and *Atlantic Monthly.* She is presently living in New York City.

JACK GILBERT (b. 1926, Richmond, Virginia) received his B.A. in 1955 from the University of Pittsburgh. He taught at San Francisco College and at the University of California at Berkeley. His first book of poems, *Views of Jeopardy,* was published by the Yale University Press in 1961 as Volume 58 in the Yale Series of Younger Poets.

ALLEN GINSBERG (b. 1926, Newark, New Jersey) graduated from Columbia College in 1948. His many books include *Howl, Kaddish, Reality Sandwiches, Planet News, Empty Mirror, Yage Letters, Wichita Vortex Sutra,* and *Indian Journals.*

LOUISE GLÜCK (b. 1943, New York City) is the author of *Firstborn.* Her poems have appeared in *The Nation, The New American Review #1, Atlantic Monthly,* and *Poetry.* In 1967 she was awarded a grant from the Rockefeller Foundation.

PAUL GOODMAN (b. 1911, New York City) is a poet, novelist, dramatist, essayist, sociologist, and community planner. His fiction includes *The Facts of Life, The Break-up of Our Camp, Parent's Day, The Empire City,* and *Making Do,* and he has also published two volumes of verse, *The Lordly Hudson* and *Hawkweed: Poems. Kafka's Prayer* and *The Structure of Literature* are books of criticism. In the area of social studies, he has written several books including *Growing Up Absurd, Com-*

pulsory Mis-Education and the Community of Scholars, and *People or Personnel.*

JOHN HAINES (b. 1924, Norfolk, Virginia) is the author of *Winter News,* which was published in 1966. His poems have appeared in such periodicals as *The Nation, Hudson Review, Massachusetts Review,* and *Poetry,* as well as in various anthologies. He was awarded the Massachusetts Review Prize for poetry in 1964, a Guggenheim Fellowship in 1965, and a grant from the National Endowment in Arts in 1967. He resides in Fairbanks, Alaska, where he has been a homesteader for the past 14 years.

DONALD HALL (b. 1928, New Haven, Connecticut) is presently professor of English at the University of Michigan as well as a consultant with Harper & Row. His books include *A Roof of Tiger Lilies, Henry Moon, String Too Short to Be Saved,* and *The Dark House.* He won the Lamont Poetry Selection in 1955 and was awarded a Guggenheim Fellowship in 1963.

KENNETH O. HANSON (b. 1922, Shelley, Idaho) is the author of *The Distance Anywhere,* which won the 1967 Lamont Award. Mr. Hanson received his B.A. from the University of Idaho and did graduate work at the University of Washington. He is currently professor of literature at Reed College.

ANTHONY HECHT (b. 1923, New York City) is the author of *A Summoning of Stones* and *The Hard Hours,* which won the Pulitzer Prize in 1968, as well as *The Seven Deadly Sins* and *A Bestiary,* both of which were published in limited editions. His many awards include the 1951 Prix de Rome, Guggenheim Fellowships in 1954 and 1959, a Ford Foundation Fellowship in 1960, and a Rockefeller Foundation Fellowship in 1967. He is on the editorial board of the *Hudson Review* and on the executive committee of the P.E.N. Club.

DARYL HINE (b. 1936, Burnaby, British Columbia, Canada), is the author of *5 Poems, The Carnal and the Crane, The Devil's Picture Book, The Prince of Darkness & Co., The Wooden Horse,* and *Minutes.* He has also published a novel, *Polish Subtitles,* and a travel diary. He is currently assistant professor of classics at the University of Chicago.

DANIEL HOFFMAN (b. 1923, New York City) received his B.A., M.A., and Ph.D. from Columbia University. He is the author of *Striking the Stones, The City of Satisfactions, A Little Geste,* and *An Armada of Thirty Whales,* as well as several critical studies. He was awarded the Yale Series of Younger Poets Award in 1954, and the 1967 award for poetry from the National Institute of Arts and Letters. He is presently professor of English at the University of Pennsylvania.

JOHN HOLLANDER (b. 1929, New York City) is presently professor of English at Hunter College. His books include *A Crackling of Thorns*, *Movie-Going*, *Visions from the Ramble*, and *The Quest of the Gole*, and his poems have appeared in *The New Yorker*, *Partisan Review*, *Poetry*, and *Harper's*, to name only a few. He was awarded a grant from the American Institute of Arts and Letters in 1963.

RICHARD HOWARD (b. 1929, Cleveland, Ohio) is the author of two books of poetry, *Quantities* and *The Damages*. In addition he has translated over one hundred books from the French and is the author of *Alone with America*, a study of American poetry since 1950.

BARBARA HOWES (b. 1914, New York City), edited *Chimera*, a literary quarterly from 1943 to 1947. Her first book, *The Undersea Farmer*, was published in 1948 and was followed by *In the Cold Country*, *Light and Dark* and *Looking Up at Leaves*. She has also edited *23 Modern Stories* and *From the Green Antilles*, writings of the Caribbean. She resides in North Pownal, Vermont.

ROBERT HUFF (b. 1924, Evanston, Illinois), currently associate professor of English at Western Washington State College, is the author of two books of poetry, *Colonel Johnson's Ride* and *The Course*. His poems have also appeared in numerous anthologies as well as in countless periodicals. He is presently at work on a new book entitled *The Ventriloquist*.

RICHARD HUGO (b. 1923, Seattle, Washington), winner of the Theodore Roethke Prize in 1963 and the Helen Bullis Award in 1965, is the author of *A Run of Jacks* and *Death of the Kapowsin Tavern*. His poems have appeared in such periodicals as *The New American Review*, *Poetry*, *Poetry Northwest*, and *Tri-Quarterly*, as well as in numerous anthologies. He is currently assistant professor of English at the University of Montana.

DAVID IGNATOW (b. 1914, Brooklyn, New York), lecturer in English at Vassar and adjunct professor at Southampton College, is the author of the following books: *Poems*, *The Gentle Weight Lifter*, *Say Pardon*, *Figures of the Human*, *Rescue the Dead*, and *Earth Hard*. He has received an award from the National Institute of Arts and Letters, a Guggenheim Fellowship, and the Shelley Memorial Award, among many other awards.

RANDALL JARRELL (b. 1914, Nashville, Tennessee), a member of the National Institute of Arts and Letters and poetry consultant to the Library of Congress, published seven books of poems, the last of which was *The Lost World*. He was also the author of two books of criticism, *Poetry and the Age* and *A Sad*

Heart at the Supermarket, and a best-selling novel, *Pictures from an Institution,* as well as numerous children's books. He died on October 14, 1965.

LeROI JONES (b. 1934, Newark, N.J.), well-known playwright and poet, has also published articles and reviews on music in publications such as *Downbeat, Metronome,* and *The Jazz Review.* His numerous published books include *Preface to a Twenty Volume Suicide Note; The System of Dante's Hell; Blues, Black and White America; Blues People; The Dead Lecturer; Tales;* and *Black Music.* His play *Dutchman* was published and produced in 1964 and won the Obie Award for that year. It was made into a motion picture in 1967.

DONALD JUSTICE (b. 1925, Miami, Florida), professor of English at Syracuse University, is the author of *The Summer Anniversaries, A Local Storm,* and *Night Light.* Editor of *The Collected Poems of Weldon Kees,* he also co-edited a volume of contemporary French poetry. He is a winner of the Lamont Award, the Inez Boulton Prize, and the Harriet Monroe Memorial Prize.

WELDON KEES (b. 1914, Beatrice, Nebraska), poet, writer, documentary film maker, painter in the abstract expressionist movement, jazz pianist, composer, and photographer, disappeared on July 18, 1955. His books of poetry include *The Last Man, The Fall of the Magicians,* and *Poems: 1947–1954,* as well as *The Collected Poems of Weldon Kees,* a collection edited by Donald Justice and published in 1960 by Stone Wall Press. This volume contains most of his published and previously unpublished poems.

X. J. KENNEDY (b. 1929, Dover, New Jersey), studied in Paris on the GI Bill of Rights and became poetry editor for the *Paris Review* in 1962. His one book of verse, *Nude Descending a Staircase,* won the 1961 Lamont Award. He is presently teaching at Tufts.

GALWAY KINNELL (b. 1927, Providence, R. I.), a graduate of Princeton University, is the author of *What a Kingdom It Was, Flower Herding on Mount Monadnock, Black Light,* and *Body Rags.* He won a Guggenheim in 1961, a National Institute of Arts and Letters Award in 1962, and a Rockefeller Grant in 1967. He is currently residing in Sheffield, Vermont.

CAROLYN KIZER (b. 1925, Spokane, Washington) is currently director of literary programs for the National Endowment for the Arts. Editor and founder of *Poetry Northwest,* her published books include *Knock upon Silence* and *The Ungrateful Garden.* She is currently working on a book of stories to be called *Love, the Butcher Bird, Lurks Everywhere.*

KENNETH KOCH (b. 1925, Cincinnati, Ohio), poet and playwright, received his B.A. from Harvard and his M.A. and Ph.D. from Columbia University. Currently associate professor of English at Columbia, he is the author of *Poems, Ko or a Season on Earth, Permanently,* and *Thank You and Other Poems.* His off-Broadway productions include *Bertha, The Election, George Washington Crossing the Delaware, The Construction of Boston,* and *Guinevere or the Death of the Kangaroo.*

AL LEE (b. 1938, Louisville, Kentucky), who teaches at the Newark College of Engineering, is the author of the volume of poetry *Them and Us.* He is a former Peace Corps Volunteer assigned to Ghana, where he taught school. His poems have appeared in *Poetry Northwest, Partisan Review, Kenyon Review,* and *Yale Review.*

DENISE LEVERTOV (b. 1923, Ilford, Essex, England), came to the United States in 1948 and is currently teaching at Berkeley. She is the author of *The Double Image, Here and Now, Overland to the Islands, With Eyes at the Back of Our Heads, The Jacob's Ladder, O Taste and See,* and *The Sorrow Dance.* Her poetry has also appeared in various publications and anthologies. During 1961, Miss Levertov served as poetry editor of *The Nation.*

PHILIP LEVINE (b. 1928, Detroit, Michigan) is presently teaching at Fresno State College. A former factory worker and truck driver, he has published poems in *Commentary, Hudson Review, Encounter,* and *Kayak,* to mention only a few. He is the author of *On the Edge,* which won the Joseph Henry Jackson Award, and *Not This Pig.*

LAURENCE LIEBERMAN (b. 1935, Detroit, Michigan), in addition to being a poet and teacher, reviews poetry regularly for the *Yale Review* as well as other periodicals. He is the author of *The Achievement of James Dickey,* and a volume of poetry, *The Unblinding.* He teaches at the University of Illinois.

JOHN LOGAN (b. 1923, Red Oak, Iowa), former poetry editor of *The Nation,* is currently teaching at the State University of New York at Buffalo. His books include *Cycle for Mother Cabrini, Ghosts of the Heart,* and *Spring of the Thief.* He is the winner of the Miles Modern Poetry Award.

ROBERT LOWELL (b. 1917, Boston, Massachusetts), is a graduate of Kenyon College. *Land of Unlikeness,* his first book of poems, was privately printed. *Lord Weary's Castle,* which was published in 1946, won the Pulitzer Prize that year. His other books include *The Mills of the Kavanaughs, Life Studies,* which won the National Book Award, *Phaedra, Imitations, For the*

Union Dead, The Old Glory, and *Near the Ocean.* In 1963, Mr. Lowell was elected by the American Academy of Arts and Letters to the chair vacated by Robert Frost.

WILLIAM H. MATCHETT (b. 1923, Chicago, Illinois) is currently professor of English at the University of Washington and editor of *Modern Language Quarterly.* He is the author of *Water Ouzel and Other Poems* and *The Phoenix and the Turtle: Shakespeare's Poem and Chester's "Loues Martyr",* as well as coauthor of *Poetry: From Statement to Meaning.* Well known for his articles, book reviews, stories, and translations, he also edited *The Life and Death of King John* by William Shakespeare for the Signet Classic line of paperback books.

E. L. MAYO (b. 1905, Boston, Massachusetts), recently advisory editor of *North American Review* and poetry editor of *Northwest Review,* is author of *The Diver, The Center Is Everywhere,* and *Summer Unbound and Other Poems.* Currently teaching at Drake University, he won the Blumenthal Prize for Poetry in 1942.

WILLIAM MEREDITH (b. 1919, New York City), has published four volumes of verse, *Love Letter from an Impossible Land, Ships and Other Figures, The Open Sea,* and *The Wreck of the Thresher and Other Poems,* as well as a translation of *Alcools: Poems 1898–1924* by Guillaume Apollinaire. Along with such poets as W. H. Auden, Robert Lowell, and Richard Wilbur, he is a chancellor of the Academy of American Poets.

JAMES MERRILL (b. 1926, New York City) is the author of two novels, *The Seraglio* and *The Diblos Notebook,* as well as four books of poetry, *First Poems, The Country of 1000 Years of Peace, Water Street* and *Night and Days,* which won the 1967 National Book Award.

W. S. MERWIN (b. 1927, New York City) in addition to his poetry and translations from French, Spanish, Latin, and Portuguese, has also written articles for *The Nation* and radio scripts for the BBC. His books of poetry include *A Mask for Janus, The Dancing Bears, Green with Beasts, The Drunk in the Furnace, The Moving Target,* and *The Lice.* His translations include *The Poem of the Cid, Spanish Ballads, The Satires of Persius, Lazarillo de Tormes,* and *The Song of Roland.*

HOWARD MOSS (b. 1922, New York City) is currently poetry editor for *The New Yorker* magazine. His books include *The Wound and the Weather; The Toy Fair; A Swimmer in the Air; A Winter Come, A Summer Gone; Finding Them Lost;* and *Second Nature.* His poems have appeared in such publications as *Poetry, Kenyon Review, The Nation, New Republic,* and *The New Yorker* as well as in countless anthologies.

STANLEY MOSS (b. 1926, New York City) has written two books. *The Wrong Angel*, published by Macmillan in 1966, and *The Wrong Angel and New Poems*, published by Anvil (Oxford). He is currently poetry editor of *The New American Review* and a Rockefeller Fellow in Poetry for 1967–1968.

LISEL MUELLER (b. 1924, Hamburg, Germany) came to America in 1939. A graduate of Evansville College, she is the author of *Dependencies*, published in 1965. Her poems have appeared in *The New Yorker*, *Quarterly Review of Literature*, *Perspective*, and *Saturday Review* as well as in a number of anthologies.

HOWARD NEMEROV (b. 1920, New York City), currently professor of English at Brandeis, received his B.A. from Harvard. A member of the National Institute of Arts and Letters and the American Academy of Arts and Sciences, he is the author of six volumes of poems, the most recent of which is *The Blue Swallows*, published by the University of Chicago Press in 1967. He has also written several novels and books of criticism.

FRANK O'HARA (b. 1926, Baltimore, Maryland) received his B.A. from Harvard and his M.A. from the University of Michigan, where he won a Hopwood Award for poetry. From 1951 until his death in 1966 he lived and worked in New York, both for *Art News* and the Museum of Modern Art, where he was associate curator of the department of painting and sculpture exhibitions. Six volumes of his poetry have been published: *A City Winter and Other Poems*, *Meditations on an Emergency*, *Second Avenue*, *Odes*, *Lunch Poems*, and *Love Poems*.

CHARLES OLSON (b. 1910, Worcester, Massachusetts), poet, essayist, and critic, was educated at Wesleyan, Yale, and Harvard. He presently holds a professorship at the State University of New York at Buffalo. His books of poems include *In Cold Hell, In Thicket*; *The Maximus Poems 1–10*; *The Maximus Poems 11–22*; *Maximus from Dogtown—1*; and *The Distances*.

ROBERT PACK (b. 1929, New York City) is presently poet in residence at Middlebury College. Among the awards he has received are the National Institute of Arts and Letters Award as well as the 1965 Borestone Mountain Poetry Award. His books of poetry include *The Irony of Joy*, *A Stranger's Privilege*, *Guarded by Women*, and *Selected Poems*.

DONALD PETERSEN (b. 1928, Minneapolis, Minnesota), former assistant editor of *Western Review*, is currently associate professor of English at the State University College in Oneonta, New York. Author of *The Spectral Boy (Poems 1948–1964)*, he has published poems in *Poetry, Furioso,* and *Paris Review.* His poetry has been anthologized in *Midland* and *New Poets of England and America.*

SYLVIA PLATH (b. 1932, Boston, Massachusetts) went to Smith College. In 1955 she won a Fulbright to Newnham College, Cambridge, where she met and married poet Ted Hughes. Author of *The Colossus* and *Ariel,* Sylvia Plath died on February 11, 1963.

ADRIENNE RICH (b. 1929, Baltimore, Maryland) published her first book of poems in 1951 while still an undergraduate at Radcliffe. For this book, *A Change of World,* she won the Yale Series of Younger Poets Prize. Her other volumes of poems are *The Diamond Cutters, Snapshots of a Daughter-in-Law,* and *Necessities of Life.* She has been the recipient of numerous awards and prizes.

THEODORE ROETHKE (b. 1908, Saginaw, Michigan) was one of America's most honored poets. Among his awards: the 1954 Pulitzer Prize, two Guggenheim Fellowships, the Bollingen Prize, the award of the American Academy of Arts and Letters, and the National Book Award, which was given posthumously in 1964 for his book *The Far Field.* Among Mr. Roethke's other works are *The Waking, Open House, The Lost Son and Other Poems, Praise to the End, Words for the Wind,* and *I Am! Says the Lamb.* In 1947, Mr. Roethke went to the University of Washington as poet in residence and professor of English, where he remained until his death in 1963.

JAMES SCHUYLER (b. 1923, Chicago, Illinois) has published *A Picnic Cantata* (with music by Paul Bowles), a novel, *Alfred and Guinevere,* and two collections of poems, *Salute* and *May 24th or So.* He is presently one of the editors of *Locus Solus,* and a frequent contributor to *Art News.*

WINFIELD TOWNLEY SCOTT (b. 1910, Haverhill, Massachusetts) graduated from Brown University and was on the staff of *The Providence Journal* from 1931 to 1951. Winner of such awards as the Harriet Monroe Award and the Shelley Memorial Award, he is the author of *Change of Weather* and *Collected Poems.* Mr. Scott died in 1968.

ANNE SEXTON (b. 1928, Newton, Massachusetts) published her first book of poetry, *To Bedlam and Part Way Back,* in 1960. This was followed by *All My Pretty Ones* in 1962 and *Live or Die,* which won the 1966 Pulitzer Prize. Her poems have also appeared in such periodicals as *Harper's, Hudson Review, The New Yorker,* and *Encounter.*

KARL SHAPIRO (b. 1913, Baltimore, Maryland) is currently professor of English at the University of California at Davis. Appointed consultant in poetry to the Library of Congress in 1946, he joined the faculty of Johns Hopkins University the following year. In 1950 he became editor of *Poetry: A Magazine of Verse.* He is the author of *Person, Place and Thing; V-Letter and Other Poems,* which won the Pulitzer Prize in 1945; and *Selected Poems,* for which he won the Bollingen Prize in 1968.

CHARLES SIMIC (b. 1938, Chicago, Illinois) is presently an editorial assistant with *Aperture,* a photography quarterly. He is a graduate of New York University. His book of poems, *What the Grass Says,* was published in 1967.

LOUIS SIMPSON (b. 1923, Jamaica, West Indies) came to the United States in 1940. Currently a professor at the State University of New York in Stony Brook, he is the author of *The Arrivistes, Good News of Death, A Dream of Governors, At the End of the Open Road,* and *Selected Poems.* In 1964 he won a Pulitzer Prize.

L. E. SISSMAN (b. 1928, Detroit, Michigan), currently vice president and creative director of Kenyon and Eckhardt Advertising in Boston, graduated from Harvard College, where he won the Garrison Poetry Prize. He is the author of *Dying: An Introduction,* which won the Lamont Award in 1968.

WILLIAM JAY SMITH (b. 1918, Winnfield, Louisiana) is the author of *Poems, Celebration at Dark, Poems 1947–1957,* and *The Tin Can and Other Poems,* as well as translations of Laforgue and Latbaud; a literary study, *The Spectra Hoax;* and a number of well-known books of poems for children. A contributor to *The New Yorker, New Republic, Atlantic Monthly,* and other magazines, he was poetry reviewer for *Harper's* for many years. In 1968 he was appointed consultant in poetry to the Library of Congress.

W. D. SNODGRASS (b. 1926, Wilkinsburg, Pennsylvania), currently teaching at Syracuse University, is the author of *Heart's Needle,* which won the 1960 Pulitzer Prize, *Gallows' Songs,* which are translations from the German poet Christian Morgenstern, and *After Experience. . . .*

GARY SNYDER (b. 1930, San Francisco, California) is a graduate of Reed College. A winner of the National Institute of Arts and Letters Award, he is the author of *Riprap, Rivers and Mountains, A Range of Poems, Poetry Myths and Texts,* and *Six Sections from Mountains and Rivers Without End.*

WILLIAM STAFFORD (b. 1914, Hutchinson, Kansas) is the author of *Down in My Heart, West of Your City, Traveling*

Through the Dark, which won the National Book Award in 1963, and *The Rescued Year*. He is presently professor of English at Lewis and Clark College.

MARK STRAND (b. 1934, Prince Edward Island, Canada), a graduate of Antioch College and Yale University, is the author of two books of poems, *Sleeping With One Eye Open* and *Reasons for Moving*.

ROBERT SWARD (b. 1933, Chicago, Illinois) received his B.A. from the University of Illinois and his M.A. from the University of Iowa. He is the author of *Kissing the Dancer, Thousand-Year-Old Fiancée, Uncle Dog and Other Poems,* and *Advertisements*. His poems have appeared in such magazines as *Paris Review, Transatlantic Review, The Activist,* and *The Nation*.

MAY SWENSON (b. 1919, Logan, Utah) is the author of five books of poetry: *Another Animal, A Cage of Spines, To Mix with Time: New and Selected Poems, Poems to Solve,* and *Half Sun Half Sleep*. A former editor at New Directions, she is presently working on a new collection of poems and a play.

JAMES TATE (b. 1943, Kansas City, Missouri) won the Yale Series of Younger Poets Award in 1966 and a National Endowment for the Arts Award in 1968. His many books of poetry include *The Lost Pilot, The Notes of Woe, The Destination, The Torches,* and *Row With Your Hair*. His latest book, *Shadowboxing,* is about to be published by Harper & Row.

CONSTANCE URDANG (b. 1922, New York City) received her B.A. from Smith and her M.F.A. from the State University of Iowa. Her book of poems, *Charades and Celebrations,* was published in 1965, and she is currently working on a novel, tentatively entitled *Natural History,* for Harper & Row.

PETER VIERECK (b. 1916, New York City) is professor of modern history at Mt. Holyoke College. His first book of poems, *Terror and Decorum,* won the 1949 Pulitzer Prize. He is also the author of a verse drama, *The Tree Witch,* and has written five scholarly books in political science and history.

DAVID WAGONER (b. 1926, Massillon, Ohio) is currently professor of English at the University of Washington and editor of *Poetry Northwest*. His books of poetry include *Dry Sun, Dry Wind; A Place to Stand; The Nesting Ground;* and *Staying Alive*. He has also published five novels, three of which are presently under option to the movies.

DIANE WAKOSKI (b. 1937, Whittier, California) received her B.A. from Berkeley. She is the author of *Coins and Coffins,*

Discrepancies and Apparitions, and *The George Washington Poems,* and her work has appeared in such periodicals as *The New Yorker* and *The Village Voice.*

THEODORE WEISS (b. 1916, Reading, Pennsylvania), currently professor of humanities at Princeton, is editor and publisher of *The Quarterly Review of Literature.* His books of poetry include *The Catch, Outlanders, Gunsight, The Medium,* and *The Last Day and the First.*

REED WHITTEMORE (b. 1919, New Haven, Connecticut) received his B.A. from Yale University. Currently senior program associate of the National Institute of Public Affairs and lecturer at the University of Maryland, he is the author of *An American Takes a Walk, Self-Made Man, Boy from Iowa, Fascination of the Abomination, Poems: New and Selected,* and *From Zero to the Absolute.*

RICHARD WILBUR (b. 1921, New York City) is currently teaching at Wesleyan University. He is the author of *The Beautiful Changes, Ceremony, Things of This World, Poems 1943–1956, Advice to a Prophet,* and *The Poems of Richard Wilbur,* as well as translations of *The Misanthrope* and *Tartuffe* by Molière. In 1956 he won both the Pulitzer Prize and the National Book Award for *Things of This World.*

CHARLES WRIGHT (b. 1935, Pickwick Dam, Tennessee) was educated at Davidson College and the State University of Iowa. A Fulbright Scholar and currently a Fulbright lecturer in Italy, he has had poetry published in such publications as *The New Yorker, The Nation,* and *Northwest Review.* He is the author of *The Dream Animal,* which was published in 1968.

JAMES WRIGHT (b. 1927, Martins Ferry, Ohio), a graduate of Kenyon College, was awarded M.A. and Ph.D. degrees from the University of Washington. His most recent collection of poetry is *Shall We Gather at the River.* He is also the author of *The Branch Will Not Break, Saint Judas,* and *The Green Wall.*

Index of First Lines

Index of Titles

401

The SIGNET CLASSIC Poetry Series

☐ **THE SELECTED POETRY OF BROWNING edited by**
George Ridenour. Includes **Pauline**, selections from **The
Ring and the Book**, **St. Martin's Summer**, **Fra Lippo
Lippi**, **Childe Roland to the Dark Tower Came**, and
longer works often omitted in standard anthologies.
Introduction, Chronology, Bibliography.
(#CY889—$1.25)

☐ **THE SELECTED POETRY AND PROSE OF BYRON edited
by W. H. Auden**. A comprehensive collection which in-
cludes **Beppo**, **Epistle to Augusta**, selections from **Don
Juan, Childe Harold, English Bards and Scotch Review-
ers**, and extracts from the journals and letters. Intro-
duction, Chronology, Bibliography. (#CW905—$1.50)

☐ **THE SELECTED POETRY OF KEATS edited by Paul de
Man**. The major long poems, all the "Odes," many son-
nets, and several letters. Introduction, Chronology,
Bibliography. (#CW901—$1.50)

☐ **THE SELECTED POETRY OF ALEXANDER POPE edited
by Martin Price**. The most famous works of the famed
poet are contained in this volume. They include **The
Rape of the Lock**, and **Eloise and Abelard** among others.
(#CW853—$1.50)

☐ **THE SELECTED POETRY AND PROSE OF SHELLEY
edited by Harold Bloom, Yale University**. All the major
and most of the minor poems. Sixty selections including
Mutability, Prometheus Unbound, Ode to the West Wind,
selections from **Hellas**, and **A Defense of Poetry**.
(#CW832—$1.50)

Ⓒ

The Complete Plays of SHAKESPEARE

Superlatively edited paperbound volumes of Shakespeare's complete plays are now available in Signet Classic editions. Under the general editorship of Sylvan Barnet of the English Department of Tufts University, each volume features a general Introduction by Dr. Barnet; special Introduction and Notes by an eminent Shakespearean scholar; critical commentary from past and contemporary authorities; and when possible, the actual source, in its entirety or in excerpt, from which Shakespeare derived his play.

☐ **KING LEAR. Edited by Russell Fraser.**
(#CY967—$1.25)

☐ **MACBETH. Edited by Sylvan Barnet.** (#CY974—$1.25)

☐ **OTHELLO. Edited by Alvin Kernan.** (#CY958—$1.25)

☐ **RICHARD II. Edited by Kenneth Muir.** (#CQ808—95¢)

☐ **THE WINTER'S TALE. Edited by Frank Kermode.**
(#CY966—$1.25)

☐ **AS YOU LIKE IT. Edited by Albert Gilman.**
(#CQ933—95¢)

☐ **HAMLET. Edited by Edward Hubler.** (#CY1022—$1.25)

☐ **JULIUS CAESAR. Edited by William & Barbara Rosen.**
(#CY983—$1.25)

☐ **A MIDSUMMER NIGHT'S DREAM. Edited by Wolfgang Clemen.** (#CY973—$1.25)

☐ **TROILUS AND CRESSIDA. Edited by Daniel Seltzer.**
(#CQ935—95¢)

☐ **THE TEMPEST. Edited by Robert Langbaum.**
(#CY994—$1.25)

THE NEW AMERICAN LIBRARY, INC.,
P.O. Box 999, Bergenfield, New Jersey 07621

Please send me the SIGNET CLASSIC BOOKS I have checked above. I am enclosing $_____(check or money order—no currency or C.O.D.'s). Please include the list price plus 35¢ a copy to cover handling and mailing costs. (Prices and numbers are subject to change without notice.)

Name_____

Address_____

City_____State_____Zip Code_____
Allow at least 4 weeks for delivery